Good Faith in Contractual Performance in Australia

Nurhidayah Abdullah

Good Faith in Contractual Performance in Australia

palgrave
macmillan

Nurhidayah Abdullah
Faculty of Economics & Administration
University of Malaya
Kuala Lumpur, Malaysia

ISBN 978-981-15-6077-4 ISBN 978-981-15-6078-1 (eBook)
https://doi.org/10.1007/978-981-15-6078-1

This Palgrave Macmillan imprint is published by the registered company Springer Nature Singapore Pte Ltd.
The registered company address is: 152 Beach Road, #21-01/04 Gateway East, Singapore 189721, Singapore

I dedicate this book to my mother, Rusizah binti Mohd Taib; my two beloved children, Mohd Al Haddad bin Mohd Hakimi and Nur Hurin Amani bin Mohd Hakimi; and my beloved family for their endless support and unconditional love.

To my late father, Abdullah bin Kassim, who passed away on the 18th of April 2018, may Allah accept him among the guided ones. Amin.

Preface

Good faith is arguably the most controversial, frustrating and poorly defined concept in contract law. Judges and scholars have different and contradicting views of the concept of good faith, both as to its operation and as to its meaning. The concept of good faith nevertheless has begun to gain recognition and continues to have an increasing influence on many types of contracts in many contexts. The concept of good faith had generally been rooted in countries that practice civil law. Only now is it beginning to be acknowledged in some common law countries.

The aim of this book is to give a detailed account of the current state of the law concerning good faith in contractual performance. In Australia, good faith is an area of law which is undergoing rapid development. The concept of good faith was introduced by Priestley J in his *obiter* comments in *Renard Constructions (ME) v Minister for Works* (1992) 26 NSWLR 234. This case paved the way for the emergence of the concept of good faith in Australian contract law. The book deals with the issues surrounding its development, its meaning and its acceptance at the international level. The empirical dimension of this book offers updated insights into the concept of good faith in Australia. It does this by building on Tyrone Carlin's study in 2005 entitled 'A Critical Analysis of the Burgeoning Good Faith Performance Doctrine in the Australian Contract Law', his unpublished master's dissertation submitted to the University of Sydney. My study examines the concept of good faith over a longer period, from 1992 to 2009. This book indicates how questions relating to good faith in contractual performance have been material to the evolution of the concept in Australia.

This book is distinct from most research conducted on good faith because it adds to the research on good faith in contractual performance using the empirical legal research approach. The scope of the research is broader in terms of the materials and the study period. This research focused on the attitude of the judges to good faith, the definition of good faith and the possibility of legislating a good faith obligation in Australian contract law.

Kuala Lumpur, Malaysia

Nurhidayah Abdullah

Acknowledgements

This book would not have been possible without the support of scholars, government officials and friends, who kindly shared with me their experiences and thoughts when I was writing this book. My research was also greatly aided by the Ministry of Higher Education Malaysia and the University of Malaya. Members of these institutions believed in my ability to pursue higher studies and provided generous financial support.

This book originates from my doctoral thesis, which I completed at the University of Sydney Business School at the University of Sydney, Australia in the Business Law Department, under the supervision of Professor Tyrone Carlin and Professor Andrew Terry. I am indeed grateful to them for the guidance they provided while I pursued my doctoral degree. I would like to thank Professor Terence Gomez, as well as my colleagues at the Faculty of Economics and Administration, University Malaya, who constantly inspired me to complete the writing of this book.

To my family and friends, I would like to express my gratitude for their unfailing support without whom I would not have completed this work. I wish to acknowledge the valuable feedback I received from various reviewers. Their suggestions helped me improve the quality and coherence of my arguments.

Finally, I must also acknowledge here that I have previously published certain sections of this book in the form of journal articles. Full publication details of these articles are as follows:

Abdullah, N., Musa, M. K & Hanafi, H. The Duty of Good Faith in Common Law: A New View on Contemporary Contract Law *PERTANIKA Journal of Social Science and Humanities (Special Issue January 2017)* (SCOPUS-Indexed).

Abdullah, N., Kari, F. & Ismail Nawang, N. The Issue of Incorporating the Concept of Good Faith in Australian Contract Law: Implication or Construction. *PERTANIKA Journal of Social Science and Humanities* 23(S) Nov.2015 (SCOPUS-Indexed).

Contents

List of Figures

List of Tables

CHAPTER 1

Introduction

1.1 Introduction

Good faith is arguably one of the most controversial, frustrating and poorly defined concepts in contract law. Judges and scholars have differing and contradicting views of the concept of good faith, in terms of both its operation and its meaning.[1] The concept of good faith nevertheless is gaining recognition and continues to have an increasing influence on many types of contracts, in many contexts. In Australia, the concept of good faith was introduced by Priestley J in his *obiter* comments in *Renard Constructions (ME) v Minister for Works*.[2] That case paved the way for the emergence of the concept of good faith in Australian contract law.

This research aims to examine the principle of good faith in the performance of contracts following the foundation laid down by Priestley J. The issue of good faith discussed in this research is timely and important. Despite Priestley J's strong belief in the position of good faith in Australia, its application remains uncertain. There remains no High Court decision regarding the position of good faith in Australia. As a consequence, the precise role of the concept of good faith in Australian contract law remains unsettled. The unresolved issues were a key motivation for this research.

[1] Carlin, T. M. The Rise (and Fall) of Implied Duties of Good Faith in Contractual Performance in Australia (2005), 25 *University of New South Wales Law Journal*, 99, 123.

[2] (1992) 26 NSWLR 234.

N. Abdullah, *Good Faith in Contractual Performance in Australia*,
https://doi.org/10.1007/978-981-15-6078-1_1

1.2 Background

Good faith is a ubiquitous but poorly understood concept in contract law. Two decades after Priestley J first introduced the concept in the Australian judicial agenda, good faith remains a confusing, nebulous and mutable concept. Good faith encompasses the theme that all parties to a contract owe a duty to each other beyond those expressly provided by the terms of the contract. In this context, it is expected that the contracting parties take into account other parties' interests when exercising their contractual rights.[3] The concept of good faith is pivotal to the contracting parties in two ways: (1) cooperation and fairness are achievable through the concept of good faith, and (2) in the absence of express terms in the contract to prevent unfairness, good faith is treated as an implicit expectation of the parties. Burrows further explained the function of good faith, stating that:

> *The concept of good faith is regularly invoked not only to condemn deception and lack of candour at the time a bargain is concluded but also to require a forthcoming attitude, to condemn chicanery and sharp practice in the carrying out of contractual obligations.*[4]

In countries where civil law is the basis of the legal system, the concept of good faith is recognised as a general and pervasive principle, as illustrated in many of the European civil codes.[5] Under common law, there is no overarching duty of good faith; nevertheless, it has a role in English law. English law takes a different approach to the concept of good faith, relying on a number of specific doctrines and achieving some of the same results as might be required by good faith without referring to that concept.

In English law, good faith is recognised in specific settings and legislation whereby the most common expression of good faith can be found in

[3] Gava, J., & Kincaid, P. (1996). Contract and Conventionalism: Professional Attitudes to Changes in Contract Law in Australia, *Journal of Contract Law*, 10, 141–150.

[4] See Burrows, J. F. (1968). Contractual Cooperation and Implied Terms. *Modern Law Review*, 31, 390, for an interesting discussion of a somewhat broader notion of good faith and an implied duty of cooperation and for a discussion of the extent to which each party has a duty to cooperate in the contractual undertaking, 395–405.

[5] See (list is not exhaustive) the *German Civil Code* s 242, the *French Civil Code* Article 1134(3), the *Italian Civil Code* Article 1375, the *Swiss Civil Code* Article 2, the *Greek Civil Code* Article 288 and the *Quebec Civil Code* Articles 61, 375 and 1434. Many of the European codes make reference to good faith in the statutory provision as mentioned above.

insurance contracts.[6] In legislation, there is increasing recognition of good faith in specific instances.[7] The general recognition of good faith as described by Lord Bingham is that it is 'the most important contractual issue of our time'.[8] It can be found in the landmark case of *Interfoto Picture Library Ltd v Stiletto Visual Programmes Ltd*, where Lord Bingham implied the concept of good faith when he held that:

> *In many civil law systems and perhaps most legal systems in the common law world, the law of obligations recognises and enforces an overriding principle that in making and carrying out contracts, parties should act in good faith. This does not simply mean that they should not deceive each other, a principle which any legal system must recognise; its effect is perhaps most aptly conveyed by such metaphorical colloquialisms as 'playing fair', 'coming clean', or 'putting one's card face upwards on the table' … English law has, characteristically, committed itself to no such overriding principle but has developed piecemeal solutions in response to demonstrated problems of unfairness. Many examples could be given. Thus equity has intervened to strike down unconscionable bargains. Parliament has stepped in to regulate the imposition of exemption clauses and the form of certain hire-purchase agreements. The common law also has made its contribution, by holding that certain classes of contracts require the utmost good faith by treating as irrecoverable what purport to be agreed to estimates of damage but are in truth disguised as a penalty for breach, and in many other ways.*[9]

A similar view is shared by other common law countries, such as Australia, New Zealand and Canada, where good faith is not recognised as an overriding obligation but is nevertheless recognised in other doctrines such as unconscionability and in specific statutory provisions. However, the approach of the US is different whereby the concept of good faith is

[6] In specific context like insurance, it is a fundamental principle of insurance law that both the insurer and the insured must observe a duty of utmost good faith towards each other. Later, the concept of utmost good faith was given a statutory recognition in S 13 of the *Insurance Contracts Act 1984* (Cth), where it is stated that 'A contract of insurance is a contract based on the utmost good faith and there is implied in such a contract a provision requiring each party to it to act towards the other party, in respect of any matter arising under or in relation to it, with the utmost good faith'.

[7] In *Bropho v Human Rights & Equal Opportunity Commission* [2004] FCAFC 16 [84], the court held that there are at least 154 federal Acts that mention the term good faith.

[8] *Interfoto Picture Library Ltd v Stiletto Visual Programmes Ltd* [1989] QB 433.

[9] [1989] QB 433, 439.

entrenched in the *Uniform Commercial Code*[10] and the *Restatement (Second) of Contracts.*[11]

The concept of good faith is widely employed at international levels, where many international trade instruments incorporate it.[12] In the *Nuclear Tests* case (*Australia v France*), the International Court of Justice claimed that 'One of the basic principles governing the creation and performance of legal obligations, whatever their source, is the principle of good faith'.[13] An example of the adoption of good faith in an international trade instrument can be found in the *United Nations Convention on Contracts for International Sale of Goods* Article 7.1, known as the Vienna Sales Convention (CISG), which provides that:

> *... in the interpretation of the Convention, regard is to be had to its international character and the need to promote uniformity in its application and the observation of good faith in international trade.*

[10] See the *Uniform Commercial Code*, ss 1-203, 201(11), 2-(103)(1) and 2-104(1).

[11] See the *Restatement (Second) of Contracts* s 205.

[12] See also the *Principles of International Commercial Contracts* (UNIDROIT Principles 2004) Article 1.7, which clearly supports the duty of good faith. It stated that:

> In the interpretation of this Convention, regard is to be had to its international character and to the need to promote uniformity in its application and the observance of good faith in international trade and prohibits the parties from limiting or excluding the duty in their contracts.

The *Vienna Convention on the Law of Treaties* Article 31(1) provides that:

> A treaty shall be interpreted in good faith in accordance with the ordinarily meaning to be given to the terms of the treaty in their context and in the light of its object and purpose.

The *Principles of European Contract Law* Article 1.201 provides that:

> in exercising his rights and performing his duties each party must act in accordance with good faith and fair dealing.

[13] [1974] ICJ REP. 253, 268.

1.2.1 Good Faith in Australian Contract Law

Good faith was put onto the agenda in Australia through *obiter* comments by Priestley J in the landmark case of *Renard* in 1992.[14] In that case, Priestley J suggested the notion of good faith in his interpretation of Australian contract law. His Honour held that:

> *The kind of reasonableness I have been discussing seems to me to have much in common with the notions of good faith which are regarded in many civil law systems of Europe and in all states in the United States as necessarily implied in many kinds of contract. Although this implication has not yet been accepted to the same extent in Australia as part of judge-make Australian contract law, there are many indications that the time may be fast approaching when the idea, long recognised as implicit in many of the orthodox techniques of solving contractual disputes, will gain explicit recognition in the same way as it has in Europe and in the United States.*[15]

Nevertheless, the concept of good faith had a significant impact on Australian contract law, with many other cases following Priestley J's opinion.[16]

There are two means by which a general term of good faith is recognised in contract law: implication and construction. There are two types of implication: the term 'implied in law' and the term 'implied in fact'. A term 'implied in law' is based on the test of necessity in a particular class of contract. A term 'implied in fact' is based on the judge's view of the actual intention of the parties. Peden argues that 'construction' is the best approach for incorporating good faith in contracts.[17] The New South Wales Court of Appeal in *Burger King Corporation v Hungry Jack's Pty Ltd* held that:

[14] (1992) 26 NSWLR 234.

[15] (1992) 26 NSWLR 234, 264.

[16] See *Hughes Aircraft Systems International v Airservices Australia* (1997) 76 FCR 151, 191–193; *Alcatel Australia Ltd v Scarella* (1998) 44 NSWLR 349, 368–369; *Garry Rogers Motors (Aust) Pty Ltd v Subaru (Aust) Pty Ltd* (1999) ¶ATPR 41–703, 43,014; *Burger King Corporation v Hungry Jack's Pty Ltd* (2001) 69 NSWLR 558, 570; and *Vodafone Pacific Ltd v Mobile Innovations Ltd* [2004] NSWCA 15 (Unreported, Sheller, Giles and Ipp JJA, 20 February 2004) [183]–[191].

[17] See Elisabeth Peden, 'Cooperation' in English Contract Law - To Construe or Imply? (2000), 16 *Journal of Contract Law* 56.

> *There ... appears to be increasing acceptance ... that if the terms of good faith and reasonableness are to be implied, they are to be implied as a matter of law.*[18]

There are instances however in which the concept of good faith is not accepted, especially in commercial contracts, where the parties have the freedom to decide on the terms of their contract. In *GSA Group Pty Ltd v Siebe Plc*, Rogers CJ commented that:

> *Against a trend toward a general obligation of good faith, fairness or reasonableness, there have been judicial comments to the effect that the court should be slow to intrude into the commercial dealings of the parties who are quite able to look after their own interests. The courts should not be too eager to interfere in the commercial conduct of the parties, especially where the parties are all wealthy, experienced, commercial entities able to attend to their own interests.*[19]

In contrast to the position, the concept of good faith is receiving particular attention in relational contracts such as franchising. In the context of franchising, good faith is now considered to be an implied duty owed by the franchisor to the franchisee to curb unethical conduct where there is an imbalance of power between them. In *Far Horizons Pty Ltd v McDonald's Australia*, Byrne J emphasised the need for an implied term of good faith to ensure a successful relationship between the franchisor and franchisee. His Honour made the following comments:

> *I do not see myself as at liberty to depart from the considerable body of authority in this country which has followed the decision of the New South Wales Court of Appeal in Renard Constructions (ME) Pty Ltd v Minister for Public Works. I proceed, therefore, on the basis that there is to be implied in a franchise agreement a term of good faith and fair dealing which obliges each party to exercise the powers conferred upon it by the agreement in good faith and reasonably...*[20]

The competing argument towards the acceptance and recognition to the concept of good faith indicates that the status of good faith in Australian contract law is still not clear. To date, there has been no High Court decision to provide comprehensive guidance on this issue. In *Royal Botanic Gardens and Domain Trust v South Sydney City Council*, the Court

[18] [2001] NSWCA 187 [164].
[19] (1993) 30 NSWLR 573, 579 (F).
[20] [2000] VSC 310 (18 August 2000).

held that 'Whilst the issues respecting the existence and scope of a "good faith" doctrine are important this is an inappropriate occasion to consider them'.[21]

Despite it being a well-known concept, there is a controversy as to the meaning of good faith, which makes defining it an almost impossible task. Most of the definitions are confusing and contradictory.[22] Some scholars and judges suggest that attaching a definition to good faith is impossible. Other scholars and judges nevertheless maintain that it is possible to define good faith. As a consequence, the precise role of the concept of good faith in Australian contract law remains unsettled.

1.2.2 Research Questions

Research Question 1: What is the attitude of Australian judges to the issue of good faith?

Since Priestley J introduced the concept of good faith in the *Renard* case in 1992, there have been diverse opinions from other judges. Justice Kirby quotes Lord Denning's view that there are two types of judges: 'timorous souls' and 'bold spirits'.[23] 'Timorous souls' refers to judges who are fearful to allow a new course of action, while 'bold spirits' refer to judges who are ready to allow a new course of action if justice so requires.[24] In dealing with the issue of good faith, the 'timorous souls' may argue that an implied obligation of good faith will add uncertainty to contract law, while the 'bold spirits' may argue that there is a need to explore good faith as necessary or desirable. These statements by the two types of judges suggest that there is a conflicting attitude regarding the concept of good faith. The first research question is aimed at determining the attitudes of Australian judges to the issue of good faith in contract law in Australia. A sample of 104 Australian cases from 1992 to 2009 was studied.

Research Question 2: What is the meaning of good faith?

There are many different interpretations of the meaning of good faith, some of which are contradictory. Justice Steyn argued that 'a definition of

[21] (2002) 240 CLR 45, 63.

[22] For further discussion, see Chap. 6.

[23] Kirby, M. (1988). Bold Spirit of the Law. Quadrant 16, 32(3).

[24] Norrie. G. (1984). *The Development of Consumer Law and Policy-Based Spirit and Timorous Souls.* Steven & Sons.

good faith and fair dealing is impossible'.[25] Therefore, the second research question aims to determine whether a precise meaning can be established and to propose a workable definition.

Research Question 3: Should a good faith obligation be legislated in Australia?

The issue of legislating a good faith obligation is on the regulators' agenda in Australia. This ongoing debate has often revolved around the issue of uncertainty associated with its meaning or lack of meaning. Given the ethical underpinnings of the concept, it is naturally difficult to define it in a single authoritative definition. It is precisely this seeming inability to define the concept that has sustained this lengthy debate. However, in this discourse, certain concrete milestones are reached that mark concrete steps in the evolution of the concept in Australia. Perhaps the most notable of these is the decision of the previous Australian government to accept the recommendation to include good faith in the specific business context of franchising.[26] The previous Australian government appointed Wein, an experienced franchisor operator and small business advisor, to review the *Franchising Code of Conduct.* The previous Australian government accepted the recommendation made by Wein to introduce an express obligation of good faith for both the franchisor and franchisee to curb any unethical conduct that is the cause of major problems in the franchising context. The Wein review recommended the incorporation of the common law duty of good faith rather than devising some new and different definition of good faith. This was decided based on the premise that the concept will not be defined but understood through 'non-discretionary reference criteria', namely in a manner similar to the unconscionable conduct prohibition set out in s 22 of the *Australian Consumer Law.*[27] The third research question, therefore, considers whether good faith should be enshrined in Australian legislation and examines the merits of the approach decided by the government.

[25] Steyn, J. (1991). The Role of Good Faith and Fair Dealing in Contract Law: A Hair-Shirt Philosophy? *Denning Law Journal*, 6, 131–140.

[26] See generally Australian Government, *Commonwealth Government Response to the Review of the Federal Franchising Code of Conduct*-Forward Looking Franchising Regulation (2013).

[27] Australian Government, *Commonwealth Government Response to the Review of the Federal Franchising Code of Conduct*-Forward Looking Franchising Regulation (2013), 13.

1.2.3 Research Rationale

This research has the following three broad objectives: (1) to analyse the attitude of Australian judges to the issue of good faith, (2) to provide clarity on the definition of good faith and (3) to consider whether a general obligation of good faith should be enshrined in Australian legislation. This research uses both qualitative and quantitative approaches to the issue of good faith in Australia. The qualitative study traces the origin and development of good faith from secondary sources. The quantitative study is based on cases between 1992 and 2009 which cite the *Renard* case that focuses on good faith in contractual performance. The study employed the longitudinal approach, where the study is framed by the 1992 to 2009 period, with the years divided into three phases, 'Introduction Phase 1992 to 1998', 'Development Phase 1999 to 2003' and 'Consolidation Phase 2004 to 2009', in order to trace the evolution and development of good faith in Australian contract law. Although there is a wide and rich literature on good faith in Australia, there are limited in-depth empirical studies on good faith or on how the concept of good faith is applied in Australia. This book describes the results of an empirical study on the reception and development of the concept of good faith in Australia across various Australian jurisdictions.

1.2.4 Research Parameters and Methods

The research sources used in this book include primary and secondary legal sources. The primary legal sources referred to are statutory provisions, including federal and state acts, and cases that focus on good faith in contractual performance. Secondary legal sources include texts, articles, research theses, reviews of research, and other publications containing factual information and commentaries.

The multidisciplinary nature of this book requires a number of approaches in order to understand the concept of good faith as a general principle in contract law and good faith in Australian contract law.

Part II (Chaps. 2, 3 and 4) of this book is based on traditional legal research methods combined with historical-comparative methodology and narrative research (discourse analysis). Each research strategy has its limitations, and no single strategy is adequate for the analysis undertaken. In-depth analysis of the good faith concept in contract law, combined with narrative research (discourse analysis), allows the most appropriate method to be applied to each specific area of the analysis. Furthermore, a comprehensive historical analysis is adopted for an international review of good faith. A similar approach is also adopted in reviewing the development of good faith in Australia.

Part III (Chaps. 5, 6 and 7) uses a combination of research approaches; theoretical and empirical approaches are adopted to identify the 'landscape' of good faith in Australia. A combination of methods is suitable for this, tracing a brief history of good faith in Australia, its development, its reception and expectations for the future. An extensive range of cases is examined to determine the overall status, definition or meaning, and judicial approach in relation to good faith. The reasons for the sample selection and data collection and analysis are set out in Chap. 5.

1.3 Book Structure and Outline

In order to present the argument in a systematic manner, this book is divided into six chapters. The following chapter will provide an overview of good faith as one of the legal concepts in contract law. It argues that good faith is inherent but ubiquitous in all common law contract principles. Unfortunately, good faith is arguably the most controversial, frustrating and a poorly understood concept in contract law. Judges and scholars have different and contradicting views of the concept. Therefore, this section will discuss the function, importance and the perspectives of good faith to further illuminate the concept.

Section 1.2 includes a discussion of different approaches of civil law and common law to good faith. In civil law countries, good faith is considered as a general and pervasive principle recognised in the civil codes. In common law, there is no overarching duty of good faith, but there are a number of legal concepts that incorporate good faith. Four related legal concepts are discussed: unconscionability, fiduciary obligation, non-derogation from grant and the common law duty to cooperate. Good faith can be traced to two sources: legislation and common law. This suggests that good faith is an important and acknowledged concept in common law, despite the varying approaches taken by judges and scholars.

Chapter 3 addresses that despite good faith being a civil law concept, it is gaining recognition in common law countries. The research analyses the reception of good faith in both civil law and common law countries. The discussion includes the background, development and reception of the concept of good faith in various jurisdictions. Germany, France and Italy represent the civil law legal system in which the concept of good faith was codified into the civil law codes. However, the United Kingdom, Canada and New Zealand represent the common law legal system, whereby good faith is recognised in a particular contract. The US, on the other hand, is the only common law country which recognises good faith in the statutory provision despite inheriting the common law legal system. On the contrary, the People's Republic of China is influenced by both the civil law and socialist law; nonetheless, the concept of good faith has been of interest due to China's economic expansion. Apart from its recognition at the national level, good faith is also recognised at the international level where many international trade instruments refer to good faith. It is self-evident that good faith is an important concept at both national and international levels.

Chapter 4 argues that there are various definitions or meanings that have evolved since the introduction of the notion of good faith. Despite it being a well-known concept, there is a controversy as to its meaning, which makes defining it an almost impossible task. Most of the definitions are confusing and contradictory. Some scholars and judges suggest that attaching a definition to good faith is impossible. Other scholars and judges nevertheless maintain that it is possible to define good faith. In analysing the definition of good faith, a new approach of a taxonomic solution is used. The collected definitions or meanings of good faith are analysed, and similar expressions or terminology are grouped together as a 'family' based on their similarity using a distinct 'label'. Each 'label' is supported by the empirical data by year and jurisdiction to detect the frequency received. The more frequency received for the 'label', the more confident is the data. The 'label' that received more support has a greater potential to serve as a definition of good faith. The findings of the definition of good faith are significant because they are based on the genuineness of the selected cases that defined good faith in Australia. Therefore, the definition chosen is reliable in that it is supported by the literature and empirical observations during the period of observation.

Chapter 5 argued that the emergence and historical development of good faith obligations in Australia is very unique. The concept of good faith was first put onto the judicial agenda in Australia through *obiter* comments by Priestley J in the *Renard* case in 1992. Despite there being no overarching duty of good faith, good faith is recognised in both common law and legislation. There are two sources of good faith: implication and construction. There are two types of implication: the term 'by law' and the term 'by fact'. A term 'implied by law' is based on the test of necessity as a legal incident of a particular class in contracts. A term 'implied by fact' is concerned with 'business efficacy'. Without a High Court decision to determine its status, good faith remains untested, presenting a key motivation for the execution of a detailed empirical analysis of good faith in Australia. In addition, this chapter will also provide an overview of the development of good faith in Australian contracts in which a more detailed review of the 'landscape' of decided cases on the issue of good faith in contractual performance during the period of review is presented, with tables and graphs to aid in the understanding of the discussion.

The book concludes with a summary of the main points and arguments as well as areas for future research. The aim is to summarise the conversation so far and provide avenues for further discussion. Key areas include legislating the concept of good faith. Suggestions have also been made to legislate good faith as a general obligation similar to the civil law code model. In the civil law code model, good faith is not defined but instead requires judicial interpretation. This research argues that good faith can be legislated in contractual performance similar to the experience in the context of franchising which provides an opportunity to legislate good faith. No doubt, the presence of an authoritative definition of good faith will resolve the issue of uncertainty. It is anticipated that this approach to the legislation of a good faith obligation will do away with the reservations arising from the issue of uncertainty.

CHAPTER 2

Good Faith Under Contract Law

2.1 Introduction

This chapter describes the evolution of the concept of good faith as a general principle in contract law. It also provides a background to the concept of good faith from both civil law and common law perspectives. It explores the relationship between the concept of good faith and the legal concepts related to the doctrine of good faith such as unconscionability, fiduciary obligation, non-derogation from grant and the common law duty to cooperate. It also surveys the perspectives of good faith from the point of view of judges and scholars.

2.2 Overview of Good Faith

In civil law, good faith is recognised as a general and pervasive principle.[1] In most European civil codes, there is a general good faith provision. However, in common law systems, there is no such general principle of good faith, but this does not mean that the rules of contract law do not generally conform to the requirements of good faith. Instead, the invocation of the concept of good faith can be reached in other ways in common law systems. While the underlying principles are found in the common

[1] See Bigwood, R. (2005). Symposium Introduction: Confessions of a Good Faith Agnostic. New Zealand Business Law Quarterly, 11, 371.

N. Abdullah, *Good Faith in Contractual Performance in Australia*,
https://doi.org/10.1007/978-981-15-6078-1_2

law, the concept is not specifically referred to.[2] For example, the equitable doctrine of unconscionability is used by the court to review unconscionable conducts, and a more liberal statutory doctrine of unconscionability is laid down in the *Australian Consumer Law*.[3] There are two sources of good faith: legislation and common law. In legislation, good faith is mentioned in different ways; in some, good faith is expressly spelt out in the legislation, while in others, the reference is more oblique. In common law, good faith is a growing concept acknowledged by many judges. There are two types of terms in the contract: express and implied. Furthermore, there are two types of implied terms recognised by the court: terms 'implied in fact' and 'implied in law'. Judges and scholars differ in their perspectives on good faith. Some scholars welcome the concept, while others are cautious due to the difficulty in understanding the concept. However, it is not surprising that the growing recognition of good faith may produce fundamental changes.

2.2.1 Civil Law and Common Law Approaches to Good Faith

There are three types of legal systems in the world that discuss the concept of good faith: civil law, common law[4] and Islamic law. The concept of good faith, which has its roots in civil law, has influenced common law. In Islamic law, the concept of good faith is an integral part of the contract. The contract is regarded as lacking in perfection without the element of good faith, in accordance with what is considered appropriate behaviour, decency and ethical standards in Islam.[5] For the purposes of this chapter, the discussion is focused on civil law and common law.

[2] See Lando, O., & Beale, H. (Eds.). (1995). *The Principles of European Contract Law, Part 1: Performance, Non-performance and Remedies.* Martinus Nijhoff Publishers.

[3] The *Australian Consumer Law* 2010, s 20 prohibits unconscionable conduct within the meaning of the unwritten law, from time to time; s 21 prohibits unconscionable conduct in connection with the supply of goods or services to a person; s 22 prohibits unconscionable conduct in connection with the supply of goods or services, or the acquisition of goods or services, in business transactions.

[4] In common law, the concept of good faith has no general foundation but is recognised in specific settings, for example, the most common expression of good faith can be found in the insurance context.

[5] Abdullah Alwi Haji Hassan. (1997). *Sales and Contracts in Early Islamic Commercial Law* (1.). DELHI: Kitabbhavan, p. 15.

Civil law has its origins in Roman law, which has influenced the continental system of law.[6] The civil law legal system has been widely adopted in Europe, as well as in Latin America, Asia, Africa and the Middle East. Common law originates in the English legal system[7] and has been adopted in the United Kingdom (UK), the US (excluding Louisiana), Canada (excluding Quebec), Australia, New Zealand and other countries colonised by the British, including India, Hong Kong, Singapore and Malaysia.

There is a fundamental difference between civil law and common law legal systems. Civil law is based on codification, where its legal rules are predominantly written.[8] In the context of civil law, the role of the judge is limited to the interpretation and application of the law based on the civil law code. In contrast to civil law, common law is developed by judges through decisions of the court or based on the doctrine of binding precedent. Both common law and civil law adopted two different legal systems. However, it is interesting to note that in the law of contract, there is a tendency of common law lawyers to refer to civil law. According to Nicholas, 'it is in the law of contract also that Common lawyers have most often looked to Roman or civil law'.[9] In civil law, the influence of Roman law can be traced back to the law of obligation, particularly in the law of contract.[10] Therefore, in the context of good faith, there is a higher chance that good faith, which was rooted in civil law, will have a big influence on common law lawyers.

2.2.2 Bona Fides *in Civil Law*

Among the features of Roman law characteristic of the civil law system is *bona fides*. The concept of *bona fides* requires that 'one's word must be kept' and 'one's conduct should be in exact conformity with it [promise]'.[11] Therefore, it is a kind of social[12] and moral concept that regulates the relationship. The underlying theme of *bona fides* is to ensure that justice and

[6] Slapper, G., & Kelly, D. (2006). *The English Legal System* (8th ed.). Cavendish.

[7] Ibid.

[8] Watkin, T. G. (1999). *An Historical Introduction to Modern Civil Law*. Ashgate Publishing Company.

[9] Nicholas, B. (1974). Rules and Terms—Civil Law and Common Law. *Tulane Law Review*, 946.

[10] Ibid.

[11] See Turpin, C. C. (1965). Bonae Fidei Judicia. *The Cambridge Law Journal*, 260–262.

[12] See Powell, R. (1956). Good Faith in Contracts. *Current Legal Problems*, 16–20.

fairness are upheld regardless of the expressed intention of the parties to the contract.

Prior to *bona fides*, the concept of *strict juris* (formal contract) had already existed in Roman contract law. *Strict juris* is a concept whereby a judge is required to decide on a contractual dispute according to the strict rules of civil law.[13] A right in the contract could only be applied when the right is expressly granted. Therefore, it is difficult to fulfil the requirement of *strict juris* when the right needs to be implied. However, the requirement of *strict juris* seems of little value regarding the rights and duties concerning everyday dealings such as sale, letting and hiring, and especially those rights and duties which were not explicitly expressed but implied.

This concept causes a problem when the plaintiff pleads breach of contract but is unable to assert a definite and express right in the contract. However, there were problems with the use of *strict juris*. Firstly, upon breach of contract, according to *strict juris*, the issue must be defined in precise Latin words, sometimes invoking the Roman god.[14] This situation was problematic to non-Roman citizens not well versed in Latin and who did not believe in the Roman gods. This made it difficult for non-Roman citizens to comply with the requirement that was set by the *strict juris concept*. Secondly, as early as the third century, with the expansion of business between Rome and other countries, there was a need for the court to provide adequate remedies for breach of contract. Therefore, in order to accommodate these two limitations, Roman law introduced the concept of *bona fides*.

There were procedural differences between the two concepts. In applying *bona fides,* the court has to consider other elements, for example, the circumstances of the case and the parties' intention, compared to when applying *strict juris*, which relies on the right given.[15] The praetor (Roman magistrate) would always reject a remedy if the person seeking it was not in good faith, without having to show any element of bad faith in the contract.[16] The ultimate effect which *bona fides* had on Roman law is described by Martin Schermaier:

[13] See Hutchinson, D. (1999). Good Faith in the South African Law of Contract. In Brownsword, R., Hind, N. J., Howells, G. (Eds). *Good Faith in Contract, Concept and Context* (p. 215): Ashgate.

[14] Ibid.

[15] See O'Connor, J. F. (1990). *Good Faith in English Law*. Darmouth Publishing Company.

[16] Watkin, above n. 34, 309.

> *The expansion of the judicial discretion in assessing the merits of a case lay at heart of the brilliant development of Roman contract law from the time of the late Republic until the end of the classical period. Before the introduction of the bonae fidei iudicia, the judge was confined to determining whether the claim asserted under the procedural formula did or did not exist. The bona fide clause enabled him to consider the parties' relationship in its origin and all its effects, within the framework of all surrounding circumstances and the conduct of the parties.*[17]

The historical origin of *bona fides* within Roman law has played a vital part in the acceptance of good faith within contemporary contract law in European civil codes. Most European civil codes contain a general good faith provision. In addition, some codes contain specific rules in which reference is also made to the concept of good faith. The inclusion of good faith both in specific code provisions and as a blanket concept of importance for entire fields of law has given good faith an 'institutional' or formal role in codified civil law systems, unlike in common law.[18] Moreover, many specific rules in the codes are said to be special applications of good faith.[19]

In Germany, a general good faith provision is enshrined in the *German Civil Code* Section 157, which provides that contracts must be interpreted in accordance with good faith, having regard to common usage. Section 242 of the *German Civil Code* provides that the debtor is bound to perform the contract in accordance with good faith, having regard to common usage.

In France, the *French Civil Code* Article 1134(3) pronounces that contracts must be performed in good faith. The Code does not define good faith or the standards by which it is to be judged. Article 1134(3) seems to impose a minimum obligation of honest conduct where duties are not prescribed by the contract or by the law.[20]

In Italian law, by virtue of the *Italian Civil Code* Article 1375, contracts are to be performed to an objective standard of good faith. In the

[17] Schermaier, M. Bonae Fides in Roman Contract Law. In Zimmermann, R., & Whittaker, S. (Eds). *Good Faith in European Contract Law* (pp. 81–82). Cambridge University Press.

[18] Schermaier, above n. 43, 85.

[19] See Hesselink, M. (1998). Good Faith. In Hartkamp, A., Hesselink, M., Hondius, E., Joustra, C., du Perron, E. (Eds). *Towards a European Civil Code* (2nd ed. revised and expanded) (p. 87). Kluwer Law International.

[20] Powell, above n. 38, 30.

Swiss Civil Code, Article 2 provides that every person is bound to exercise their rights and fulfil their duties as well as act in accordance with good faith. In addition to that, the *Greek Civil Code* and the *Dutch Civil Code* (Article 6:248) both make reference to the concept of good faith.

2.2.3 Common Law: The Common Law Approaches to Good Faith

Unlike civil law, there is no overriding general positive duty of good faith imposed on the parties to a contract either in negotiation or performance in common law. Lord Ackner commented that:

> *...[T]he concept of a duty to carry on negotiations in good faith is inherently repugnant to the adversarial position of the parties when involved in negotiations. Each party to the negotiations is entitled to pursue his (or her) own interest, so long as he avoids making representations. A duty to negotiate in good faith is as unworkable in practice as it is inherently inconsistent with the position of the negotiating parties.*[21]

In the context of performance, common law confers the parties' rights as stipulated in the contract. In *James Spencer & Co Ltd v Tame Valley Padding Co Ltd*, Potter LJ commented that:

> *[t]here is no general doctrine of good faith in the English law of contract. The Plaintiffs are free to act as they wish provided that they do not act in breach of a term of the contract.*[22]

This parallels the features of common law itself, which is based on precedent. The development of good faith in common law stems from English law through the Court of Chancery.[23] In the Court of Chancery, the first chancellors were ecclesiastics well versed in canon law. The principle of good faith is inherent in canon law (the law of the Church of England). Therefore, canon law has been significant in the development of common law. Canon law emphasised that every promise was binding on the

[21] See *Walford v Miles* [1992] 2 AC 128,138.

[22] See *James Spencer & Co Ltd v Tame Valley Padding Co Ltd* (Court of Appeal, 8th April 1998, unreported).

[23] Powell, above n. 38, 22.

conscience of the person who made it and that failure or refusal to keep it was a breach of that person's duty to God.[24]

The jurisdiction of common law courts over contracts was limited during the Middle Ages and was no remedy for the breach of a simple contract. However, the ecclesiastical courts were willing to enforce such contracts. For this reason, common law courts issued writs of prohibition to prevent recourse to the Court of Chancery as a means to avoid conflict.

Due to the rapid development of international trade in the thirteenth century, a general remedy for breach of contract was needed. Even though there were many available statutes and petitions that were addressed to the King that called for contracts to be honoured, the available statutes and petitions were insufficient to provide a remedy for breach of contract. In the sixteenth century, the Court of Chancery progressed and developed from a court of conscience to being a court of equity. This event led to the development of the concept of good faith. It also implies that the concept of good faith is separate from the concept of conscience.[25] Thus, it would appear that the basic obligation of good faith arising from a promise or an agreement (*pacta sunt servanda*), which was enforced on grounds of conscience in the Court of Chancery, became the basis of the general remedy for breach of contract in common law. In view of this, it is beyond dispute that the Court of Chancery was mainly responsible for the development of good faith in common law courts.

By the eighteenth century, under the influence of Lord Mansfield, it seemed that good faith might emerge as a broad principle of significance in English contract law.[26] Lord Mansfield emphasised basic fairness and the intentions of the parties as governing principles.[27] In his famous decision in *Carter v Boehm*, Lord Mansfield, relying on the idea of good faith bargaining in contract formation, held that:

> *The governing principle is applicable to all contracts and dealings. Good faith forbids either party from concealing what he privately knows, to draw the other into a bargain, from his ignorance of that fact, and his believing the contrary.*[28]

[24] Powell, above n. 38, 21.

[25] O'Connor, above n. 41, 8.

[26] Atiyah, P. S. (2005). Implied Terms (A Duty to Act in Good Faith?). In *Atiyah, P. S. Atiyah's Introduction to the Law of Contract* (pp. 1–168). Oxford University Press.

[27] See Oldham, J. (2004). *English Common Law in the Age of Mansfield, Contract and Quasi Contract*. The University of North California Press.

[28] [1766] 3 Burr. 1905, 1910.

Despite the strong advocacy of Lord Mansfield, the concept of good faith is still in its infant stages. English contract lawyers are familiar with the concept of subjective good faith in the sense of honesty in fact or a clear conscience. However, until very recently, the idea of a general doctrine of good faith, in the sense of an overriding and objective requirement of fair dealing, has not been part of the established norms of English contract law.[29] There has been relatively little support for the concept of good faith in common law. For example, Lord Steyn observed that there is no need for English law to introduce a general duty of good faith as it is unnecessary as long as the courts respect the reasonable expectations of the parties 'in accordance with [English law's] own pragmatic tradition'.[30]

From the above discussion, it can be concluded that the perception of good faith as an important legal principle appears to be much clearer in civil law systems compared to common law systems. The application of good faith in common law is still ambiguous.

2.2.4 *Good Faith and Related Doctrine*

As mentioned earlier, in civil law, the concept of good faith is well recognised through the term *bona fides*, and many of the European codes have adopted the concept. While there is no general duty of good faith in common law, this does not mean that the concept of good faith is unable to deal with the problems of unfairness, contractual injustice or unequal bargaining. Nor does it fail in making clear the benefit of the contract or carry out the common intention of the parties as clearly stated in the contract.

In common law, there are other legal concepts that can overcome these problems. This section discusses the most important relevant legal concepts: unconscionability, fiduciary obligation, non-derogation from grant and the common law duty to cooperate. These legal concepts are well established as well as longstanding, and the setting of each legal concept is stable compared to the broad concept of good faith. This means that the idea of good faith may be an unnecessary addition to Australian contract law. It has been stated by Gummow J in *Service Station Association Ltd v Berg Bennett & Associates Pty Ltd* (in relation to specific equitable

[29] See generally Beatson, J., & Friedmann, D. (Eds). (1995). *Good Faith and Fault in Contract Law*. Oxford University Press.

[30] Steyn. J. (1997). Contract Law: Fulfilling the Reasonable Expectations of Honest Men. *Law Quarterly Review*, 113, 442.

interventions in Anglo-Australian contract law where notions of good conscience play a part) that:

> *...it requires a leap of faith to translate these well-established doctrines and remedies into a new term as to the quality of contractual performance, implied by law.*[31]

The concepts of good faith, unconscionability and fiduciary obligation were explained in *Shelanu Inc v Print Three Franchising Corporation*, where the Court of Appeal for Ontario quoted Finn (formally Finn J of the Federal Court of Australia):

> *'Unconscionability' accepts that one party is entitled as of course to act self interestedly in his actions towards the other. Yet in defence to that other's interests, it then proscribes excessively self-interested or exploitative conduct. 'Good faith', while permitting a party to act self-interestedly, nonetheless qualifies this by positively requiring that party, in his decision and action, to have regard to the legitimate interests therein of the other. The 'fiduciary' standard for its part enjoins one party to act in the interests of the other-to act selflessly and with undivided loyalty. There is, in other words, a progression from the first to the third: from selfish behaviour to selfless behaviour. Much of the most contentious of the trio is the second 'good faith'. It often goes unacknowledged. It does embody characteristics to be found in the other two.*[32]

This shows a blurred dividing line between the concepts. This inevitably contributes to a lack of clarity in definition and reflects the fact that good faith is a context-dependent notion.[33] The following subsections discuss these concepts in more depth.

Good Faith and Unconscionability

The equitable doctrine in relation to unconscionable conduct is a long-standing doctrine. It operates to protect parties with special disadvantages[34] from a stronger party trying to enforce some unfair bargain or gain some benefit. The equitable doctrine was given statutory recognition in

[31] (1993) 45 FCR 84, 97.

[32] (2003) 64 OR (3d) 533, 555–6.

[33] *Bropho v Human Rights & Equal Opportunity Commission* [2004] FCAFC 16 [84].

[34] The requirement of 'special disadvantages' was explained in *Blomley v Ryan* (1956) 99 CLR 362, 415. Kitto J held that:

Trade Practices Act 1974 (Cth) in s 51AA[35] to extend the statutory remedies to equitable unconscionability cases. However, the equitable doctrine is limited by the restricted meaning given to special disadvantage. In *Commercial Bank of Australia v Amadio*, Mason J explained that a court would grant relief to:

> *…the class of case in which a party makes unconscientious use of his superior position or bargaining power to the detriment of a party who suffers from special disability or is placed in some special situation of disadvantages, e.g. a catching bargain with an expectant heir or an unfair contract made by taking advantage of a person who is seriously affected by an intoxicating drink.*[36]

A mere inequality of bargaining power was held by the court not to constitute a special disadvantage. Therefore, the legislature introduced a new and more liberal doctrine of unconscionability. The statutory unconscionability which was enacted in s 51AB for consumer unconscionability and s 51AC for business-to-business unconscionability freed unconscionability from the equitable requirement of a special disability. Today, the unconscionability provisions are contained in the *Australian Consumer Law*, which was given legislative effect as schedule 2 of the *Competition and Consumer Act 2010* (Cth), which came into effect on 1 January 2011.

The key issue in the unconscionability provision is the meaning of unconscionable conduct. The *Australian Consumer Law* does not define unconscionability—indeed, a government report relating to this issue found that defining unconscionability is impossible because it is a wide and vague concept.[37] Instead, the *Australian Consumer Law* includes in s 22 a list of 12 'non-exclusive discretionary factors' which the court may

> This is a well-known head of equity. It applies whenever one party to a transaction is at a special disadvantage in dealing with the other party because of illness, ignorance, inexperience, impaired faculties, financial needs or other circumstances affect his ability to conserve his own interest, and the other party unconscientiously takes advantage of the opportunity thus placed in his hands.

[35] After the amendment, this section is now referred to as s 20-22 of *Australian Consumer Law*.

[36] (1983) 46 ALR 402,412.

[37] See Senate Standing Committee on Economics, Parliament of Australia, *The Need, Scope and Content of a Definition of Unconscionable Conduct for the Purpose of Part IVA of the Trade Practices Act 1974* (Cth) (2008).

take into account in determining whether a conduct is unconscionable. One of the factors considered is the extent to which the supplier/acquirer and the customer/supplier acted in good faith.

Without a definition of unconscionable conduct in the statutory provision, the requirement for unconscionability to be established is broad and vague. In *Antonovic v Volker*, Mahoney JA suggested that the concept of unconscionability was better described than defined because the principle is stated in very general terms.[38] However, several cases have attempted to define the meaning of unconscionability. In *Australian Competition & Consumer Commission v CG Berbatis Holdings*, Gummow and Hayne JJ state that:

> *The term 'unconscionable' is used as a description of various grounds of equitable intervention to refuse enforcement of or to set aside transactions which offend equity and good conscience. The term is used across a broad range of the equity jurisdiction. Thus, a trustee of a settlement who misapplies the trust fund and the fiduciary agent who makes and withholds an unauthorised profit may properly be said to engage in unconscionable conduct.*[39]

In a similar vein, in *Hurley v McDonald's Australia Ltd*, Dowsett J proposed that:

> *For conduct to be regarded as unconscionable, serious misconduct or something clearly unfair or unreasonable, must be demonstrated—Cameron v Qantas Airways Ltd … (1994) 55 FCR 147 at 179. Whatever 'unconscionable' means in Section 51AB and 51AC, the term carries the meaning given by the Shorter Oxford English Dictionary, namely actions showing no regard for conscience, or that are irreconcilable with what is right or reasonable-Qantas Airways Ltd v Cameron … (1996) 66 FCR 246 at 262. The various synonyms used in relation to the term 'unconscionable' import a pejorative moral-Qantas Airways Ltd v Cameron … at 183-4 and 298.*[40]

The difficulty of defining unconscionability was noted four decades earlier by Fullagar J. His Honour stated that the concept of unconscionability is incapable of a precise definition:

[38] (1986) 7 NSWLR 151, 165.
[39] (2003) 214 CLR 51, 72[42].
[40] (2000) ATPR 41-741, 40, 585.

> *Circumstances adversely affecting a party, which may induce a court of equity either to refuse its aid or to set a transaction aside, are of great variety and can hardly be satisfactory classified.*[41]

The dividing line between unconscionability and good faith is still unclear. In *Renard*, Priestley J stated that 'there is a close association of ideas between the terms unreasonableness, lack of good faith and unconscionability'.[42] This statement by Priestley J confirmed that there is a relationship between the concept of good faith and unconscionability. Zumbo, in giving his opinion to the Senate Standing Committee on Economic Affairs,[43] proposed a definition to unconscionability by including a list of no fewer than nine terms to guide the courts, which include unfair, unreasonable, harsh, oppressive, (or contrary to the concepts) of fair dealing, fair trading, fair play, good faith and good conscience. He also commented that the definition of unconscionability is non-exhaustive where the courts can consider other guideposts. In addition to that, Finn also broadly defined unconscionable conduct as a conduct which is unfair, in breach of faith, in circumstances where fairness or good faith are properly to be expected.[44]

Seddon and Ellinghus also noted that 'a breach of good faith must often also constitute unconscionable dealing or unconscionable conduct'.[45] Some courts have equated the two concepts, as illustrated in *Australia Pty Ltd v Bruness Pty Ltd*:

[41] *Blomley v Ryan* (1956) 99 CLR 362, 405.

[42] (1992) 26 NSWLR 234, 265.

[43] See Senate Standing Committee, Parliament of Australia, *The Need, Scope and Content of a Definition of Unconscionable Conduct for the Purpose of Part IVA of the Trade Practices Act 1974* (Cth), 2008, 33.

[44] Finn, P. (1994). Unconscionable Conduct. *Journal of Contract Law*, 8, 37–38. His Honour referred to the definition from the Oxford English Dictionary, where it is given as 'showing no regard for conscience; not in accordance with what is right or reasonable', and also the definition given by Spence, Chancery's historian:

> [t]he term Conscience, as denoting a principle of judicial decision, appears to have been of clerical invention; it seems to have embraced the obligations which resulted from a person being placed in any situation, as regards another that gave to the one a right to expect, on the part of the other, the exercise of good faith towards him.

[45] See Seddon, N., & Ellinghaus, M. (2002). *Cheshire & Fifoot's Law of Contract* (8th ed.). LexisNexis Butterworths.

> *The law does not prescribe a precise meaning of the term 'good faith' and it is probably no more than a prohibition on acting unconscionably. In that respect, it is significant that s 51AC of the Trade Practices Act 1974 (Cth) refers to the requirement for both parties to act in good faith in their dealings with each other.*[46]

Good Faith and Fiduciary Obligation

A fiduciary relationship is where one party owes a duty to act with care and in good faith in the interests of the other party. It is a kind of special relationship existing in certain relationships such as between principal and an agent, bank and borrower, lawyer and client, doctor and patient, as well as between brokers and other intermediaries of financial services. These kinds of relationship impose on each party the duty to act in the best interests of the other party to whom the obligations are owed and not just for self-interest. In other words, to act as a fiduciary is to serve in a relationship of trust and confidence that carries with it duties of loyalty, due care and utmost good faith.

The particularity of the fiduciary relationship is illustrated in the High Court of Australia's rejection to any suggestion of a fiduciary relationship in *Hospital Products Ltd v United States Surgical Corporation*, which relates to a commercial relationship between a manufacturer and a distributor. Gibbs CJ, Wilson and Dawson JJ placed much importance on the fact that the distributorship contract was essentially a commercial arrangement.[47] Gibbs CJ held that:

> *the fact that the arrangement between the parties was of purely commercial kind and that they had dealt at arm's length and on an equal footing has consistently been regarded by this court as important, if not decisive, in indicating that no fiduciary duty arose.*[48]

In *Kiwi Gold NL v Prophecy Mining NL*,[49] Thomas J held that a fiduciary obligation arose as a natural consequence of the relationship of joint ventures and thus the fiduciary duty was breached. However, Casey,

[46] [2002] WASC 286 (Unreported, Hasluck J, 4 December 2002) 372.
[47] (1984) 55 ALR 417.
[48] (1984) 55 ALR 417, 433.
[49] (Unreported 18 July 1991, Court of Appeal, CA/30/91).

McGechan and McKay JJ reversed that decision in that same case on appeal. McKay J held that:

> *We do not regard the relationship between the parties in the present case as being sufficient of itself to establish fiduciary obligations, but we agree with Thomas J that similar duties to act reasonably and in good faith can be implied into the contract itself.*[50]

It was argued that whenever a contract involves a fiduciary acting in this capacity, that person will owe a very wide range of duties of good faith to the other person simply as a result of this status.[51] A fiduciary relationship is a kind of relationship in which the duty of good faith arises after the contract has been made by reason of the fiduciary position of one or both of the parties.[52] This statement is in line with the view of Finn, who draws the concept of 'loyalty' from the fiduciary obligation of the parties.[53] Loyalty is often associated with the concept of good faith, as emphasised by Luke:

> *Good faith is defined as loyalty, where loyalty will not completely abandonment of self-interest. Many rules of our existing contract law can quite plausibly be seen as manifestations of good faith as loyalty. Good faith as loyalty finds an even simpler and more fundamental expression in the recognition of a legal duty to perform contractual undertakings: pacta sunt servanda.*[54]

It is interesting to note that when Sir Anthony Mason defined good faith, the notions his Honour included were cooperation or loyalty, honesty and to regard the interests of the parties.[55] In *United Dominions Corporation Ltd v Brian Pty Ltd*,[56] it was held that the joint venture agreement constituted a form of partnership among the United Dominions Corporation (UDC), Security Projects Ltd (SPL) and Brian, giving rise to

[50] (Unreported 18 July 1991, Court of Appeal, CA/30/91), 12.
[51] Schermaier, above n. 43, 47.
[52] Powell, above n. 38, 25.
[53] Finn, P. (1989). Contract and the Fiduciary Principle. *University of New South Wales Law Journal*, 12, 76–84.
[54] See Lucke, H. K. (1987). Good Faith and Contractual Performance. In Finn, P. (Ed). *Essays on Contract*. The Law Book Co.
[55] Mason, A. (2000). Contract, Good Faith and Equitable Standards in Fair Dealing. *Law Quarterly Review*, 116, 66–69.
[56] (1985) 157 CLR 1.

a duty of good faith that prevented UDC from taking the benefit of the collateralisation clause at the expense of the other partner. Mason, Brennan and Deanne JJ held that the relationship between them had plainly assumed a fiduciary character:

> *A fiduciary relationship can arise and fiduciary duties can exist between parties who have not reached, and who may never reach, agreement upon the consensual terms which are to be governed by the arrangement between them. In particular, a fiduciary relationship with attendant fiduciary obligations may, and ordinarily will, exist between prospective partners who have embarked upon the conduct of the partnership business or venture before the precise terms of any partnership agreement have been settled. Indeed, in such circumstances, the mutual confidence and trust which underlie most consensual fiduciary relationships are likely to be more readily apparent than in the case where mutual rights and obligations have been expressly defined in some formal agreement.*[57]

Fiduciary duties impose high standards of behaviour on the parties, while the duty of good faith is highly context specific. The underlying premise is that parties are unable to have a complete contract. Therefore, the law is required to promote an efficient outcome. In this way, the concepts of fiduciary duty and good faith are considered as a means to promote efficiency by providing the parties with the terms they would have contracted for in a world of zero transaction costs and unlimited foresight.[58] It is argued in the US that:

> *Contract law includes a principle of good faith in implementation-honesty in fact under the Uniform Commercial Code, plus an obligation to avoid (some) opportunistic advantage taking. Good faith in contract merges into fiduciary duties, with a blur and are not in line…*[59]

Hence, it is argued that good faith is similar to the fiduciary duties on the basis of their special relationship. Both obligations owe a duty to take care of the interests of the other parties without abandoning one's own interest. In this regard, there is a high expectation of the parties' duty as a

[57] (1985) 157 CLR 1,12.

[58] See Pargendler, M. (2008). Modes of Gap Filling: Good Faith and Fiduciary Duties Recognised. *Tulane Law Review*, 82, 1315–1318.

[59] See Easterbrook, F. H., & Fischel, D. R. (1993). Contract and Fiduciary Duty. *Journal of Law and Economics*, 36, 425–438.

consequence of their special relationship apart from those spelt out in the contract.

Good Faith and Non-derogation from Grant

The doctrine relating to derogation from the grant is an ancient and established concept in property law.[60] However, it is surprisingly not a well-known concept due to the scarcity of case law. Derogation from grant occurs when one party agrees to grant rights to another but then does something which detracts from this grant.[61] The most commonly cited definition of the maxim is given by Bowen LJ in *Birmingham Dudley & District Banking Company v Ross*:

> *The principle will be applied in a proper case by the law that a grantor having given a thing with one hand is not to take away the means of enjoying it with the other. And this principle will be carried out by a necessary implication of whatever fiction is required to support the origin of the right not to be interfered with by the grantor.*[62]

The scope is uncertain, and the main guiding principle is to look into the facts of the case and the circumstances of the parties at the time of the grant. For example, if a lessee leases part of the lessor's property for carrying on a particular business, the lessor is bound to abstain from doing anything on the remaining portion of the property which would render the leased premises unfit for conducting the lessee's business in a way that is ordinarily carried out,[63] and one cannot grant land to another and yet retain rights that are necessary for the use of the land granted.[64]

This is demonstrated by Lord Denning MR in *Molton Builders Ltd v City of Westminster London Borough Council* when his Lordship commented that non-derogation from grant:

[60] See also Duncan, W. D. (1998). Non-derogation from Grant and Tenant Mix. *Australian Property Law Journal*, 6, 2.

[61] See Sykes, J. (2009). Taken for Granted on the Scope of the Doctrine of Non-derogation from Grant. *New Law Journal*.

[62] (1888) 38 Ch D295, 312.

[63] See *Aldin v Latimer Clark, Muirhead & Co* [1984] 2 Ch 437, 444 per Stirling J.

[64] See *Wheeldon v Burrows* (1879) 12 Ch D 31, 49.

> *[It] is a general principle of law that, if one man agrees to confer a particular benefit on another, he must not do anything which substantially deprives the other of the enjoyment of that benefit: because that would be to take away with one hand what is given with the other.*[65]

An interesting case is *JLCS Pty Ltd v Squires Loft City Steakhouse Pty Ltd*,[66] where a restaurant licensee argued that there is an implied term in the licence which provides that the use of a similar trademark by another restaurant is not allowed to protect the goodwill of the restaurant.[67] Finkelstein J refers to the concept of non-derogation from grant as 'he must not seek to take away with one hand what he had given with the other'. This is 'a principle which merely embodies in a legal maxim a rule of common honesty'.[68] His Honour held that the licensor is required to ensure that the licensee can use the trademark without 'undue interference' as it is the hope of the parties to operate a successful business. His Honour also clearly stated that the obligation on the licensor is 'not to use, or permit the use of the similar trademark in a location so close to the current restaurant that it would likely result in a significant adverse effect on the goodwill of the licensee'.[69]

An analogy can be drawn from this: an expectation from the licensee to the licensor to ensure that the intention of the parties is implemented based on any agreement made. In simple terms, the concept of good faith exists in the contract to protect the parties' interests, that is to protect the licensee from the unscrupulous behaviour of the licensor. From the above discussion, it is clear that the doctrine of non-derogation from grant is significant to contracting parties so that they do what is right in dealing with each other. Terry and Di Lernia claim that:

[65] (1975) 30 P & CR 182, 186.

[66] 78 IPR 319.

[67] Ibid.

[68] See *Harmerv Jumbil (Nigeria) Tin Areas Ltd* [1921] 1 Ch 200, 225, where sometimes it is said that the principle rests on an implied term.

[69] Ibid. Interestingly, the non-derogation from grant doctrine does not seem to have been raised by the parties but by Finkelstein J, who stated that: 'Harold and Saul [the directors of the licensee] have not sought relief based on the rule that a person may not derogate from his grant. Were they to apply to amend their cross-claim to include relief in that regard I would accede to the application'.

> *Based on the current expectation of what a duty of good faith would achieve, the doctrine of non-derogation from grant could potentially cover the field and provide the knights of good faith with what they seek.*[70]

Good Faith and Common Law Duty to Cooperate

A duty to cooperate, as a general moral standard, has long existed in common law as one of the principles to ensure a contract is executed based on the parties' intention to the contract. This duty is derived from the nature of the contract itself. When the contracting parties make a contract, the court assumes the parties intended the contract to be effective by applying a duty to cooperate. It is clear that the duty to cooperate could be part of the intention of the contract unless the parties express a contrary intention,[71] which is rare.

The duty of cooperation has been accepted as part of the law as early as 1881. In *Mackay v Dick*, the duty to cooperate was found to be part of the obligation of good faith. Lord Blackburn stated:

> *Where in a written contract it appears that both parties have agreed that something shall be done, which cannot effectually be done unless both concur in doing it, the construction of the contract is that each agrees to do all that is necessary to be done on his part for the carrying out of that thing, though there may be no express words to that effect. What is the part of each must depend on circumstances.*[72]

The above statement indicates that the duty of cooperation is performed when both parties agree to do something to the benefit of the contract even though it is not expressly stated. A contract will not be effective without the duty of cooperation, without which the parties are deprived of the benefit of the contract. A duty of cooperation is imposed to the extent that is necessary to make the contract workable. In the context of business, the parties must rely on the desire to validate the interests

[70] Terry, A., & Cary. D. L. (2009). Franchising and the Quest for the Holy Grail: Good Faith or Good Intentions. *Melbourne University Law Review*, 33, 542–554.

[71] Peden, E. (2000). Co-operation in English Contract Law—To Construe or Imply. *Journal of Contract Law*, 16, 56.

[72] (1881) 6 App Cas 251, 263.

of both parties in a way that the business is normally run,[73] which is analogous to the concept of good faith, where one is expected to help one's contractual partners. It was further explained in the following statement drawn from *Butt v McDonald:*

> *It is a general rule applicable to every contract that each party agrees, by implication to do all such things as are necessary on his part to enable the other party to have the benefit of the contract.*[74]

On the other hand, an implied duty to cooperate applies to acts which are necessary for the performance of fundamental obligations under the contract. However, when the acts are not fundamental, although necessary to entitle the other party to a benefit under the contract, the implication of a duty to cooperate depends on the intentions of the parties. Thus, there is a need for the court to decide. This was discussed in *Secured Income Real Estate (Australia) Ltd v St Martin's Investments Pty Ltd*, in which it was held that:

> *Whether the contract imposes a duty to cooperate on the first party or whether it leaves him at liberty to decide for himself whether the acts shall be done, even if the consequence … is to disentitle the other party to a benefit.*[75]

Cooperation includes (1) an obligation not to hinder or prevent the fulfilment of the other party's purpose,[76] (2) an obligation to do all such things that are necessary to enable the other party to have the benefit of the contract and (3) an obligation that neither party will prevent the other from performing the contract. It is further argued by Carter, Peden and Tolhurst that:

[73] See *Mona Oil Equipment Co v Rhodesia Railways Ltd* [1949] 2 All E.R1014, 1018. Devlin J also refers to Lord Blackburn, who spoke of 'necessity' in *Mackay v Dick*, arguing that he perhaps did not mean it in the strictest sense, but he did mean to emphasise that there are definite limits on what a man is expected to do to help his contractual partners.

[74] (1896) 7 QLJ 68, 70–71.

[75] (1979) 144 CLR 596, 607 per Mason J.

[76] *Shepherd v Felt & Textiles of Australia Ltd* (1931) 45 CLR 359, 378.

> *[g]ood faith is inherent in all common law contract principles, and any attempt to imply an independent term requiring good faith is unnecessary and a retrograde step.*[77]

Peden argued that the introduction of good faith overlaps the duty of cooperation because both concepts require parties to do all that is reasonably necessary to facilitate the performance of contracts. Furthermore, the expected outcome of the duty of cooperation is similar to that of the duty of good faith. Therefore, Peden contends that cooperation is analogous to good faith:

> *'Cooperation' is sometimes seen as equivalent to 'good faith', and this seems appropriate. The effect of requiring cooperation often overlaps with what is trying to be achieved by the newly created obligation of 'good faith'. Cooperation (or good faith if that term is preferred) basically must embrace a duty to act honestly and a duty to have regard to the legitimate interests of the other party.*[78]

Similarly, when Sir Anthony Mason formulated the definition of good faith, his Honour defined good faith from three notions: honesty, the interests of the parties and cooperation/loyalty (that is loyalty to the contract where a contract is treated as a promise).[79] This definition affirms Peden's view that good faith is analogous to the duty of cooperation.[80]

On the other hand, Burrows argued that the duty to cooperate is a vague term and can be used to cover a wide range of situations that rest on each party to a contract.[81] While good faith is a broad principle that covers a wide range of definitions in different contexts,[82] the duty to cooperate, although vague, is well established in the common law doctrine and has a clearer foundation when compared to good faith.

[77] Peden, E., Tolhurst, G. J., Carter, J. W. (2007). *Contract Law in Australia, Good Faith.* LexisNexis Butterworths.

[78] Peden, E. (2003). *Good Faith in the Performance of Contract.* LexisNexis Butterworths.

[79] Mason, above n. 81, 69.

[80] Peden, E., & Carter, J. W. (2003). Good Faith in Australian Contract Law. *Journal of Contract Law*, 19, 155–162.

[81] Burrows, J. F. (1968). Contractual Cooperation and Implied Terms. *Modern Law Review*, 31, 390.

[82] See Chap. 8 for further discussion of the various meanings of good faith.

2.3 Sources of Good Faith

2.3.1 Legislation and Common Law

There are two sources of law in the common law legal system: law enacted by Parliament, referred to as legislation, and law developed by decisions of the court. In this context, both are aimed to provide a solution to the problem of unfairness due to lack of good faith. Both sources of law have made distinct contributions to the concept of good faith, as discussed below.

2.3.2 Legislation

There are at least 154 federal Acts in Australia that mention the term 'good faith'.[83] These Acts apply good faith in different ways: in some, good faith is expressly spelt out in the legislation, while in others, the reference is more oblique. One of the well-known examples of legislation of good faith is found in the *Insurance Contracts Act 1984* (Cth) s 13:

> *A contract of insurance is a contract based on the utmost good faith and there is implied in such a contract a provision requiring each party to it to act towards the other party, in respect of any matter arising under or in relation to it, with the utmost good faith.*

It is clear that there is an expectation that parties to the insurance contract have a duty to disclose the required information to each other in order to ensure the sanctity of the contract. The concept of utmost good faith in the insurance contract is a longstanding one.

In other legislation, reference to the obligation of good faith is oblique. For example, in s 181(1) of the *Corporations Act 2001* (Cth), it is explained that:

> *a director or other officer of a corporation must exercise their powers and discharge their duties in good faith in the best interests of the corporation and for a proper purpose.*

The existence of such a wide range of legislative references to good faith suggests that there is a strong indication from the legislature that the good faith obligation is a commonly expected norm.

[83] *Bropho v Human Rights & Equal Opportunity Commission* [2004] FCAFC 16 [84].

2.3.3 Good Faith as a Term of the Contract

A duty of good faith may be assumed by the parties either expressly or by implication. While the parties can expressly incorporate a term requiring performance in good faith, most of the cases on good faith have been based on implied terms.

Express Term

An express term of the contract refers to a term in the contract which the parties intend to be binding. The terms of the contract govern the relationship between the contracting parties and determine their rights and obligations. Express terms concerning good faith can be included in the contract. However, there has been a judicial debate as to the effect of an obligation to negotiate in good faith. In *Walford v Miles*, Lord Ackner, with regard to reasons of uncertainty and policy, commented that:

> *The concept of a duty to carry on negotiations in good faith is inherently repugnant to the adversarial position of the parties involved in negotiations ... A duty to negotiate in good faith is as unworkable in practice as it is inherently inconsistent with the position of a negotiating party.*[84]

On the other hand, in *Thiess Contractors Pty Ltd v Placer (Granny Smith) Pty Ltd*,[85] the Full Court faced a dispute over a mining contract, which contained a clause in these terms:

> *The successful operation of this contract requires that [Thiess] and [Placer] agree to act in good faith in all matters relating both to carrying out the works, derivation of rates and interpretation of this document.*[86]

The Full Court took this to mean that the parties were obliged to agree on rates in advance of work done and were required to cooperate in the establishment of rates based, as far as reasonably possible, on actual costs. This meant that Thiess had to disclose all facts relevant to the establishment of rates based on actual costs. This was the 'content' of the obligation of good faith. When Thiess knowingly misrepresented to Placer that certain costs were its genuine estimate of costs but the truth of the matter

[84] [1992] 2 AC 128, 131.
[85] [2000] WASCA 102.
[86] [2000] WASCA 102 [22].

was that they actually included profits, this was in breach of the express terms to act in good faith.

Thus, the express term of good faith is a mechanism to ensure the parties adhere to the agreed contract whereby the contracting parties are required to behave in good faith as expressly stated in the contract.

Implied Term

There are two types of implied terms: term 'implied by law' and term 'implied by fact'. In *Castlemaine Tooheys Ltd v Carlton & United Breweries Ltd*,[87] Hope JA discussed two kinds of implication of terms in a contract. It is either based on the legal incidence of a particular class of the contract or based on the test of necessity to give business efficacy to the contract. The former is commonly called implication as a matter of law, and the latter is known as implication as a matter of fact. The term is prima facie implied in all contracts of a particular class, but its implication may be excluded due to the express terms of the contract and 'the relevant surrounding circumstances of the case'.[88] His Honour observed that the classes of contracts in which the law will imply terms is not limited and considered[89] a test for deciding for the first time whether a term should be implied in a particular class of contract.

Term 'Implied in Fact'

As a general proposition, in cases where parties intend a term or terms to be part of a contract but where, for one reason or another, such a term or terms failed to be drafted into the final contract, the court may imply such a term or terms into the contract. This is known as implication in fact. In ascertaining the intention of the parties, the courts use the objective test of what a reasonable person would conclude as to the parties' intentions. The implication of a term in fact allows the courts to fill contractual 'gaps' created by the silence of the contract on a particular subject. The court has to infer the actual intention of the parties from the contract. The traditional test for implication, in fact, was enunciated in *BP Refinery (Westernport) Pty Ltd v Shire of Hastings*, in which it was established that the implied term must be

[87] (1987) 10 NSWLR 468 (see particularly 486–7).

[88] Ibid, 487.

[89] Ibid, 487–9.

1. Reasonable and equitable;
2. Necessary to give business efficacy to the contract, so that no term will be implied if the contract is effective without it;
3. So obvious that 'it goes without saying';
4. Capable of clear expression and
5. Must not contradict any express term of the contract[90]

The task of the court must be undertaken with a degree of caution enjoined by Giles JA (with whom Heydon JA and Ipp JJA agreed) in *State Bank of New South Wales Ltd v Currabubula Holdings Pty Ltd*[91] as stated by Mason J in *Codelfa Construction Pty Ltd v State Rail Authority of New South Wales*, the courts are slow to imply a term. It is not enough that it is reasonable to imply the term. It must be necessary to do so in order to give business efficacy to the contract. The term must also be obvious that it goes without saying: 'Further, there is the difficulty of identifying with any degree of certainty the terms which the parties would have settled upon had they considered the question.'[92]

In such a case, it is necessary to arrive at some conclusion as to the actual intention of the parties before considering any presumed or imputed intention of the parties. Implied term by fact gives little scope for good faith. It is only in rare situations that the contract will be ineffective without it.

Term 'Implied in Law'

Good faith has been treated as a term implied in law[93] in relation to a particular class of contract. A term is implied by law where the courts consider that the imposition of a particular obligation in a particular class of contract[94] is necessary to prevent 'the enjoyment of the rights conferred by the contract' from being 'rendered nugatory, worthless, or perhaps being seriously undermined'.[95]

[90] (1977) 180 CLR 266, 283.

[91] (2001) 51 NSWLR 399.

[92] (1982) 149 CLR 337, 346.

[93] See *Alcatel Australia v Scarella* (1998) 44 NSWLR 349, 369; *Garry Rogers Motors Aust Pty Ltd v Subaru (Aust) Pty Ltd* (1999), ¶ATPR 41-703, 43,014; *Commonwealth Bank of Australia Ltd v Spira* (2002) 174 FLR 274 [140]; *Commonwealth Development Bank of Australia v Cassagrain* [2002] NSWSC 965 [210].

[94] *Liverpool City Council v Irwin* [1977] AC 239.

[95] *Bryne Australia v Australian Airlines Ltd* (1995) 185 CLR 410, 450.

In *Breen v Williams*,[96] in a passage adopted in the High Court in *Australis Media Holdings Pty Ltd v Telstra Corporation Ltd*, Gaudron and McHugh JJ said:

> *A term implied by law, on the other hand, arises from the nature, type or class of contract in question ... Some terms are implied by statutes in contracts of a particular class, for example, money lending and home building contracts. Such terms give effect to social and economic policies which the legislature thinks are necessary to protect and promote the rights of one party to that class of contract. Other terms are implied by the common law because, although originally based on the intentions of parties to specific contracts of particular descriptions, they became so much a part of the common understanding as to be imported into all transactions of the particular description.*[97]

It is easier to identify good faith from the term 'implied by law' based on a particular type of contract. To satisfy the requirement of implied term by law is less controversial, not because of what the parties intended but because the court or legislature thinks it is for the fair functioning of the contract.

2.3.4 *Perspectives of Good Faith*

Judges and scholars are divided as to the desirability of qualifying the concept of good faith. Some scholars welcome the concept of good faith in contracts because it helps to overcome gaps in them. Good faith was put onto the judicial agenda in Australia through obiter comments by Priestley J in the landmark case of *Renard* in 1992. His Honour held that:

> *The kind of reasonableness I have been discussing seems to me to have much in common with the notions of good faith which are regarded in many civil law systems of Europe and in all States in the United States as necessarily implied in many kinds of contract. Although this implication has not yet been accepted to the same extent in Australia as part of judge-make Australian contract law, there are many indications that the time may be fast approaching when the idea, long recognised as implicit in many of the orthodox techniques of solving contractual disputes, will gain explicit recognition in the same way as it has in Europe and in the United States.*[98]

[96] (1996) 186 CLR 71.
[97] (1998) 43 NSWLR 104, 122.
[98] (1992) 26 NSWLR 234, 264.

However, some scholars disagree with the introduction or acceptance of the concept of good faith as it will overwrite the essence of the contract. One of them is Bristow, who claims that 'defining the concept of what good faith actually encompasses is an exercise that frequently proves to be frustratingly circular'.[99] The following subsections outline the varying perspectives adopted in relation to the concept of good faith.

2.3.5 Good Faith Goes Against Parties' Intentions

The recognition of an implied duty of good faith has been seen as an unnecessary and undesirable judicial intervention, especially for commercial parties. English law takes the view that, in general, it is for the parties themselves to allocate risk through the terms of their contract, and it is not the role of the courts to do it for them.[100] Thus, it gives freedom and autonomy to the commercial parties to the contract.[101] The court's duty is to respect and enforce the parties' intentions in the contract. This was supported by Rt. Hon Sir Robert Goff:

> *[w]e [the United Kingdom Commercial Court] are there to help businessmen not to hinder them: we are there to give effect to their transactions, not to frustrate them: we are there to oil the wheels of commerce, not to put a spanner in the works, or even grit in the oil.*[102]

When parties bargain, there is an expectation of an outcome similar to the intention of the contract. Therefore, implying a requirement that the parties deal with each other in good faith may go against the parties' intention and consequently make the contracting process no longer reflect their intention.

Furthermore, the fear is that good faith will interfere with the commercial conduct of the parties where the parties have equal bargaining power

[99] Bristow, D. I., & Seth, R. (2000). Good Faith in Negotiations. *Dispute Resolution Journal*, 55, 16–18.

[100] Ibid. 20.

[101] Bristow, above n. 125, 19. Fear that an ambiguous good faith doctrine would somehow jeopardise the Anglo-Canadian legal tradition of individual autonomy and free to contract. The tension between the individual and the society is clearly illustrated in a recent House of Lords case, *Walford v Miles* [1992] 2 AC 128.

[102] Goff, R. L. A. (1984). Commercial Contracts and the Commercial Court. *Llyod's Maritime and Commercial Law Quarterly*, 382–391.

and where the expected outcome is consistent with the contract agreed. It was held by Rogers CJ in *GSA Group Pty Ltd v Siebe Plc* that:

> *Against a trend towards a general obligation of good faith, fairness or reasonableness, there have been judicial comments to the effect that the courts should be slow to intrude into the commercial dealings of the parties who are quite able to look after their own interests. The courts should not be too eager to interfere in the commercial conduct of the parties, especially where the parties are all wealthy, experienced, and commercial entities [who] are able to attend to their own interests.*[103]

2.3.6 Good Faith Creates Uncertainty

Contract law must provide parties with certainty.[104] However, good faith creates uncertainty because it has no definite meaning.[105] Over two decades ago, Professor Roy Goode told an Italian audience that:

> *...[we] in England find it difficult to adopt a general concept of good faith. He seemed not at all overcome by regret and added that we do not know quite what [good faith] means.*[106]

Good faith is often associated with the concept of honesty, reasonableness, fairness and cooperation. These concepts are believed to be too subjective and uncertain.[107] Therefore, the concept of good faith has been described as a 'mystery' with its meaning susceptible to 'change', which shows that there is a lack of clarity around the concept of good faith.

[103] (1993) 30 NSWLR 573, 579 (F).

[104] See Bigwood, R. (2006). Conscience and the Liberal Conception of Contract: Observing Basic Distinctions Part 1. *Journal of Contract Law*, 16, Special Issue: 1–36. See also Phang, A. (2000). Security of Contract and the Pursuit of Fairness. *Journal of Contract Law*, 16, 158.

[105] See a detailed discussion on the meaning of good faith in Chap. 8. See also Goode, R. (1997). International Restatements of Contract and English Contract Law. *Uniform Law Review*, 2, 239. Steyn, J. (1991). The Role of Good Faith and Fair Dealing in Contract Law: A Hair-Shirt Philosophy? *Denning Law Journal*, 6, 131–140.

[106] Goode, R. (1992). *The Concept of Good Faith in English Law*. Paper presented at the Centro di Studi e Ricerche di Diritto Comparato e Straniero, Rome, 3, cited by Cole, T. R. H. (1994). The Concept of Reasonableness in Construction Contracts. *Building and Construction Law Journal*, 10, 7–12.

[107] Arlen, D. (2007). A Universal Duty of Good Faith: An Economic Perspective. *Monash University Law Review*, 33, 182–199.

According to Farnsworth, an eminent American commentator, the doctrine of good faith performance has produced a 'tangled case law' and has had an 'uncertain development'.[108] However, the term good faith is rich in connotation and even among laymen is regarded as highly expressive,[109] meaning that it is a fruitful exercise to identify the various contexts in which a flexible approach can be taken in order to provide benefit to all parties in a contract. It is important to note, however, that just because a term cannot be exhaustively defined, it does not mean that it is uncertain. On the contrary, Summers expounded the idea of good faith as an 'excluder', that is, as a phrase that has no general meaning or meanings of its own but which serves to exclude many heterogeneous forms of bad faith.[110] He suggested that:

> *In case of doubt, a lawyer will determine more accurately what the judge means by using the phrase 'good faith' if he does not ask what good faith itself means, but rather asks: What does the judge intend to rule out by his use of this phrase?*[111]

According to Summers, it is easier to identify bad faith than good faith. Even though Lucke recognised this explanation as having 'an agnostic flavour',[112] Summers' definition of good faith was recognised and adopted in Section 205 *Restatement (Second) of Contracts* s 205, Comment (d), which notes:

> *A complete catalogue of types of bad faith is impossible, but the following type are among those which have been recognised in judicial decision: evasion of the spirit of the bargain, lack of diligence and slacking off, willful rendering of imperfect performance, abuse of power to specify terms, and interference with or failure to cooperate in the other party's performance.*

Hence, similar to unconscionability, good faith is a difficult concept to define. Due to the problem in defining the concept, unconscionability was

[108] See Farnsworth. E. A. (1995). Good Faith in Contract Performance. In Beatson, J., & Friedmann, D. (Eds). *Good Faith and Fault in Contract Law* (p. 158). Oxford University Press.

[109] See Holmes, E. M. (1977). A Contextual Study of Commercial Good Faith: Good Faith Disclosure in Contract Formation. *University of Pittsburgh Law Review*, 39, 381–408.

[110] Summers, R. (1968). Good Faith in General Contract Law and the Sales Provision of the Uniform Commercial Code. *Virginia Law Review*, 54, 195–196.

[111] Ibid. 200.

[112] See Lucke, H. K. (1987). Good Faith and Contractual Performance. In Finn, P. (Ed). *Essays on Contract.* The Law Book Co.

given a legislative effect whereby the meaning was determined by a set of 'non-discretionary reference criteria', as prescribed in s 22 of the *Australian Consumer Law*, as guidance to assist its meaning. Therefore, having a guideline like 'non-discretionary reference criteria' will help make defining good faith much easier.

2.3.7 *Good Faith as the Essence of Contract Law*

Carter and Peden argue that 'Every aspect of contract law is, or should be, consistent with good faith because good faith is the essence of contract'.[113] Because good faith is inherent in all contract doctrines, it seems obvious that if a court implies a term of good faith, the court is either implying a redundant term or implying a term which by definition must impose a more onerous requirement.[114]

Carter and Peden explain that one of the criticisms of recent cases is the failure to acknowledge the good faith element of contract rules.[115] For example, in the law of contract, many elements to enforce a valid contract underlie the concept of good faith. One of them is the contract between the offeror and the offeree, where there is a concern from the law of contract that the offeror acts in good faith. Any revocation must be communicated to the offeree prior to the time of the acceptance. Because an offer does not create any legal obligations, can there be a justification for the requirement that the revocation is communicated? Carter and Peden view that it can only be in good faith that elementary considerations of honesty and fairness have the right of revocation.[116]

Thus, although it has sometimes been recognised that many rules of contract law give expression to ideas that can only be explained in terms of good faith, the implications of this may not have been fully understood or appreciated in recent Australian cases.[117]

[113] Peden and Carter, above n. 106, 162.

[114] Ibid.

[115] Ibid.

[116] Carter, J. W., & Peden, E. (2004). Good Faith in Australian Contract Law. *Australian Construction Law Newsletter*, 94, 6–8.

[117] Peden, E. (2005). When Common Law Trumps Equity: The Rise of Good Faith and Reasonableness and the Demise of Unconscionability. *Journal of Contract Law*, 21, 226–248.

2.3.8 *Good Faith Is Not a Concept in English Law*

Good faith is regarded as a foreign rule in English law.[118] This statement was supported by Harrison, who claimed that 'it is customary for English lawyers to say … "we do not have a principle of good faith in English law"'.[119] The concept of good faith is rooted in civil law via the concept of *bona fides*. Many European countries adopted the requirement of good faith in their civil codes, some of which are s 242 of the *German Civil Code*, Article 1375 of the *Italian Civil Code*, Article 1134 (3) of the *French Civil Code* and more recently Article 6:2 of the *Dutch Civil Code*.[120] Adopting good faith in English law will implant a 'foreign rule' which may be applied differently. For example, in the *German Civil Code*, good faith is applied in many aspects of the contract, from the negotiation process, performance, to the enforcement of a contract.

There is no general duty of good faith in the making of contracts in English law in relation to performance as well as the formation of contracts.[121] The underlying reason against the adoption of a general principle of good faith in English contract law is to apply a specific legal concept rather than a general principle to police unfairness. There are various specific legal concepts that clearly govern behaviour, such as the doctrine of economic duress. One of the elements in the doctrine of economic duress is the improper or illegitimate nature of the pressure used.[122] In this context, a general doctrine cannot be appropriate when contracting contexts vary so much. In particular, a general doctrine of good faith would make little sense in those contracting contexts in which the participants regulate their dealings in a way that openly tolerates opportunism.[123] In addition, good faith is recognised in specific classes of contract, for example, in

[118] Teubner, G. (1998). Legal Irritants: Good Faith in British Law or How Unifying Law Ends Up in New Divergence. *Modern Law Review*, 61, 11.

[119] Harrison, R. (1997). *Good Faith in Sales*. London: Sweet & Maxwell.

[120] See Kötz, H. (1998). Towards a Europe Civil Code. In Cane, P., & Stapleton, J. (Eds.). *The Law of Obligation; Essays in Celebration of John Fleming* (pp. 243–244). Oxford University Press.

[121] Atiyah, above n 52, 164.

[122] Whittaker, S., & Zimmermann, R. (2000). Good Faith in European Contract Law: Surveying the Legal Landscape. In Zimmermann, R., & Whittaker, S. (Eds.). *Good Faith in European Contract Law* (pp. 7–45). Cambridge University Press.

[123] Hird, N. J., Howells, G. G., Brownsword, R. (Eds). (1999). *Good Faith in Contract, Concept and Context*. Ashgate.

insurance contracts[124] and fiduciary contracts.[125] In legislation, there is increasing recognition in specific instances, like the *Unfair Terms in Consumer Contract Regulations 1999*, which was introduced to protect the presumed weaker parties.[126] Furthermore, Bridge also shared a similar view in his article on the doctrine of good faith performance and speculated that good faith is '[F]ar from involving the community ethic in the day to day task of law-making and decision-making … good faith is more likely to produce idiosyncratic judgments'.[127]

On the other hand, common law has long used recourse to interpret parties' intentions to achieve a variety of normative results,[128] with the aim of ascertaining the actual intentions of the parties by looking at the typical intentions or expectations of the parties to the type of contract in question. In this context, it means that the interpretation of expressed contractual terms or the implication of terms where one of the parties is held to be responsible to the other for defects in the subject matter of the contract, whereby some information was not disclosed before the contract took place, will lead to legal consequences. In such circumstances, other systems are dealt with by a general requirement of good faith.[129] Thus, there is strong support by Lord Steyn, who stated that 'there is not a world of difference between the objective requirement of good faith and the reasonable expectation of the parties'.[130]

In 1991, in a lecture on good faith at Oxford University, Lord Steyn explained that due to the lack of a doctrine of good faith, 'English law has to resort to the implication of terms'.[131] His Honour urged that 'in using the high techniques of common law, the close attention paid to the purpose of the law of contract is to promote good faith and fair dealing'.[132] His Honour asserted that there is no need for a good faith concept because common law prefers to look at the intention and the expectation of the

[124] The contract of insurance is an example of that special class of contracts known to the common law as contracts *uberrimae fidei* that is the utmost good faith, requirement imposed both on the insurer and the insured.

[125] See Sect. 2.3.2 for a discussion of the relationship between fiduciary duty and good faith.

[126] See Chap. 3 for further details.

[127] Bridge, M. (1984). Does Anglo-Canadian Contract Law Need a Doctrine of Good Faith? *Canadian Business Law Journal*. 9, 385–413.

[128] Whittaker and Zimmermann, above n. 148, 45.

[129] Nicholas above n. 35, 950.

[130] Steyn (1997), above n. 56, 450.

[131] Steyn (1991), above n. 131, 133.

[132] Ibid.

parties. Therefore, implying good faith resulted in implanting a 'foreign language' in English law.

Good faith is a foreign concept. Therefore, good faith is still not the favourable concept in English law. English law has its own way of dealing with the issue of unfairness in a contract. This is evident in available specific legal concepts which have achieved an outcome similar to that of good faith when policing unfairness. Despite the specific legal concept, English law emphasises the interpretation of the parties' intention to understand the parties' expectations, which they believe provides a better outcome. When parties draft a contract, they should understand what is expected from the contract.

2.3.9 Good Faith as a Universal Term

Cooperation and reasonableness are two underlying concepts in contracts that imply good faith. Therefore, good faith is regarded as a universal term.[133] Thus, it can be said that there is no need for the concept of good faith because the current legislation and legal concepts discussed earlier, such as unconscionability, duty of cooperation, non-derogation from grant and fiduciary duty, are sufficient to tackle issues of unfairness and injustice. On the contrary, there is a need to have good faith as a universal term to act as a gap filler in the absence of an express term of the contract.

2.4 Conclusion

Good faith in civil law countries is a well-established concept and has been adopted in the civil law codes. In common law, there is no general duty of good faith, but good faith is recognised in discrete settings and contexts. This does not mean that common law operates in a 'vacuum' when considering issues of unfairness and injustice. The four related legal concepts—unconscionability, fiduciary obligation, non-derogation from grant and common law duty to cooperate—provide an alternative to the concept of good faith in common law.

Common law prefers to apply specific doctrines rather than a general concept (such as good faith) where the application of specific concepts

[133] Seddon and Ellinghaus above n. 71, 419.

generates the same result.[134] For example, where there is unequal bargaining power between the parties, the statutory of unconscionability is available to settle the problem, as clearly stated in the *Australian Consumer Law*, which was given a legislative effect as schedule 2 of the *Competition and Consumer Act 2010* (Cth), which came into effect on 1 January 2011. Certain problems relating to property law may be addressed under the concept of non-derogation from grant, which may make available remedies to the injured parties. Therefore, to say that common law is handicapped due to the absence of a general duty of good faith in contract law is an overstatement as the existing legal concepts are available to police an unfair contract.

Although the concept of good faith is uncertain, frustrating and meaningless, it has been adopted in some legislation and in common law. Insurance is the obvious example, where the concept of *uberrimae fidei* or utmost good faith has long been in existence where it is expected that the parties to the insurance contract must disclose all relevant information. The expression of good faith can be seen as an express term and an implied term in the contract. When good faith is expressly stated as a term or clause of the contract, the parties are expected to behave in good faith as expressly stated in the contract. However, there are some instances where much of the context of the contract may not be spelt out but is left to implication. There are two types of implied terms: term 'implied by law' and term 'implied by fact'. Good faith is considered as a term 'implied by law' rather than a term 'implied by fact'. It is easier to satisfy the requirement of term 'implied by law' based on a particular class of contract than the modern test for term 'implied by fact'. Sometimes the modern test for term 'implied by fact', as discussed in *BP Refinery (Westernport) Pty Ltd v Shire of Hastings*,[135] is too difficult to be satisfied.

Therefore, it is not surprising that there remains a range of different perspectives among scholars and judges as to the concept of good faith. It is a fairly new concept in common law and therefore is open for further debate and interpretation.

[134] See McKendrick, E. (1997). English Contract Law—A Rich Past, an Uncertain Future? *Current Legal Problems*, 50, 25–35 and 42–44.

[135] (1977) 180 CLR 266, 283.

CHAPTER 3

Good Faith in International Context

3.1 Introduction

As discussed in the earlier chapter, good faith, a civil law concept, is gaining recognition in common law countries. Many common law countries have recognised the concept of good faith, but the recognition is in limited situations such as in the insurance context. In the insurance context, good faith is a well-known concept. The concept of utmost good faith and its relationship in the insurance contract has been recognised for more than 250 years from the case of *Carter v Boehm*.[1] There is an expectation that both the insured and the insurer should behave in utmost good faith to effectuate the insurance contract. In addition, there are some specific legal concepts in common law which illustrate the execution of good faith, for example, the common law duty of cooperation achieves the same result as might be required by good faith without explicitly referring to that concept. When the contracting parties make a contract, the court assumes that the parties intend the contract to be effective by applying a duty to cooperate. This is similar to the concept of good faith to express the parties' intentions. In *Butt v McDonald*, the concept of common law duty to cooperate further explained that 'it is a general rule applicable to every contract that each party agrees, by implication to do all such things as are

[1] (1766) 3 Burr 1905, 1910.

N. Abdullah, *Good Faith in Contractual Performance in Australia*,
https://doi.org/10.1007/978-981-15-6078-1_3

necessary on his part to enable the other party to have the benefit of the contract'.[2]

In civil law countries, the concept of good faith is clearly expressed in the civil law codes. In the civil law codes, good faith is recognised as a general and pervasive principle in all phases of contract from negotiation to performance as well as enforcement. This means that good faith is treated as a standard of behaviour which is expected from the parties in a contract. In civil law codes, good faith is mentioned but no definition is given. The definition of good faith depends on the facts of each case.[3] The position taken by these countries is explained by the Commission on European Contract Law in the statement below:

> *The principle of good faith and fair dealing is recognised or at least appears to be acted on as a guideline for contractual behaviour in all EC countries. There is, however, a considerable difference between the legal systems as to how extensive and how powerful the penetration of the principle has been. At the one end of the spectrum figures a system where the principle has revolutionised the contract (and other parts of the law as well) and added a special feature to the style of that system (GERMANY). At the other end, we find systems which do not recognise a general obligation of the parties to conform to good faith in the performance of a contract, but which in many cases by specific rules reach the results which the other systems have reached by the principle of good faith (ENGLAND and IRELAND).*[4]

In civil law countries, notably Germany, France and Italy, the concept of good faith is well recognised as a general and pervasive principle in the civil law codes. Common law countries, however, tend to be suspicious of the idea that parties must act in good faith. In common law countries, there is no overarching duty of good faith but good faith is recognised in particular contexts. Other common law countries have adopted a similar position, for example, Canada and New Zealand. The situation, however, is different in the US. The US has inherited a similar common law background, yet, the concept of good faith has been given a statutory

[2](1896) 7 QLJ 68, 70–71.

[3]Woo, P. Y. (2001). Protecting Parties' Reasonable Expectations: A General Principle of Good Faith. *Oxford University Commonwealth Law Journal*, 1, 195–221.

[4]See Lando, O. (1995). Article 1.201: Good Faith and Fair Dealing. In Lando, O., & Beale, H. (Eds.). *The Principles of European Contract Law, Part 1: Performance, Non-Performance and Remedies* (p. 113.). Martinus Nijhoff Publishers.

provision as demonstrated in the *Uniform Commercial Code* and *Restatement (Second) of Contracts*. Uniquely, the People's Republic of China is influenced by both civil law and socialist law, whereby there is an emerging interest in the concept of good faith. In China, good faith is considered as a general principle in contract law and is also given statutory recognition in the *Contract Law of the People's Republic of China*. The concept of good faith is also well recognised in many international trade instruments, where the concept of good faith is used as the expected behaviour of the contracting parties in dealing with international business transactions.

This chapter considers the significance of good faith in selected civil law countries such as Germany, Italy and France. This chapter also reviews the development and reception of good faith in the UK, where no general principle of good faith has been recognised. This chapter will also highlight the concept of good faith in the US. This is because, despite the US inheriting the common law, good faith is found in its statutory provisions, as mentioned in the earlier chapter. This chapter also discusses the issue of good faith in Canada and New Zealand. At the end of this chapter, the emerging interest in good faith in the Peoples' Republic of China due to the transitional business activities is examined. Finally, international trade instruments that recognise good faith are discussed.

3.2 Good Faith in Civil Law Countries

The concept of good faith is well established in civil law countries through its inclusion in their civil codes.[5] The civil law approach to good faith is derived from a general philosophy of contract where it 'focuses on the relationship between the parties'[6]; this means the contracting parties are generally expected to behave in good faith. For example, the approach of the drafter of the *German Civil Code* to the role of good faith, which is also applicable to other civil law systems, has been described as follows:

[5] See, for example, the *Italian Civil Code* Article 1375, which provides for contracts to be performed to an objective standard of good faith. The *Swiss Civil Code* Article 2 provides that every person is bound, in exercising their rights and fulfilling their duties, to act in accordance with good faith. The *Greek Civil Code* by virtue of Article 288, the *Quebec Civil Code* by virtue of Article 6, 1375 and 1434 and the *Dutch Civil Code* by virtue of Article 6:248 all made references to the concept of good faith.

[6] Klein, J., & Bachechi, C. (1994). Precontractual Liability and the Duty of Good Faith Negotiations in International Transactions. *Hous Journal International Law*, 17, 1–17.

> Utilizing the general concepts developed by civil-law theory, they sought to lay down abstractly formulated rules, couched in terms of rigidly defined concepts and comprising as many individual's solutions as possible, which were to be binding on the judges. Still, they had sufficient insight into the variety and variability of life-situations to insert in the Code a number of blanket concepts modelled after the *bona fidei* interpretation and the *boni mores* of Roman Law, such as good faith (*Treu und Glauben*), 'good morals' (*güte Sitten*), 'fairness' (*Billigkeit*), and the like, which left some lee-way for judicial law-finding.[7]

In the civil law codes, contracts must be performed and interpreted in accordance with the requirement of good faith with the aim of creating a 'gapless' system of law.[8] In this context, good faith is regarded as a fundamental principle of the law of contract, where every phase of the contract from negotiation to performance and enforcement must be carried out with good faith.

There are two types of reference to good faith in the civil law codes: general clauses and specific clauses. A general clause is a clause where good faith is generally applicable to all contracts and all parties in a contract. An example of a general clause can be found in the *Swiss Code* Article 2, where 'every person is bound, in exercising their rights and duties, to act in accordance with good faith'. A specific clause, on the other hand, is a clause where good faith is limited to a particular context or circumstance. An example could be in the case of a debtor. To illustrate, a specific clause in the *German Civil Code* Article 242 states that 'the debtor is bound to perform the contract in accordance with good faith having regard to common usage'.[9] The significance of the inclusion of good faith in both a specific clause and a general clause provides a formal role for good faith in the civil law code, which is lacking in the common law systems.[10] The Civil Codes of Germany, Italy and France are now discussed in more detail.

[7] Wandlungen, R. E. (1930). Wissenschaft and Lehre. In Schoch, M. M. (Ed). *Jurisprudence of Interests: Selected Writings* (pp. 17–18) cited in O'Connor, J. F. (1990). *Good Faith in English Law*. Darmouth Publishing Company.

[8] Styles, S. C. (1999). Good Faith: A Principled Matter. In Forte, A. D. M. (Ed), *Good Faith in Contract and Property* (pp. 157–158). Oxford: Hart Publishing.

[9] In Germany, the *German Civil Code* Article 242 has been expanded far beyond the actual wording to become the legal foundation for the courts to develop the law.

[10] O'Connor, J. F. (1990). *Good Faith in English Law*. Darmouth Publishing Company.

3.2.1 Germany

In German contract law, good faith plays an important role in regulating the contract. The principle of good faith is essentially enshrined in Article 242, which relates specifically to the manner in which an obligation is to be performed. The *German Civil Code* Article 242 (specific clause) provides that '[t]he debtor is bound to perform the contract in accordance with good faith having regard to common usage'. Article 242 focuses on the behaviour of the contracting parties in commerce by taking into consideration the general practice in commerce. Article 242 describes the duty of good faith as *Treu und Glauben*, which can be translated to mean faith and credit.[11] Therefore, good faith is evidently taken into consideration when dealing with the fair balancing of interests and needs of the parties in a contract.[12] Historically speaking, the concept of *Treu und Glauben* is deeply rooted in the *bona fides* of Roman law which is equivalent to *bonne foi* in French, which is, in essence, good faith.[13] The concept of *Treu und Glauben* was further explained by Whittaker and Zimmerman:

> '*Treu*' … signifies faithfulness, loyalty, fidelity, reliability; '*Glauben*' means belief in the sense of faith or reliance. The combination of '*Treu und Glauben*' is sometimes seen to transcend the sum of its components and is widely understood as a conceptual entity. It suggests a standard of honest, loyal and considerate behaviour, of acting with due regard for the interests of the other party, and it implies and comprises the protection of reasonable reliance. Thus, it is not a legal rule with specific requirements that have to be checked but may be called an 'open' norm. Its content cannot be established in an abstract manner but takes shape only by the way in which it is applied.[14]

In deciding whether the debtor has an obligation to perform his/her contract in the manner required by good faith giving consideration to

[11] Powers, P. J. (1999). Defining the Undefinable: Good Faith and the United Nations Convention on the Contracts for the International Sale of Goods. *Journal of Law and Commerce*, 18, 333–337.

[12] Waas, B. (2010). Good Faith in the Law of the Employment Relationship: Germany. *Comparative Labor Law & Policy Journal*, 32, 603–605.

[13] Ibid.

[14] Whittaker, S., & Zimmermann, R. (2000). Good Faith in European Contract Law: Surveying the Legal Landscape. In Zimmermann, R., & Whittaker, S. (Eds.). *Good Faith in European Contract Law* (pp. 7–45). Cambridge University Press.

common usage within the parameter of Article 242, Article 157 was invoked to deal with this issue. Article 157 provides that '[c]ontracts shall be interpreted according to the requirements of good faith, ordinary usage being taken into consideration'. Article 157 deals with the standard for contractual interpretation. This means the determination of the content of a contract should be interpreted in light of good faith. Therefore, the combination of Article 242 and Article 157 suggests that good faith is required in all aspects of the contract.

Although Article 242 requires good faith to be specifically related to how the debtor is to perform, the specific provision has evolved due to the process of interpretation far beyond its actual wording, particularly in the area of private law.[15] This is because German courts have used this provision in a wider scale, compared to its originally narrow scope, as the statutory basis for deriving a new general principle of law when existing rules of law proved to be inadequate in adjudicating actual cases. Courts also rely on Article 242 to create additional duties for the parties that were not expressly provided for in the statute or in the contract. This modification to Article 242 has been done to settle the economic and social problems that arose after the two world wars and the reunification of Germany, as well as to suit the social and moral attitudes that change in the society.[16] Therefore, Article 242 is regarded as a universal application to solve contractual problems occurring between contracting parties.[17] Schlechtriem commented:

> *You can find a source (be it a court decision or a scholarly theory) for every solution imaginable or wanted, BGB Article 242 [German civil code good faith provision] serving as the legal anchor to even the wildest propositions and results.*[18]

This provision had a profound effect on the development of German contract law by courts that created a number of obligations to ensure a

[15] O'Connor, above n. 171, 85.

[16] Kötz, H. (1998). Towards a Europe Civil Code. In Cane, P., & Stapleton, J. (Eds.). *The Law of Obligation; Essays in Celebration of John Fleming* (pp. 243–244). Oxford University Press.

[17] Styles, above n. 169, 175.

[18] Schlechtriem, P. (February 1996). Good Faith in German Law and in International Uniforms Law. Retrieved from http://www.uniromal.it/idc/ventro/publications/24sclectriem.pdf.

loyal performance of a contract such as a duty of the parties to cooperate, to protect each other's interests and to give information. However, even though good faith is mentioned and has a central role in the *German Civil Code*, there is no formal definition of good faith. This evidently shows that judges in the civil law system like Germany are more frequently engaged in creativity to interpret the meaning of good faith on a case-by-case basis.

3.2.2 Italy

In Italy, the *Italian Civil Code* also mentions the concept of good faith. The drafting of the *Italian Civil Code* was influenced by Article 242 of the *German Civil Code*, where good faith is considered as an important concept.[19] In the *Italian Civil Code*, the concept of *buona fede* has been interpreted as synonymous to the German *Treu und Glauben*, where the Italian court gives consideration to the principle of freedom of contract to the contracting parties.[20] This means good faith is the expected behaviour of the contracting parties with an aim to protect the relationship in the contract. Therefore, it can be said that Italy has a well-developed concept of good faith in the same way as Germany has. It covers pre-contractual negotiations, formation as well as performance.

In the *Italian Civil Code*, good faith is considered as a tool to regulate the conduct of the parties in a contract. Therefore, the *Italian Civil Code* highlights the importance of good faith in different stages of a contractual relationship in several articles of the code. For example, Article 1337 provides that 'the parties, in the conduct of negotiations and the formation of a contract, should conduct themselves according to good faith'. It was further explained by Palmieri that 'good faith is a limitation on private autonomy that restricts, during negotiation as well as in the execution of a contract, the freedom of the parties; private control of legal transactions is not indiscriminate freedom to act, but freedom to act in good faith'.[21] In the context of negotiation, good faith acts as a tool to protect the relationship of the contracting parties by creating a legal obligation between them.

[19] Musy, A. M. (2001). The Good Faith Principle in Contract Law and the Precontractual Duty to Disclose: Comparative Analysis of New Differences in Legal Cultures. *Global Jurist Advances*, vol. 1, no. 1, 2001, https://doi.org/10.2202/1535-1661.1007.

[20] Ibid., 8.

[21] Palmieri, N. W. (1993). Good Faith Disclosures Required During Precontractual Negotiations. *Seton Hall Law Review*, 24, 70, 200–201.

Besides Article 1337, there are other articles that clearly mention good faith, for example, Article 1366 provides that a 'contract must be interpreted in good faith', and Article 1375 states that a 'contract must be executed in good faith'. It also covers the relationship between the debtor and the creditor to behave in good faith, as illustrated in Article 1175: 'debtor and creditor must behave according to good faith and fair dealing rules'. Article 1460 provides that:

> *[I]n contracts providing for mutual counter-performance, each party can refuse to perform his obligation if the other party does not perform his own at the same time unless different times for performance have been established by the parties or otherwise stipulated by the nature of the contract. However, performance cannot be rejected if, considering the circumstances, such rejection is contrary to good faith.*

Despite the fact that good faith has been mentioned in many of the articles, the *Italian Civil Code* does not contain any definition of good faith. In the *Italian Civil Code*, good faith is recognised as a broader ethical idea between the contracting parties.[22] The ethical ingredient of good faith is explained thus:

> *The need for good faith, taken in its ethical sense, constitutes one of the hinges of the legal discipline of obligations and establishes a legal duty in the true sense of the word … which is violated not only if one of the parties has acted maliciously to the other party's detriment but also when the conduct of said party was not guided by openness, diligent fairness, and a sense of social solidarity, which are integral parts of good faith; thus, even if the result of mere negligence, or even silence … such constitute a transgression of the duty of good faith if suitable to induce reasonable reliance on the other party.*[23]

In general, good faith is defined as 'openness, diligent fairness and a sense of social solidarity'.[24] This definition compels the contracting parties to acknowledge the importance of good faith and, at the least, to act reasonably.[25] In the *Italian Civil Code*, good faith is analogous to an ethical obligation, which is an integral part of public policy.[26] In this context,

[22] Ibid.
[23] Ibid.
[24] Powers, above n. 172, 338.
[25] Ibid.
[26] Ibid., 387.

parties must acknowledge the public policy behind good faith and value its importance when contracting. The Italian scholars, however, are sceptical about the concept of good faith as it is too abstract and it might vest judges too broad a discretionary power in interpreting the concept.[27] Due to this problem, the concept of good faith has not been able to offer the judges a clear picture of the definition of good faith.

3.2.3 France

In France, good faith was mentioned in the *French Civil Code*. The obligation of good faith is enshrined in Article 1134 of the French Civil Code, which states that:

> *Agreements lawfully formed take the place of law for those who have made them. They cannot be revoked except by mutual consent or on grounds allowed by law. They must be performed in good faith.*

According to Article 1134 of the *French Civil Code*, all contractual obligations must be performed in good faith. In the first paragraph of Article 1134 of the *French Civil Code*, it is clearly stated that '[a]greements lawfully formed take the place of law for those [contracting parties] who have made them'. In that same paragraph, the word 'good faith' is mentioned to emphasise the importance of the contracting parties to behave in good faith in their agreements. However, good faith is evidently not defined. This seems to force French judges to find a creative way to impose the good faith principle on the contracting parties.[28] In this sense, the obligation of good faith has provided a creative instrument for the French judges to determine the content of the contract. Unfortunately, it has made a big impact on the concept of good faith as the meaning of good faith is now open for further interpretation by the French judges. The Obligation Section in the *French Civil Code*, by virtue of Article 1135 of the *French Civil Code*, does not contain other explicit references to the good faith principle:

[27] Musy, above n. 180, 9.

[28] Vigneau, C. (2010). The Obligation of Good Faith in France. *Comparative Labor Law & Policy Journal*, 32, 593–594.

Agreements obligate not only to what is expressed in the agreement creating them but also to the consequences which equity, custom or the law (loi) give to the obligation in accordance with its nature.

The concept of good faith in the *French Civil Code* appears to be undeveloped due to the fact that it does not define good faith.[29] This is because French jurists are somewhat uncertain with regard to the idea of good faith. Some of the jurists who support the idea of good faith warned that the concept should not be allowed to lead to the idea of an 'absolute altruism negating one's own interest'.[30] Thus, it also made good faith a broad principle. As explained by Jourdain:

In the end, good faith remains a hazy notion, which is expressed effectively only when it runs into the legal mould of other concepts with more precise contents. This congenital weakness stems from the vague nature of a notion which in practice remains essentially moral and which has been made into a norm of behaviour governing pre-contractual relations. But if the notion of good faith appears to be of somewhat restrained utility as an instrument of legal technique, no one would contest that the idea of good faith inspires many actual solutions to legal problems. For this reason, should one at least raise it to the rank of a general principle of law? The debate on this question though remains open.[31]

Article 1134 and Article 1135 of the *French Civil Code* serve as an open-ended concept that is open to considering the concept of good faith rather than having good faith as a criterion for a contractual agreement. One of the reasons for the lack of development of good faith in France is that French lawyers are 'more inclined to view the law in terms of the legal rules used in practice and applied by the court and place less emphasis on statements of general principle and rules of ideal conduct'.[32] Therefore, despite being mentioned in the *French Civil Code*, there is no definition of good faith.

The above discussion indicates that good faith is a well-recognised concept in civil law countries in all phases of a contract, from negotiation to

[29] O'Connor, above n. 171, 95.

[30] Whittaker and Zimmermann, above n. 175, 38.

[31] Whittaker and Zimmermann, above n. 175, 38–39.

[32] Ibid., cites David, R. (1972). French Law, Its Structure, Sources and Methodology. *Louisiana State University Press*. p. 76, in support of this proposition.

performance as well as enforcement, indicating that good faith can be relied upon by both parties to the contract.[33] However, despite its wide recognition in civil law countries, good faith is not defined in civil law codes but has developed based on the interpretation of the judge on a case-by-case basis. Therefore, an attempted search for an all-encompassing definition of good faith may be pointless because good faith is an abstract concept that depends on the facts of each case.[34]

3.3 Good Faith in Common Law Countries: United Kingdom

There is no general principle of good faith in the English law of contract. Powell upheld that 'there is in English law today "no overriding general positive duty of good faith imposed on the parties to a contract"'.[35] In saying that there is no duty of good faith in this context means there is no general duty to negotiate a contract in good faith or any general duty to perform the contract in good faith or to renegotiate in good faith in the event of a significant change of circumstances affecting the balance of the contract or any general duty on contracting parties to exercise good faith in their rights arising under the contract. For example, the position of the duty of good faith in negotiation is discussed in *Walford v Miles*, where Lord Ackner held that:

> *The concept of a duty to carry on negotiations in good faith is inherently repugnant to the adversarial position of the parties when involved in negotiations. Each party to the negotiations is entitled to pursue his (or her) own interests, so long as he avoids making misrepresentations. A duty to negotiate in good faith is as unworkable in practice as it is inherently inconsistent with the position of the negotiating parties.*[36]

[33] Powers, above n. 172, 338.
[34] Woo, P. Y. (2001). Protecting Parties' Reasonable Expectations: A General Principle of Good Faith. *Oxford University Commonwealth Law Journal*, 1, 195–221.
[35] Powell, R. (1956). Good Faith in Contracts. *Current Legal Problems*, 16–20.
[36] [1992] 2 A.C 128, 138.

The position of English law in relation to the principle of good faith can be found in the landmark case of *Interfoto Picture Library Ltd v Stiletto Visual Programmes Ltd*,[37] where Lord Bingham held that:

> *In many civil law systems and perhaps most legal systems in the common law world, the law of obligations recognises and enforces an overriding principle that in making and carrying out contracts, parties should act in good faith. This does not simply mean that they should not deceive each other, a principle which any legal system must recognise; its effect is perhaps most aptly conveyed by such metaphorical colloquialisms as 'playing fair', 'coming clean', or 'putting one's card face upwards on the table' ... English law has, characteristically, committed itself to no such overriding principle but has developed piecemeal solutions in response to demonstrated problems of unfairness. Many examples could be given. Thus equity has intervened to strike down unconscionable bargains. Parliament has stepped in to regulate the imposition of exemption clauses and the form of certain hire-purchase agreements. The common law also has made its contribution, by holding that certain classes of contracts require the utmost good faith by treating as irrecoverable what purport to be agreed on estimates of damage but are in truth as disguised penalty for breach, and in many other ways.*[38]

Despite good faith being a well-recognised principle in civil law legal systems and also in many common law legal systems, English law takes a different position. English law's preference for pragmatic solutions means that no such overriding principle of good faith has been adopted. The fact that English law does not recognise a duty of good faith does not mean that the rule of contract law does not generally conform to the requirements of good faith. Instead, English law responds to perceived cases of unfairness by developing piecemeal solutions in which good faith is implied.

[37] [1989] QB 433. In this case, the issue started when the plaintiff had omitted to draw intention to the defendants about Condition 2 of the delivery note that states that the consequences in the event of the defendant's failure to return the photographs. Dillon L J held that Condition 2 is an onerous clause and therefore the defendants should be alerted by the plaintiff as the defendant had to pay an extortionate holding fee for photographs returned after the due date. Since the plaintiff had done nothing to draw the attention of the defendant, Condition 2 was not a part of the contract.

[38] [1989] QB 433,439.

Firstly, apart from the philosophy of *caveat emptor*,[39] English courts prefer to apply a specific legal concept rather than a general principle as the application of specific legal concepts generates the same results.[40] For example, misrepresentation, duress, undue influence and mistake are specific legal concepts available to police specific issues of fairness rather than fairness generally in contracts and their performance. In *New Zealand Shipping Co Ltd v A.M. Satterthwaite & Co Ltd*, Lord Wilberforce characterised English law as follows:

> *English law, having committed itself to a rather technical and schematic doctrine of contract, in application takes a practical approach, often at the cost of forcing the facts uneasily into the marked slots of offer, acceptance and consideration.*[41]

Secondly, the common law of contract has been transformed over the last half of the twentieth century or so by statutory intervention, sometimes at a general level but more often at a particular level. Although the concept of good faith has no general foundation in English law, in specific instances, good faith is recognised in specific settings in legislation.

In legislation, there is increasing recognition of good faith in specific instances, for example, in the UK consumer contract, the *Unfair Terms in Consumer Contracts Regulations 1999*. The primary aim of the regulation is to protect the presumed weaker party. This is by virtue of clause 5(1) of the *Unfair Terms in Consumer Contracts Regulations 1999*, which provides that:

> *A contractual term which has not been individually negotiated shall be regarded as unfair if, contrary to the requirement of good faith, it causes a significant imbalance in the parties' right and obligations arising under the contract, to the detriment of the consumer.*

Schedule 2 of the *Unfair Terms in Consumer Contracts Regulations 1999* contains an indicative and non-exhaustive list of terms that may be

[39] Steyn, J. (1991). The Role of Good Faith and Fair Dealing in Contract Law: A Hair-Shirt Philosophy? *Denning Law Journal*, 6, 131–140.

[40] See McKendrick, E. (1997). English Contract Law—A Rich Past, an Uncertain Future? *Current Legal Problems*, 50, 25–35 & 42–44.

[41] [1975] QB 154.

regarded as unfair.[42] The requirement of good faith was clearly mentioned in the *Unfair Terms in Consumer Contracts Regulations 1999*, with the definition of an unfair term in Regulation 5(1). There are two conditions that must be satisfied: the term must be 'contrary to the requirement of good faith' and the term must 'cause a significant imbalance in the parties' rights and obligations arising under the contract' to the detriment of the consumer. The difficulty lies in distinguishing between good faith and 'significant imbalance'. This is not a simple issue in English law because there is no general principle on which to rely in English courts. Therefore, the court must draw upon the European origin of good faith.

The issues are explored in more detail by the House of Lords in *Director General of Fair Trading v First National Bank*.[43] The decision represents an important step towards further integrating the concept of good faith in English law. In this case, the bank included a term in its common form loan agreement that upon default of the borrower's repayment, the bank is entitled to recover from the borrower the whole balance of the customer's loan together with the outstanding interest and the costs of seeking judgement. The trial judge held that the term was fair. On appeal, the Court of Appeal concluded that the term was unfair and believed that:

> *The bank, with its strong bargaining position as against the relatively weak position of the customer, has not adequately considered the consumer's interest in this respect. In our view, the relevant term in that respect does create unfair surprises and so does not satisfy the test of good faith; it does cause a significant imbalance in the rights and obligations of the parties by allowing the bank to obtain interest after judgement…*[44]

[42] Schedule 2 states that particular regard shall be had to (a) the strength of the bargaining positions of the parties, (b) whether the consumer had an inducement to agree to the term, (c) whether the goods or services were sold or supplied to the special order of the consumer and (d) the extent to which the seller or supplier has dealt fairly and equitably with the consumer. The list is significant to establish the criteria of good faith.

[43] [2000] 1 All ER 97. This case is actually concerned with the interpretation of the 1994 rather than 1999 Regulations, but the differences between the two sets of Regulations are immaterial for the purpose of the case. Therefore, this decision is relevant to the interpretation of the 1999 Regulations.

[44] *Director General of Fair Trading v First National Bank* [2000] QB 672, 688 [16].

The Court of Appeal relied on the requirement of fairness elaborated by Lord Bingham in *Interfoto Picture Library Ltd v Stiletto Visual Programmes Ltd*.[45] His Honour further elaborated that:

> *The requirement of good faith in this context is one of fair and open dealing. Openness requires that the terms should be expressed fully, clearly and legibly containing no concealed pitfalls or traps. Appropriate prominence should be given to terms which might operate disadvantageously to the customer. Fair dealing requires that a supplier should not, whether deliberately or unconscionably, take advantage of the consumer's necessity, indigence, lack of experience, unfamiliarity with the subject matter of the contract, weak bargaining position or any other factor listed in or analogous to those listed in Schedule 2 to the Regulations.*[46]

Lord Steyn agreed with Lord Bingham that the term of the agreement was unfair. Lord Bingham also commented that good faith looks to good standards or commercial morality.[47] Lord Steyn observed in his opinion that in this context, the notion referred to is good faith and fair dealing. Lord Bingham also briefly described a significant imbalance where:

> *The requirement of significant imbalance is met if a term is so weighted in favour of the supplier as to title the parties; rights and obligations under the contract are significantly in his favour. This may be by granting to the supplier of a beneficial option or discretion or power, or by imposing on the consumer of a disadvantageous burden or risk or duty … This involves looking at the contract as a whole.*[48]

From the *Interfoto* case, it is clear that good faith is now firmly embedded in consumer law in the UK.[49] Despite the fear of a foreign concept, Goode claimed that once the courts have become familiarised with the application of this wider concept of good faith, as well seen in the *Unfair*

[45] [1989] QB 433, 439.

[46] *Director General of Fair Trading v First National Bank* [2000] QB 672, 688 [17].

[47] *Director General of Fair Trading v First National Bank* [2000] QB 672, 688 [17].

[48] *Director General of Fair Trading v First National Bank* [2000] QB 672, 688 [17].

[49] Adams, J. N., & Brownsword, R. (2004). Understanding Contract Law. In Brownsword, R (Ed.). *Understanding Contract Law* (4th ed). p. 116. Sweet & Maxwell.

Terms in Consumer Contracts Regulations 1999, they may well find that to use it on a broader basis is simple and satisfactory.[50]

The law of special contracts is far less hostile to the idea of good faith than its general counterpart. The common law developed the law of special contract in which good faith is a recognised principle in contract law. There is a 'special kind of relationship' established by the contract which carries an implied obligation of good faith via mutual trust and confidence. Various popular contracts involved duties expressly put in terms of good faith, whether this results directly from a rule of law applicable to the contract such as insurance, fiduciary or employment by way of the implication of a term.

In the insurance context, good faith is a well-known concept. The duty of good faith in insurance law was introduced almost 250 years ago in *Carter v Boehm*,[51] in which Lord Mansfield commented that:

> *Insurance is a contract of speculation. The special facts upon which the contingent chance is to be computed lie most commonly in the knowledge of the assured only; the underwriter trusts his representation and proceeds upon confidence that he does not keep back any circumstance in his knowledge to mislead the underwriter into a belief that the circumstances do not exist. The keeping back of such circumstances is fraud, and therefore the policy is void. Although the suppression should happen through mistake, without any fraudulent intention, yet still the underwriter is deceived and the policy is void; because the risqué run is really different from the risqué understood and intended to be run at the time of the agreement … The policy would be equally void against the underwriter if he concealed … Good faith forbids either party, by concealing what he privately knows to draw the other into a bargain from his ignorance of the fact, and his believing the contrary.*[52]

Later, the concept was codified in the *Insurance Act 2015* by virtue of s 14 of the *Insurance Contracts Act 2015* (Part 5), which provides that:

> *Any rule of law permitting a party to a contract of insurance to avoid the contract on the ground that the utmost good faith has not been observed by the other party is abolished.*

[50] Goode, R. (1997). International Restatements of Contract and English Contract Law. *Uniform Law Review*, 2, 231–240.

[51] (1766) 3 Burr 1905.

[52] (1766) 3 Burr 1905, 1910.

A fiduciary relationship is a relationship in which one party undertakes or agrees to act for or on behalf of, or in the interests of, another person in the exercise of a power or discretion that will affect the interests of that other person in a legal or practical sense. It is a kind of relationship of trust and confidence or confidential relationship, viz. trustee and beneficiary, agent and principal, solicitor and agent, employee and employer, director and company and partners. It is a requirement to act in the interests of another as a consequence of a 'special kind of relationship'.

The employment of such a relationship was recognised as one of the categories of relationship in which fiduciary duties were implied by the implication of terms without the need for the fiduciary epithet. Employees may owe fiduciary duties to their employers; this is similar to the duty of good faith and fidelity. Hence, in *Pearce v Foster*, the English Court of Appeal held that an employee had breached an implied contractual duty because he 'had deliberately placed himself in that position which rendered his interest conflicting with his duty'.[53] The duty was implied because 'the relation of master and servant implies necessarily that the servant shall be in a position to perform his duty duly and faithfully'.[54]

In this context, the special relationship requires trust and confidence that carries with it an expectation of utmost loyalty and good faith.[55] In the partnership agreement, there is a relationship of trust and mutual confidence that gives rise to a fiduciary duty of full disclosure on the part of both parties. The partners are bound to exercise the utmost good faith in their dealings with one another. The requirement of trust and mutual confidence was observed in *Helmore v Smith*,[56] where Bacon VC observed that 'their mutual confidence is the life-blood of the concern. It is because they trust one another that they are partners in the first instance; it is because they continue to trust one another that the business goes on.'[57]

In employment, the duty of good faith is implied from the relationship between the employer and the employee. It was clearly stated in *Wessex Dairies Limited v Smith* that 'it is a necessary implication which must be engrafted on such a contract (employment) that the servant undertakes to

[53] (1886) 17 QBD 536, 541–542 (Lindley LJ).

[54] (1886) 17 QBD 536, 539 (Lord Esher MR).

[55] See Adler, R. S., & Mann, R. A. (1995). Good Faith: A New Look at an Old Doctrine. *Akron Law Review*, 28, 31–34.

[56] (1886) 35 ChD 436.

[57] (1886) 35 Ch D 436, 44.

serve his master with good faith and fidelity'.[58] Riley argues that the duty of good faith in the employment context is consistently implied as a duty of 'mutual trust and confidence' where both parties are expected to act in the best interests of maintaining trust in the relationship.[59] This statement is elaborated further in *Eastwood v Magnox Electric Plc*, where Lord Nicholls held that 'the trust and confidence in an implied term mean, in short, that an employer must treat his employers fairly. In his conduct of his business and his treatment of his employees, an employer must act responsibly and in good faith.'[60]

Good faith appears to be implied in many of the contexts of English law. However, it is evident that good faith is not defined. This is most probably because good faith is an abstract concept. English courts have expressed concern about the lack of certainty in defining the content of a duty of good faith in the context of the relationship between contracting parties. Many legal experts have also expressed concern over the ambiguity of the meaning of good faith. Steyn J has argued that '[a] definition of good faith and fair dealing is impossible',[61] Goode laments that '[w]e do not know quite what it means',[62] while White and Summers have warned that '[w]e caution anyone who is confident about the meaning of good faith to reconsider'.[63] There is a reluctance to imply a condition of good faith on the ground that it will introduce uncertainty into contract law. In *Union Eagle Ltd v Golden Achievement Ltd*, Lord Hoffman held that:

> *The principle that equity will restrain the enforcement of legal rights when it would be unconscionable to insist upon them has an attractive breadth. But the reasons why the courts have rejected such generalisations are founded not merely upon authority ... but also upon consideration of business. These are, in summary, that in many forms of transaction it is of great importance that if something happens for which the contract has made express provision, the parties*

[58] [1935] 2 KB 80.

[59] See Riley, J. (2003). Mutual Trust and Good Faith: Can Private Contract Law Guarantee Fair Dealing in the Workplace? *Australian Journal of Labour Law*, 16, 1–4.

[60] [2005] 1 AC 503 [11].

[61] Steyn, J. (1991). The Role of Good Faith and Fair Dealing in Contract Law: A Hair-Shirt Philosophy? *Denning Law Journal*, 6, 131–140.

[62] Goode, R. (1992). *The Concept of Good Faith in English Law*. Paper presented at the Centro di Studi e Ricerche di Diritto Comparato e Straniero, Rome, 3 cited by Cole, T. R. H. (1994). The Concept of Reasonableness in Construction Contracts. *Building and Construction Law Journal*, 10, 7–12.

[63] *Uniform Commercial Code*, Vol 1 (4th ed) 5, 187.

> *should know with certainty that the terms of the contract will be enforced. The existence of an undefined discretion to refuse to enforce the contract on the ground that this would be 'unconscionable' is sufficient to create uncertainty.*[64]

Thus, introducing the concept of good faith would cause much dissatisfaction among legal jurists due to its vagueness. A contract requires clear definitions of legal concepts in order to avoid uncertainty and confusion among parties. Without a comprehensive and concise definition, the contract becomes meaningless.

3.4 Good Faith in the US

In the US, good faith is well recognised as a fundamental concept in modern contract jurisprudence. At an earlier stage, the US courts were slow to recognise the duty of good faith in common law contract cases.[65] Later, the concept of good faith was acknowledged in the *Uniform Commercial Code* and was later adopted by the American Law Institute as part of the *Restatement (Second) of Contracts*. Since the middle of the twentieth century, good faith has attracted the attention of American legal scholars to employ the concept, particularly in commercial cases.[66]

The case of *Wood v Lucy, Lady Duff-Gordon*, is a significant illustration of the good faith principle in American contract law. This case is important because it illustrates that there is an implied promise within a contract in which a party will use their best effort to fulfil the terms of the contract. In this case, Cardoza J held that:

> *The law has outgrown its primitive stage of formalism when the precise word was the sovereign talisman, and every slip was fatal. It takes a broader view today. A promise may be lacking and yet the whole writing may be 'instinct with an obligation', imperfectly expressed.*[67]

Later in 1933, in *Kirke La Shelle Co v Paul Armstrong Co*, the New York Court of Appeals recognised that:

[64] [1997] AC 514 [218–219].

[65] Dubroff, H. (2006). The Implied Covenant of Good Faith in Contract Interpretation and Gap-Filling: Reviving a Revered Relic. *St. John's Law Review*, 80, 559–587.

[66] Ibid., 561.

[67] 222 NY 88,118 NE 214, 214(1917).

> *In every contract, there is an implied covenant that neither party shall do anything which will have the effect of destroying or injuring the right of the other party to receive the fruits of the contract, which means that in every contract there exists an implied covenant of good faith and fair dealing.*[68]

Although its existence is no longer questioned as an important principle in the US, there is still an issue pertaining to its definition and American scholars still cannot agree on a precise definition. Several scholars have attempted to define good faith by the function it serves. Summers argues that good faith cannot be defined.[69] He proposed the theory of 'excluder', where it excludes any form of bad faith, and claimed that '[i]t is a phrase which has no general meaning or meanings of its own, but which serves to exclude many heterogeneous forms of bad faith'.[70] Burton introduced a 'foregone opportunity analysis', where good faith is a standard based on the expectation of the parties,[71] and argued that good faith:

> *limits the exercise of discretion in performance conferred on one party by the contract, so it is bad faith to use discretion to recapture opportunities forgone upon contracting as determined by the other party's expectations-in other words, to refuse to pay the expected cost of performance.*[72]

Despite the fact that there is still no unanimous definition to good faith, the concept of good faith gained increased acceptance when it was incorporated into the *Uniform Commercial Code* and *Restatement (Second) of Contracts*. The following sections further illustrate the increased recognition of good faith in the US.

3.4.1 Uniform Commercial Code

The *Uniform Commercial Code* was the product of a collaborative effort by the National Conference of Commissioners of Uniform State Laws and the American Law Institute in the 1960s. The *Uniform Commercial Code*

[68] 188 NE 163, 167 per Hubbs J (NY, 1933).

[69] Summers, R. S. (1982). The General Duty of Good Faith—Its Recognition and Conceptualization. *Cornell Law Review*, 67, 810–819.

[70] Ibid.

[71] Burton, S. J. (1980). Breach of Contract and the Common Law Duty to Perform in Good Faith. *Harvard Law Review*, 94, 369.

[72] Ibid., 372–373.

is a set of laws that provide legal rules and regulations governing commercial or business dealings and transactions. The *Uniform Commercial Code* regulates the transfer or sale of personal property such as cars, rice and alcohol but does not address dealings in real property such as the sale of land, services and stocks. The underlying purpose and policy of the *Uniform Commercial Code* is to create uniform laws among the various state jurisdictions in the US.[73] The concept of good faith plays a significant role in the *Uniform Commercial Code*. Indeed, good faith is referenced in at least 50 different *Uniform Commercial Code* provisions.[74]

The concept of good faith is the requirement for all Code transactions as set out in the General Provisions chapter in s 1–203 of the *Uniform Commercial Code*, which provides that 'Every contract or duty within the Act imposes an obligation of good faith in its performance or enforcement'.[75] Good faith is defined in s 1–203 of the *Uniform Commercial Code* to mean 'honesty in fact in the conduct or transaction concerned'. An exclusive definition of good faith concerning merchants is provided in Article 2 (Sales), s 2–103 (1) (b) of the *Uniform Commercial Code*, which provides that:

> *In this article, unless the context otherwise requires ... good faith in the case of a merchant means honesty in fact and the observance of reasonable commercial standards of fair dealing in the trade.*

It is evident that good faith is mentioned in those sections but the definition is nebulous. It is important to highlight that 'there is an express mention of good faith in some fifty out of the four hundred sections of the code'.[76] For example, s 2–311(1) expressly mentions good faith in a specific fact situation such as in the sale contract, whereby:

> *An agreement for sale which is otherwise sufficiently definite (s 2–204(3)) to be a contract is not made invalid by the fact that it leaves particulars of performance to be specified by one of* the *parties. Any such specification must be made in good faith and within limits set by commercial reasonableness.*

[73] *Uniform Commercial Code*, s 1 102.

[74] Powers, above n. 172, 339.

[75] It should be noted that this provision does not apply to the negotiation or formation stage.

[76] Farnsworth, E. A. (1963). Good Faith Performance and Commercial Reasonableness Under the Uniform Commercial Code. *University of Chicago Law Review*, 30, 666–667.

Despite the express provision of good faith, there is also an implied term requiring parties to behave in good faith, for example, in s 2–601, buyers' rights on improper delivery where the buyer may reject the whole or accept the whole or accept any commercial unit or units and reject the rest.

As a result, the *Uniform Commercial Code* has two varying definitions of good faith. In this context, Farnsworth classified good faith into two senses: (i) good faith purchase and (ii) good faith performance or enforcement.[77] In the first sense and in a larger group of provisions, good faith is described as a 'state of mind' whereby:

> *A party is advantaged only if he acted with innocent ignorance or lack of suspicion. This meaning of good faith is very close to that of lack of notice … In addition, the Code also uses good faith-as did prior law-in substantially the same sense in protecting others, the purchasers, and these situations will be included in this discussion under the generic term 'good faith purchase'.*[78]

This approach looks only to the actual belief of the party. In the second sense and in a smaller group of the Code, in which good faith is used to describe performance or enforcement, it is stated that:

> *In this sense, good faith has nothing to do with a state of mind … Here the inquiry goes to decency, fairness or reasonableness, or notice. This sense of the term may be characterized as 'good faith performance' to distinguish it from 'good faith purchase' and is the sense in which 'good faith' is used in the general obligation of good faith. It is also the sense in which that term is used in a number of more specific sections. … resulting in an implied term of contract requiring cooperation on the part of one party to the contract so that another party will not be deprived of his reasonable expectations.*[79]

The former approach focused only on the actual belief of the party. The latter approach includes not only the actual belief of the party but also the reasonableness of the belief and conduct. These divergent views have created an unclear definition of good faith in the *Uniform Commercial Code*. Dobbins cautioned the fear it would cause when 'the inability to

[77] Ibid., 668.
[78] Ibid.
[79] Ibid., 669.

define good faith leaves contracting parties with no clear understanding of their obligation', which resulted in uncertainties to the contract.[80]

Although the *Uniform Commercial Code* requirements of good faith are stated in the vaguest of terms, in practice, most courts find their way to a reasonable construction of the obligation following litigation.[81] A few courts have used the doctrinal vagueness as a pretext to impose unprecedented liabilities on commercial parties. This is because the abstractness of good faith allows advocates of the term to suggest many different meanings which create an obligation.

In certain situations, good faith might require a contracting party to act as a good and upright person under the same set of circumstances, while to others, it might require a party of the contract to work in the best interests of both parties. In other circumstances, good faith imposes a moral obligation on the contracting parties in order to effectuate a contract which did not arise from the parties' agreement.

3.4.2 Restatement (Second) of Contracts

The *Restatement (Second) of Contracts* is a legal treatise from the second series of the *Restatements of the Law*,[82] which intends to inform judges and lawyers about the general principles of contract common law. It covers particularly the areas of contracts and commercial transactions but is non-binding. The American Law Institute began work on the second edition in 1962 and completed it in 1979. The *Restatement (Second) of Contracts* first emerged in 1980 and, like the *Uniform Commercial Code*, constitutes another fundamental and important source of the duty of good faith in contractual relations. The *Restatement (Second) of Contracts* imposes a duty of good faith in performance and enforcement upon each contracting party,[83] which is acknowledged in s 205, which provides that:

[80] Dobbins, T. J. (2005). Losing Faith: Extracting the Implied Covenant of Good Faith from (Some) Contracts. *Oregon Law Review*, 84, 227–230.

[81] Burton, S. J. (1993). Good Faith in Articles 1 and 2 of the UCC: The Practice View. *William and Mary Law Review*, 35, 1533–1536.

[82] *Restatements of the Law* are essentially model laws, designed to explain the common law in a particular field of law. *Restatements* are published by the American Law Institute.

[83] See Summers, R. (2000). The Conceptualisation of Good Faith in American Contract Law: A General Account. In Zimmermann, R., & Whittaker, S. (Eds.). *Good Faith in European Contract Law* (pp. 118–119). Cambridge University Press.

Every contract imposes upon each party a duty of good faith and fair dealing in its performance and its enforcement.[84]

Unlike the *Uniform Commercial Code*, the *Restatement (Second) of Contracts* mentions the terms 'good faith and fair dealing'. Robert Braucher, the chief drafter of the *Restatement*, commented that the section is very general and very abstract and needs more explanation of the concept of good faith. Summers' formulation of good faith, the 'excluder' approach, which suggests that good faith is anything that excludes bad faith, was then incorporated.[85] Using the 'excluder' approach, the comments to s 205 of the *Restatement* proceeds to define good faith by what constitutes 'bad faith'.[86] It states that:

A complete catalogue of types of bad faith is impossible, but the following types are among those which have been recognised in judicial decisions: evasion of the spirit of the bargain, lack of diligence and slacking off, willful rendering of imperfect performance, abuse of power to specify terms, and interference with or failure to cooperate in the other party's performance.[87]

As a consequence, good faith has no definition but relies on any type of bad faith to constitute a good faith definition. Indeed, the scope of the duty of good faith depends on the 'nature of the agreement', along the line with the notion of fairness, thus leading to uncertainty. Farnsworth also commented on the duty of good faith in the *Restatement (Second) of Contracts* and stated that:

…the duty [good faith] may not only proscribe undesirable conduct but may require affirmative action as well. A party may thus be under a duty[good faith] not only to refrain from hindering or preventing the occurrence of conditions of the party's own duty or performance of the other party's duty but also to take some affirmative steps to co-operate in achieving these goals….[88]

[84] It should be noted that this provision, like those in the *Uniform Commercial Code*, only applies to contractual performance and not to contract negotiation.

[85] Summers, R. (1968). Good Faith in General Contract Law and the Sales Provision of the Uniform Commercial Code. *Virginia Law Review*, 54, 195–196.

[86] Burton, S. J. (1984). More on Good Faith Performance of a Contract: A Reply to Professor Summers. *Iowa Law Review*, 69, 497–499.

[87] *Restatement (Second) Contracts* s 205, Comment (d).

[88] Summers, above n. 244, 134.

Although the *Restatement (Second) of Contracts* does not have the force of legislation, which is distinct from the *Uniform Commercial Code*, it had a substantial influence on the courts in the US, and by the 1980s, the state court systems of many US states had explicitly adopted a general obligation of good faith in a contractual relationship.[89]

It is evident that both the *Uniform Commercial Code* and the *Restatement (Second) of Contracts* are compelling authoritative sources of the duty of good faith in commercial contracts. Despite the pervasiveness of the concept of good faith throughout the statutory provision and the attempt by some of the American scholars to define good faith, there is still no firm definition and guidelines for the concept of good faith.

3.5 Good Faith in Canada

In Canada, there is no acceptance of a duty of good faith applying to all contracts as of yet.[90] The courts are generally reluctant to apply the principle of good faith in contracts when asked to override express contractual provisions and the reasonable expectations of the parties. Consequently, the acceptance of good faith is identified in specific categories of contracts, for instance, in franchise, employment, tendering, joint ventures, enterprise and other relational contracts. In the context of employment, the case of *Wallace v United Grain Growers* held that employers owe a duty of good faith and fair dealing in the dismissal of the employees.[91] In the context of tenders, the case of *Tarmac Canada Inc v Hamilton Wentworth (Regional Municipality)* held that there was a long line of authority for the proposition that not only was the Municipality obligated to treat all tenders fairly, but it must also act in good faith.[92]

However, there also appears to be a degree of extrajudicial support for good faith in Canadian contract law. In 1979, the Ontario Law Reform Commission's Report on Sale of Goods recommended the adoption of a good faith standard of fair dealing.[93] Later, in the *Report on Amendment of the Law of Contract (1987)*, the Ontario Law Reform Commission stated:

[89] Farnsworth. E. A. (1995). Good Faith in Contract Performance. In Beatson, J., & Friedmann, D. (Eds). *Good Faith and Fault in Contract Law* (p. 158). Oxford University Press.

[90] Cohen, J., & Weinberg, L. (2002). Good faith and Fair Dealing: A Primer on the Differences Between the United States and Canada. *Franchise Law Journal*, 22, 37–40.

[91] [1997] 3 SCR 701.

[92] O.J. 3273 (1999).

[93] Ontario Law Reform Commission, *Report on Sale of Goods* (1979), Vol. 1, 163–71.

While good faith is not yet an openly recognized contract law doctrine, it is very much a factor in everyday contractual transactions. To the extent that the common law of contracts, as interpreted and developed by our Courts, reflects this reality, it is accurate to state that good faith is part of our law of contracts. In this vein, a great many well-established concepts in contract law reflect a concern for good faith, fair dealing and the protection of reasonable expectations, creating a legal behaviour baseline.

In this report, the Commission recommended that the legislation recognise the doctrine of good faith in the performance of contracts generally. Reitier commented that good faith is an important norm in contract law.[94] He further argued that 'the pervasiveness of good faith in contracts has important implications for theories of contract law, for the relationship between law and society, and for the law in its practical, day to day operation'.[95] In *Gateway Realty v Arton Holdings (No.3)*, Kelly J opined that '…the insistence of a good faith requirement in discretionary conduct in contractual formation, performance and enforcement is only the fulfilment of the obligation of the courts to do justice in the resolution of disputes between the contracting parties'. It is evident that there has been an interest to recognise a general obligation of good faith in Canadian law of contract.

However, there is statutory recognition to the concept of good faith in Quebec, where the influence of civil law stems from its distinct French inheritance. The acceptance of the concept of good faith is clearly stated in the *Quebec Civil Code*. Article 6 states that 'Every person is bound to exercise his civil rights in good faith'; Article 7 states that '[n]o right may be exercised with the intent of injuring another or in an excessive and unreasonable manner which is contrary to the requirements of good faith' and Article 1375 states that '[t]he parties shall conduct themselves in good faith both at the time the obligation is created and at the time it is performed or extinguished'. Even though good faith seems to play a central role in the *Quebec Civil Code*, as mentioned in the three general provisions above, a clear definition of good faith is still not given.

The issue of the meaning of good faith is controversial in Canada. O'Bryne argues that attempts to define it continually prove to be futile because '…good faith can have no absolute meaning: it simply assumes its

[94] Reitier, B. (1983). Good Faith in Contracts. *Valparaiso University Law Review*, 17, 705–707.

[95] Ibid., 706.

contents from the facts of each particular case'.[96] It is self-evident that defining good faith is a frustrating task as 'it is impossible to take into account all the situations, types of behaviour, tactics or conducts that may in a given situation constitute a departure from 'good faith'.[97]

Although good faith is not defined, it has been expressly incorporated into the franchising legislation in Canada. In franchise, breaches of terms of good faith are an increasingly common feature of modern pleadings.[98] In Canada, franchising is purely a province matter, and currently, only five provinces have franchise legislation in place, namely, Alberta, Ontario, Prince Edward Island, New Brunswick and Manitoba. Manitoba is the newest province to enact franchise-specific legislation with a passage in its Franchise Act. The franchise legislation of each province includes a covenant of fair dealing which also carries an obligation to act in good faith between the franchisor and franchisee.[99]

In Canada, under the common law, good faith is regarded as a general principle and recognised in a specific category of contract, while under civil law, specifically in Quebec, good faith is given statutory recognition. Despite being acknowledged under both common law and civil law, there is still no definition of the concept. As a consequence, the concept of good faith does not appear to be uniformly applied and remains subject to the vagaries of judicial interpretation.

3.6 Good Faith in New Zealand

The position of good faith in New Zealand is similar to that of the UK and Canada, where there is no general obligation of good faith in all types of contracts. The status of good faith in New Zealand is discussed in the landmark case of *Livingstone v Roskilly*.[100] In this case, Thomas J agreed

[96] O'Byrne, S. K. (1995). Good Faith in Contractual Performance: Recent Developments. *Canadian Bar Review*, 74, 70–73.

[97] David I. Bristow and Reva Seth, 'Good Faith in Negotiations' (2000) 55 *Dispute Resolution Journal*, 16, 18.

[98] Bristow, D. I., & Seth, R. (2000). Good Faith in Negotiations. *Dispute Resolution Journal*, 55, 16–18.

[99] *Franchises Act*, RSA 2000, c F-23, s 7 (Alberta); *Franchises Act*, SNB 2007, c F-23.5, ss 3(1), (3) (New Brunswick); *Arthur Wishart Act (Franchise Disclosure)*, SO 2000, c 3, ss 3(1), (3) (Ontario); *Franchises Act*, RSPEI 1988, c F-14.1, ss 3(1), (3) (Prince Edward Island); and *Franchises Act*, CCSMc F156 s 3 (Manitoba).

[100] [1992] 3 NZLR 230.

with the decision made by Lord Bingham in *Interfoto Picture Library Ltd v Stiletto Visual Programme*[101] in which his Honour commented that:

> *I would not exclude from our [New Zealand] common law the concept that, in general, the parties to a contract must act in good faith in making and carrying out the contract ... [Lord Mansfield's] tradition was never swamped in the United States as it was in England by the formalism of the 19th and 20th centuries. But the principle has survived, I suggest, as the latent promise of much of our law relating to the formation and performance of contracts.*[102]

Despite it being a civil law concept, Thomas J has advocated a general doctrine of good faith to be implied into contracts in which 'parties to a contract must act in good faith in making and carrying out the contract'. The duty of good faith is recognised in obvious areas such as in the insurance context, whereby good faith is the underlying duty.[103] This position is stated in *Archibald Barr Motor Company Ltd & Anor v ATECO Automotive New Zealand*, where Allen J suggested that:

> *New Zealand courts are unlikely to incorporate an obligation of good faith into all contracts generally, particularly those commercial contract where the parties have spelt out their obligations in detail, and where a good faith requirement would not fit comfortably with those detailed express term.*[104]

[101] [1989] QB 433, 439. In this case, Lord Bingham had acknowledged a general recognition of good faith in English law whereby his Lordship held that '...English law has, characteristically, committed itself to no such overriding principle but has developed piecemeal solutions in response to demonstrated problems of unfairness. Many examples could be given. Thus equity has intervened to strike down unconscionable bargains. Parliament has stepped in to regulate the imposition of exemption clauses and the form of certain hire-purchase agreements. The common law also has made its contribution, by holding that certain classes of contract require the utmost good faith by treating as irrecoverable what purport to be agreed estimates of damage but are in truth as disguised penalty for breach, and in many other ways.'

[102] [1992] 3 NZLR230, 238.

[103] Rick Bigwood, 'Symposium Introduction: Confessions of a Good Faith Agnostic' (2005) 11 *New Zealand Business Law Quarterly*, 371. In the insurance context, the good faith characteristic to insurance contracts has been recognised for more than 250 years. The application of good faith within insurance law is predominantly focused on the disclosure of information applicable to both the insurer and the insured.

[104] (High Court, Auckland, CIV 2007-404-5797, 26 October 2007) [79].

Nonetheless, cases where a duty of good faith has been applied are largely confined to relational contracts, such as franchise, partnership, joint ventures and employment. In *Bobux Marketing Ltd v Raynor Marketing Ltd*,[105] Thomas J, in the course of the dissenting judgement, discussed comprehensively on the academic and judicial comment that relates to good faith in contract law. In this case, his Honour continued to display vigilance to recognise a duty to exercise good faith in the performance of a contractual obligation, particularly in the case of relational contracts. His Honour commented that:

> *There can be little doubt that the contract between Bobux and Raynor is predicated upon mutual trust and confidence and gave rise to a reasonable expectation of communication, cooperation and predictable performance. These features become all the more important when the contract is for an indefinite period ... It, therefore, seems to me that it would be open to Bobux to assert that the parties' obligations under the contract are subject to an obligation to act in good faith.*[106]

His Honour explained that a relational contract is a type of contract which is often a long-term contract. Therefore, there is a need to maintain the relationship because these types of contracts are often exposed to uncertainty and unforeseen factors that cannot readily be provided for in advance due to long engagement. It was further explained by Thomas J that:

> *...The norms of the ongoing relationship, of necessity, tend to supplement the express contractual obligations. Good faith is required to ensure that the requisite communication, cooperation and predictable performance occur for the advantage of both parties.*[107]

In the joint venture, the duty of good faith requires the parties to act at most only with due care and/or in good faith towards each other. Joint ventures are business arrangements whereby parties collaborate by contributing money, property or skill in a particular trading, commercial or other financial undertakings to achieve certain outcomes in the business agreement. The parties are bound by the express and implied terms of the agreement between them. If one of the parties breaches the agreement,

[105] [2002] 1 NZLR 506.
[106] Ibid., 508.
[107] [2002]1 NZLR 506, 518.

the remaining parties are left to their traditional and well-established remedies for breach of contract. The leading case in respect of the obligation owed by joint venture parties is the decision of the Supreme Court in *Chirnside v Fay*.[108] In this case, the court held that 'the relationship between partners is one which has traditionally been regarded as a classic example of a fiduciary relationship in that the parties owe to each other duties of loyalty and good faith'.[109]

In the employment context, there is a statutory requirement of good faith in the employment relationship with the aim of promoting a productive employment relationship. The *Employment Relations Act 2000* (ERA) expressly recognises a duty of good faith in s 3 of the *Employment Relations Act 2000* (ERA). It is stated that the object of this Act is:

> *(a) to build productive employment relationships through the promotion of good faith in all aspects of the employment environment and of the employment relationship-by recognising that employment relationships must be built not only on the implied mutual obligations of trust and confidence but also a legislative requirement for good faith behaviour.*

Section 4 of the *Employment Relations Act 2000* (ERA) mentioned good faith as the expected behaviour of the parties in the employment relationship. It is stated that:

> *The parties to an employment relationship must deal with each other in good faith.*

Although good faith was recognised in the relational contract and in the statutory provisions, nonetheless the courts have not yet incorporated the concept of good faith into the law in New Zealand. In *Gibbons Holdings Ltd v Wholesale Distributors Ltd*, Thomas J agreed that good faith is a prevalent concept in most common law and civil law countries, but the courts are careful in accommodating the concept of good faith into the law in New Zealand. His Honour stated that:

> *There is a widespread belief that existing concepts of judicial services already encompass a requirement of good faith. It would, it is said, add nothing to the*

[108] [2007] 1 NZLR, 433.
[109] [2007] 1 NZLR, 459 per Tipping J.

> *existing tools and principles of the common law, such as estoppels and implied terms. This case serves to demonstrate that this belief is misplaced.*[110]

One of the problems is with the definition of good faith. Good faith has many meanings; therefore, it is difficult to attach a precise definition to it. The fear is that defining it could result in an insufficient meaning of good faith, which may cause vagueness to the concept itself.[111] In *Vero Insurance New Zealand Ltd v Fleet Insurance & Risk Management Ltd*, Asher J stated:

> *Although a number of New Zealand cases have considered the circumstances in which a term of good faith will be implied, the application and meaning of good faith in contracts have not as yet been thoroughly considered in New Zealand.*[112]

Despite the fact that good faith is mentioned in New Zealand contract law, particularly in relational contracts, the issue of its meaning evidently remains unsettled.

3.7 Good Faith in the People's Republic of China

The People's Republic of China is influenced by both the civil law and the socialist law. Chinese scholars generally consider good faith as the fundamental principle in the contract law and also a fundamental principle of civil law. Recently, China legislated a new *Contract Law of the People's Republic of China*, which covers a wider scope compared to the previous contract law. One of the major fundamental guiding principles of the new contract law is the concept of good faith. The concept of good faith is considered as a general principle in contract law and is given statutory recognition.[113] The new contract law comprises three types of contract:

[110] [2008] 1 NZLR 277, 316–317.
[111] Bigwood, above n. 264, 372.
[112] (High Court, Auckland, CIV 2007-404-1438, 21 May 2007) [44].
[113] Leonhard, C. (2010). A Legal Chameleon: An Examination of the Doctrine of Good Faith in Chinese and American Contract Law. *Connecticut Journal of International Law*, 25, 305–306.

Economic Contract Law,[114] Foreign Economic Contract Law[115] and Technology Contract Law.[116] This new *Contract Law of the People's Republic of China* came into effect on 1 October 1999 and seeks to establish a more advanced, systematic and comprehensive contract law which is better suited to the particular needs of China's transitional economy.

Good faith was given statutory recognition under the new contract law as a general principle, which is illustrated in Article 6, which begins with:

> *The parties should abide by the doctrine of good faith when exercising their rights to fulfilling their obligations.*

The recognition given to the principle of good faith has brought the law in China in line with international business practice. It is argued that Article 1.7 of the International Institute for the Unification of Private Law (UNIDROIT) Principles[117] is similar to Article 6 of the *Contract Law of*

[114] The Economic Contract Law was adopted on the Fifth National People's Congress on 13 December 1981. The Economic Contract Law applied to any domestic economic contract.

[115] The Foreign Economic Contract Law was adopted by the National People's Congress on 21 March 1985. The Foreign Economic Contract Law addressed the issues of foreign interest such as the application of the law when settling disputes involving foreign economic contracts, confirmation of the invalidation and revocation of foreign economic contracts, dealing with foreign economic contracts after confirmation of invalidation or revocation and liability for breach of foreign economic contracts.

[116] The Technology Contract Law was adopted by the National People's Congress on 23 June 1987. The Technology Contract Law was implemented to encourage foreign investment projects that involve the importing of high technology into China and also to guide technology transfer associated with economic development.

[117] Article 1.7 of the International Institute for the Unification of Private Law (UNIDROIT) Principles stated that:

> Each party must act in accordance with good faith and fair dealing in international trade.

the People's Republic of China,[118] which emphasised the obligation of good faith to encourage more business opportunities at the international level.[119]

Apart from Article 6, Articles 42, 60, 92 and 125 explicitly require parties to adhere to the concept of good faith in all stages of the contract. Article 42 deals with the issue of negotiation in bad faith and the duty of confidentiality, where it stipulates:

> *A party shall be liable for damages if, in concluding the contract, it acted under one of the following circumstances, thereby causing a loss to the other party: (1) pretending to conclude a contract, and negotiating in bad faith; (2) intentionally concealing a fact relevant to the contract or providing wrong information; (3) any other circumstance which runs counter to the principle of good faith.*

Article 60 states that there is a duty to perform a contract in good faith:

> *Parties are expected, in addition to performing their obligations according to the terms of the contract, to abide by the principle of good faith and to perform implied obligations such as notice, assistance, confidentiality etc. based on the nature and purpose of the contract or on usages.*

In Article 90, there is also a duty of good faith when the contract is terminated:

> *Upon the termination of contractual rights and duties, the parties shall follow the principle of good faith and fulfil duties such as notification, assistance, confidentiality, etc. in accordance with business customs.*

Article 125 deals with an interpretation of a contract clause, which is based on its true meaning:

[118] Article 6 of *Contract Law of the People's Republic of China* stated that:

> The parties should abide by the doctrine of good faith when exercising their rights of fulfilling their obligations.

[119] See Zhang, Y., & Huang, D. (2000). The New Contract Law in the People's Republic of China and the UNIDROIT Principles of International Commercial Contracts: A Brief Comparison. *Uniform Law Review*, 5, 429–431.

> *Shall be determined according to the terms and expressions used in the contract, the contents of the relevant clauses, the purposes of the contract, usages and the principle of good faith.*

In interpreting an ambiguous contract, the court should uphold the principle of good faith by taking into account relevant factors such as the nature and purpose of the contract as well as the business customs of the place where the contract was formed. This is to derive the parties' true intentions and the meaning of the contract.

The enforcement of the concept of good faith is parallel with the People's Republic of China's traditional moral and commercial ethics.[120] Traditional moral values in China are influenced by Confucianism, which advocates the concept of good faith as part of everyday life. Many bad commercial ethics are condemned such as unethical business activities like false advertising, forgery and corruption.[121] The Chinese court recognises good faith as the 'highest guiding principle' or the 'royal principle' for legal obligations, where it requires parties to act honourably and responsibly in performing duties, to avoid abusing the rights of other parties and to adhere to business law practices.[122] According to this principle, the parties shall not try 'to evade law or contracts but to perform duties under the contract voluntarily'.[123] Parties are also required to exercise their rights and fulfil their duties in strict accordance with the principle of good faith in every stage of their transactions, which include negotiations, formation and performance. There is an expectation that in each of the transactions, the parties are expected to act in good faith, which includes keeping promises, loyalty, honesty and non-deception, as well as respecting confidentiality.

In sum, good faith is not only regarded as a traditional moral value but is also taken seriously in commercial ethics. One of the major impacts of the concept of good faith in China is on business activities. Business activities are highly dependent on contract law to govern contractual activities between parties. The new contract law represents the achievement of a uniform law for contracts where good faith, as one of the fundamental principles, is given a clear statutory recognition in the new contract law.

[120] Wang Liming and Xu Chuanxi, 'Fundamental Principles of China's Contract Law' (1999) 13 *Columbia Journal of Asian Law*, 1, 16.

[121] Ibid., 22.

[122] Wang Liming and Xu Chuanxi, above n. 281, 16.

[123] Wang, C., & Zhang, X. (Eds.). (1997). *Introduction to Chinese Law*. Sweet & Maxwell.

Even though good faith is mentioned at every stage of the contract, a definition of the meaning of good faith is still lacking.

3.8 Good Faith in International Law

Apart from the recognition of good faith at the national level, good faith is recognised internationally with many international trade instruments imposing an obligation of good faith, as discussed below.

3.8.1 *The* United Nations Convention on Contracts for International Sale of Goods

The *United Nations Convention on Contracts for International Sale of Goods,* known as the Vienna Sales Convention (hereinafter CISG), is a tool to harmonise international sales law. It was drafted to govern international sales between contracting parties. The CISG was developed by the United Nations Commission on International Trade Law (UNCITRAL) and was signed in Vienna in 1980. After the debates and conferences in resolving the parameters of good faith in CISG, the concept of good faith was finally mentioned by Article 7(1), which states that:

> *In the interpretation of the Convention, regard is to be had to its international character and the need to promote uniformity in its application and the observation of good faith in international trade.*

Despite its inclusion in Article 7(1), there is an argument about whether good faith is relevant only as an interpretative tool or as a standard of behaviour for the contracting parties.[124] A plain reading of the provision embodied in Article 7(1) provides that good faith is to be used as a principle for interpreting the provisions of the CISG. Farnsworth commented that 'this provision does no more than instruct a court interpreting the Convention's provision to consider the importance of the listed factors'.[125] The list of factors includes (1) regard to the international character of the convention, (2) the need to promote uniformity in its application and (3)

[124] Ferrari, R. (1994). Uniform Interpretation of the 1980 Uniform Sales Law. *The Georgia Journal of International and Comparative Law*, 24, 183–210.

[125] Farnsworth, E. A. (1995). Duties of Good Faith and Fair Dealing Under the UNIDROIT Principles, Relevant International Conventions and National Laws. *Tulane Journal of International and Comparative Law*, 3, 47–55.

observance of good faith. This also means that Article 7(1) does not impose on the parties an obligation to act in good faith. This situation is also confirmed in the International Chamber of Commerce (ICC) Award No 8611 of 1997, where the court stated that:

> *Observance of good faith (observation by an arbitrator) that the principle of good faith mentioned in Article 7(1) is applicable to the interpretation of the CISG only, and is not to be referred to as a source of the parties' rights and duties with respect to performance of the contract.*[126]

Despite good faith being regarded as an interpretative tool, the principle of good faith also gives an impact on the parties' behaviour. This means that promoting the observance of good faith in international trade can only be achieved by requiring the parties to act in good faith. If the parties did not act in good faith, the principle of good faith in Article 7(1) would be meaningless. Koneru strongly supports that good faith is the standard of behaviour of contracting parties, whereby 'good faith cannot exist in a vacuum and does not remain in practice as a rule unless the actors are required to participate'.[127] Bonell similarly believes that good faith is a standard of behaviour for the contracting parties. He pointed out that 'the need to promote … the observance of good faith in international trade is also necessarily directed to the parties as a standard of behaviour to be maintained throughout the life of the contract'.[128]

The main reason for the argument of whether good faith is relevant only as an interpretative tool or as a standard of behaviour for the contracting parties is the lack of definition of good faith. The lack of a definition will lead to ambiguity. The CISG fails to define it; thus, it causes uncertainty to the international contract. Good faith is an elusive term which results in no uniform interpretation. Thus, when good faith cannot expressly define the intention of the provisions, it becomes meaningless.

[126] ICC Arbitral Award No 8611 of 1997, URL: http://cisgw3.law.pace.edu/cases/978611i1.htm.

[127] Koneru, P. (1997). The International Interpretation of the UN Convention on Contracts for the International Sale of Goods: An Approach Based on General Principles. *Minnesota Journal of Global Trade*, 6, 105–140.

[128] Bonell, M. H. (1987). Article 7: Interpretation of the Convention. In Biance, C. M., & Bonell, M. J. (Eds). *Commentary on the International Sales Law—The 1980 Vienna Sales Convention*. Milan.

3.8.2 *The* Principles of International Commercial Contracts

Despite the vagueness of the concept of good faith in the CISG, good faith is also mentioned in the *Principles of International Commercial Contracts* (hereinafter UNIDROIT Principles 2004). In 1994, the Governing Council of the International Institute for the Unification of Private Law (UNIDROIT) gave its imprimatur to the publication of the *Principles of International Commercial Contracts.* UNIDROIT is an independent intergovernmental organisation that aims specifically to harmonise international commercial contracts between merchants and other professionals with a territorial scope.

The general duty to act in good faith is expressly stated in the UNIDROIT Principles 2004. This means that good faith is the expected behaviour of the parties in international commercial contracts. The UNIDROIT Principles 2004 Article 1.7 clearly supports the duty of good faith:

> *(1) Each party must act in accordance with good faith and fair dealing in international trade.*

The reference to 'good faith and fair dealing in international trade' means that the standard which has ordinarily been adopted within the different national legal systems should not be applied unless commonly accepted by all legal systems.[129] Indeed, the duty of good faith is also found in a number of articles of the UNIDROIT Principles 2004, which constitute a direct or indirect application of the principle of good faith and fair dealing in all phases of the contract.[130] These articles make it clear that good faith and fair dealing are considered as fundamental principles underlying the UNIDROIT Principles 2004. For these reasons, there is still no meaning to the principle of good faith as the meaning of good faith will be constructed in the light of the special conditions of the international commercial contract. However, the general duty to act in good faith is not binding unless chosen by the parties to be the governing rules in the international commercial contract relationship.

[129] Zaccaria, E. C. (2004) The Dilemma of Good Faith in International Commercial Trade. *Macquarie Journal of Business Law*, 1, 101–110.

[130] See, for instance, Articles 2, 2.4(2)(b), 2.15, 2.16, 2.18, 2.20, 3.5, 3.8, 3.10, 4.1(2), 4.2(2), 4.6, 4.8, 5.2, 5.3, 6.1.3, 6.1.5, 6.1.16(2), 6.1.17(1), 6.2.3(3)(4), 7.1.2, 7.1.6, 7.1.7, 7.2.2.(b)(c), 7.4.8 and 7.4.13.

3.8.3 *The* Vienna Convention on the Law of Treaties

The *Vienna Convention on the Law of Treaties* (hereinafter VCLT) was opened for signature on 23 May 1969. VCLT is the law that guides the interpretation of international treaties that include its formation and operation of treaties. One of the principles in the VCLT observed that the principles of good faith and the *pacta sunt servanda*[131] rule are universally recognised. The *Nuclear Tests* case (*Australia v France*) illustrates that good faith is an integral part of the rule of *pacta sunt servanda*, whereby the International Court of Justice held that:

> *One of the basic principles governing the creation and performance of legal obligations, whatever their source, is the principle of good faith. Trust and confidence are inherent in international co-operation, in particular in an age when this co-operation in many fields is becoming increasingly essential. Just as the very rule of pacta sunt servanda in the law of treaties is based on good faith, so also is the binding character of an international obligation assumed by unilateral declaration.*[132]

The concept of good faith is particularly relevant in the performance of treaties. It is illustrated in Article 26 of VCLT which states that 'Every treaty in force is binding upon the parties to it and must be performed by them in good faith'. This means that good faith is the foundation for the rule of *pact sunt servanda*. It is always an implicit expectation that whenever states enter into a contract, they have willingly committed themselves to its terms to ensure the success of a contract. In drafting the VCLT, the Special Rapporteur referred to this provision by commenting that:

> *the intended meaning was that a treaty must be applied and observed not merely according to its letter but in good faith. It was the duty of the parties to the treaty not only to observe the letter of the law but also to abstain from acts which would inevitably affect their ability to perform the treaty.*[133]

[131] *Pacta sunt servanda* means agreements are to be kept; treaties should be observed. According to customary international law of treaties, *pacta sunt servanda* is the foundation of international law. Without such an acceptance, treaties would become worthless.

[132] [1974] ICJ REP. 253, 268.

[133] 'Report of the International Law Commission Covering Its 16th Session, 727th Meeting (20 May 1964)' [1964] 1 *Yearbook of International Law Commission* [70], 32.

Article 31(1) mentioned that 'A treaty shall be interpreted in good faith in accordance with the ordinary meaning to be given to the terms of the treaty in their context and in the light of its object and purpose'. This means that all obligations deriving from treaties are to be interpreted in good faith. According to O'Connor, the provision above means that the requirement of good faith shall be interpreted by considering the literal meaning of the treaty to reflect the principle of *pacta sunt servanda*.[134] In this context, good faith focused on what the parties actually agreed on.

The literal meaning approach, unfortunately, fails to interpret the meaning of good faith, which has resulted in an unclear meaning.[135] Therefore, in interpreting good faith, the requirement of honesty, fairness and reasonableness was used to prevent unintentional literal interpretation that can cause an unfair or unjust advantage over another party.[136] In VCLT, good faith is considered as the foundation for the rule of *pacta sunt servanda*. This suggests that good faith is an important concept in the VCLT, but unfortunately there is still no definition of good faith.

3.8.4 *The* Principle of European Contract Law

The Commission on European Contract Law produced the *Principles of European Contract Law* (hereinafter Principles) with an aim to harmonise the law of contract in the international business community by taking into account the requirements of the European domestic trade. The Principles are based on the concept of a uniform European contract law system. Their scope of application is only limited to the member states of the European Union.

The Principles also mention the concept of good faith. The general obligation of good faith is clearly mentioned in Article 1.201 (General Obligations), whereby 'Each party must act in accordance with good faith and fair dealing and the parties may not exclude or limit this duty'. This is a clear indication that good faith is the basic principle which is required in the performance and enforcement of the contractual duties in the contract. The formula of 'good faith and fair dealing' is used in the Principles in which this proposition is made plain by the commentary in the Principles

[134] O'Connor, J. F. (1990). *Good Faith in English Law*. Darmouth Publishing Company.
[135] Ibid., 109.
[136] Ibid., 110.

relating to Comment E in Article 1.201 that distinguishes the two concepts in the following manner:

> *'Good faith' means honesty and fairness in mind, which are subjective concepts. A person should, for instance, not be entitled to exercise a remedy if doing so is of no benefit to him and his only purpose is to harm the other party. 'Fair dealing' means observance of fairness in fact which is an objective test.*[137]

Although good faith is mentioned in the Principles, it still has not been defined. Thus, it is open for further debate in terms of its definition.

Article 1.102 (Freedom of Contract) states that 'Parties are free to enter into a contract and to determine its contents, subject to the requirements of good faith and fair dealing, and the mandatory rules established by these Principles'. Furthermore, Article 1.106 laid down guidelines for the interpretation and supplementation of the Principles, which include the promotion of good faith. It is clearly illustrated in Article 1.106 that 'These Principles should be interpreted and developed in accordance with their purposes. In particular, regard should be had to the need to promote good faith and fair dealing, certainty in contractual relationships and uniformity of application.'

The Principles are a non-binding application as it only offers protection to those parties who choose for such protection in their contract. Unfortunately, there is still an issue of a lack of definition of good faith which causes uncertainty to the contracting parties who opt for the protection under the Principles.

Despite the differences in its purpose, these international trade instruments show that good faith plays an important role in international contracts. However, there is a major problem to its application because there is still a lack of a clear definition of good faith which causes reservations to the international parties.

3.9 Conclusion

Although good faith has its roots in civil law countries, it has now extended beyond its geographical borders to common law countries. The brief review of good faith in various jurisdictions confirms that good faith is a

[137] Dixon, B. (2007). Can the Common Law Obligation of Good Faith Be Contractually Excluded? *Australian Business Law Review*, 35, 110–113.

highly versatile concept due to its adaptability in both civil law and common law countries. However, the concept of good faith differs in its scope and application, depending on which legal tradition governs the particular commercial transaction.

In civil law countries, good faith is regarded as a general and pervasive principle in contract law. As a general and pervasive principle, it has found its expression in the civil law codes and is recognised in all phases of the contract: negotiation, performance and enforcement. This means that good faith is served as a standard of behaviour which is expected from the parties in a contract. In common law, there is no overarching duty of good faith but good faith is recognised in certain specific contexts, for example, insurance. In the insurance context, the duty of utmost good faith was recognised for a long time in which there is an expectation of behaviour to effectuate the insurance contract. Unlike other common law countries, good faith has a different status in the US legal system, as illustrated by the recognition of good faith in the *Uniform Commercial Code* and the *Restatement (Second) of Contracts*. It is observed that the perception of good faith as an important principle in civil law appears to be much clearer compared to common law countries.

At the international level, good faith is an important concept, as illustrated in many international trade instruments, to regulate the behaviour of the international contracting parties. Despite its recognition at both the national and international levels, they all have one common problem with regard to its definition. It is evident that there is a lack of a definition despite it being a well-known concept.

CHAPTER 4

Good Faith Under Australian Contract Law

4.1 Introduction

This chapter provides a context for understanding the concept of good faith in Australia. Although the concept of good faith is widely discussed in the country, it is without a definitive guide in Australian contract law. Nevertheless, despite the absence of an underlying obligation of good faith in Australian law, the concept is still relevant to Australian contract law. In fact, there is an increasing body of literature on good faith in Australia, which suggests that good faith has a role in Australian contract law.[1]

[1] See, for example, Jeannie Marie Paterson, 'Terms Implied in Fact: The Basis for Implication' (1998) 13 *Journal of Contract Law* 103; John H Farrar, 'Good Faith and Dealing with Dissent in Prospectuses' (1999) 1 *U. Notre Dame Austl. L.Rev* 27; Jeannie Marie Paterson, 'Duty of Good Faith Does It Have a Place in Contract Law?' (2000) *Law Institute Journal* 48; Elisabeth Peden, 'Co-operation in English Contract Law—To Construe or Imply' (2000) 16 *Journal of Contract Law* 56; Jeannie Marie Paterson, 'Good Faith in Commercial Contracts? A Franchising Case Study' (2001) 29 *Australian Business Law Review* 270; Elisabeth Peden, 'Incorporating Terms of Good Faith in Contract Law in Australia' (2001) 23 *Sydney Law Review* 222; Elisabeth Peden, 'The Meaning of Contractual Good Faith' (2002) 22 *Australian Bar Review* 235; John Carter and Elisabeth Peden, 'Good Faith in Australian Contract Law' (2003) 19 *Journal of Contract Law* 155; Elisabeth Peden, *Good Faith in the Performance of Contract Law* (LexisNexis Butterworths, 2003); Elisabeth Peden, 'Good Faith in the Performance of Contract Law' (2004) *Law Society Journal* 64; Angelo Capuano, 'Not Keeping the Faith: A Critique of Good Faith in Contract Law in Australia and the United States' (2005) 17 *Bond Law Review* 29; Paul Finn, 'Good Faith and Fair Dealing: Australia' (2005) 11 *New Zealand Business Law Quarterly* 378;

N. Abdullah, *Good Faith in Contractual Performance in Australia*,
https://doi.org/10.1007/978-981-15-6078-1_4

4.2 Early History of Good Faith in the Australian Domain

One of the earliest discussions of good faith in Australia was in the opening speech at the Second Annual Journal of Contract Law conference in 1991. Lord Goff of Chieveley commented that English and Australian lawyers have a lot in common and that the principle of good faith is an issue for both jurisdictions.[2] His Lordship commented that:

> *We know that there is such a principle [good faith] in one of the most famous provisions of the German BGB. I think that I am right saying that there is also such a principle [good faith] in the United States Uniform Commercial Code. Do we need such a principle [good faith] as this in our commercial law?*[3]

His Lordship further commented that he was unsure of the position taken by Australian judges and practitioners but believed that there were some academic lawyers who were sympathetically inclined towards the idea of good faith.[4] Lord Goff was of the opinion that because of the conservative attitude of English judges, good faith could only exist if introduced by a commercial code akin to that introduced by the US. His Lordship further commented on the position of good faith in Australia, saying:

Elisabeth Peden, 'When Common Law Trumps Equity: The Rise of Good Faith and Reasonableness and the Demise of Unconscionability' (2005) 21 *Journal of Contract Law* 226; Bill Dixon, 'Can the Common Law Obligation of Good Faith Be Contractually Excluded?' (2007) 35 *Australian Business Law Review* 110; Elisabeth Peden, 'Implicit Good Faith' or Do We Still Need an Implied Term of Good Faith?' (2009) *Journal of Contract Law* 50; Andrew Terry and Cary Di Lernia, 'Franchising and the Quest for the Holy Grail: Good Faith or Good Intentions?' (2009) 33*Melbourne University Law Review* 542; The Hon Marilyn Warren AC, 'Good Faith: Where Are We At?' (2010) 34 (1) *Melbourne University Law Review* 344; Bill Dixon, 'Good Faith in Contractual Performance and Enforcement—Australian Doctrinal Hurdles' (2011) 39 *Australian Business Law Review* 227; James Allsop, 'Good Faith and Australian Contract Law: A Practical Issue and a Question of Theory and Principle'(2011) 85 *Australian Law Journal* 341.

[2] See Goff, R. L. A. (1992). Opening Address (Second Annual Journal of Contract Law Conference in London in September 1991). *Journal of Contract Law*, 5, 4.

[3] Ibid.

[4] Ibid.

> *In this country [Australia], we are more likely to see a gradual refinement and development of a recognised concept such as estoppel, which perhaps has yet to achieve its full potential.*[5]

In his opening address at the Fourth Journal of Contract Law conference two years later, Lord Staughton noted the uncertain position of good faith in Australia.[6] His Lordship affirmed that good faith is of importance in some commercial contexts, such as insurance contracts, but noted that common law does not proceed too readily from a series of examples to the adoption of a general principle of good faith.[7]

The concept of good faith was first judicially considered in 1992 by Priestley J in New South Wales (NSW) Court of Appeal in *Renard Constructions (ME) Pty Ltd v Minister for Public Works* (*Renard*).[8] Priestley J was clearly of the opinion that the appropriate course was towards the development of a general principle of good faith and fairness.[9] His Honour stated that:

> *people generally, including judges and other lawyers, from all strands of the community, have grown used to the courts applying standards of fairness to contract which are wholly consistent with the existence in all contracts of a duty upon the parties of good faith and fair dealing in its performance. In my view, this is in these days the expected standard, and anything less is contrary to prevailing community expectations.*[10]

His Honour reviewed the influence of the *Uniform Commercial Code* and the *Restatement (Second) of Contracts* of US case law and considered that there were strong arguments 'for recognition in Australia of [such] a duty'.[11] Despite Priestley J's strong belief in the position of good faith in Australia, its application remains uncertain. There remains no High Court decision regarding the position of good faith in Australia.

[5] Ibid.

[6] See Staughton, C. (1994). Good Faith and Fairness in Commercial Contract Law. *Journal of Contract Law*, 7, 193.

[7] Ibid.

[8] (1992) 26 NSWLR 234.

[9] Despite Priestley J's strong support for good faith, it should be noted that his comments were obiter.

[10] (1992) 26 NSWLR 234, 268.

[11] (1992) 26 NSWLR 234, 268.

This chapter proceeds as follows. In Australia, the concept of good faith was first introduced in the case of *Renard*, which will be discussed in Sect. 4.2. Although there is no overarching duty of good faith in Australian law, good faith is recognised in both common law and legislation, as discussed in Sect. 4.3. Section 4.4 elucidates the two important sources of good faith: 'implication' and 'construction'. Section 4.5 elaborates the implication in fact, which is concerned with business efficacy, and Sect. 4.6 examines implication in law based on the test of necessity as a legal incident of a particular class of contract. Section 4.7 discusses the developing concept of good faith in Australia subsequent to the watershed case of *Renard*.

4.3 The Watershed Decision: *Renard Constructions (ME) Pty Ltd v Minister for Public Works*

The judgement of Priestley J in *Renard* has paved the way for the emergence of the concept of good faith in Australian contract law. The *Renard* case did not establish the doctrine of good faith because Priestley J's comments were obiter, but it has no doubt influenced many cases.[12] *Renard* has been a catalyst for debate about the doctrine of good faith.

Renard concerned a dispute that arose between *Renard Constructions* (the contractor) and *Minister for Public Works* (the principal) over the construction of sewerage works. Clause 44.1 of NPWC3-1981 General Conditions of Contract stated that:

> *If the contractor defaults in the performance or observance of any covenant, condition or stipulation in the Contract or refuses or neglects to comply with any direction as defined in clause 23 but being one which either the principal or the Superintendent is empowered to give, make, issue or serve under the Contract and which is issued or given to or served or made upon the contractor by the principal in writing or by the Superintendent in accordance with clause*

[12] Some of the cases which refer to *Renard* (not exhaustive); *Service Station Association Ltd v Berg Bennet & Associates Pty Ltd* (1993) 45 FCR 84, *Vroon BV v Foster's Brewing Group Ltd* [1994] 2 VR 32, *Vodafone Pacific Ltd v Mobile Innovations Ltd* (2004) NSWCA 15 (Unreported, Sheller, Giles and Ipp JJA, 20 February 2004), *Alcatel Australia Ltd v Scarcella* (1998) 44 NSWLR 349, *Gary Rogers Motors (Aust) Pty Ltd v Subaru (Aust) Pty Ltd* (1999) FCA 903, *Burger King Corp v Hungry Jack's Pty Ltd* (2001) 69 NSWLR 558, *Esso Australia Resources Pty Ltd v Southern Pacific Petroleum NL* (2005) VSCA 228 (Unreported, Warren CJ, Buchanan JA and Osborn AJA, 15 September 2005).

> *23, the principal may suspend payment under the Contract and may call upon the contractor, by notice in writing, to show cause within a period specified in the notice as to why the powers hereinafter contained in this clause should not be exercised.*

The clause provided that if the contractor defaulted, the principal was entitled to call upon the contractor by notice in writing to 'show cause within a period specified in the notice' as to why the powers set out in the clause 'should not be exercised'. The clause also conferred on principal the power to take over the whole, or any part, of the work and to exclude the contractor from the site.

When the contractor did not complete the work on time, the principal served a notice under clause 44.1. One of the reasons for the contractor not completing the work on time was due to the failure of the principal to supply the required material at the agreed time of the contract. The information about the failure of the principal to supply the required material at the agreed time of the contract was unknown to the officer, who had the power to make final decisions to terminate the contracts and sign the appropriate notices. At the same time, the contractor had also enlarged its workforce, worked longer hours and engaged an experienced foreman in response to the show-cause notice. For these reasons, the contractor regarded the principal's conduct as repudiatory. The arbitrator found that the principal was unreasonable in exercising the power under clause 44.1. By virtue of s 38 of the *Commercial Arbitration Act 1984* (NSW), the principal appealed the award of the arbitrator.

Cole J held that the decision of the arbitrator should be reversed on the basis that clause 44.1 did not carry an implied obligation upon the principal to the effect that the power to take over the work and exclude the contractor from the site must be exercised reasonably. The contractor then appealed against Cole J's order. In the Court of Appeal, the issue that needed to be considered was whether the principal was under a duty to act reasonably, which permitted the principal to take over the builder's work. The three judges who heard the appeal, Priestley J, Handley JA and Meagher JA, delivered separate judgements.

4.3.1 Priestley J

In Priestley J's view, a requirement of reasonableness is implied in clause 44.1. His Honour suggested that the requirement could be either implied in fact[13] or implied in law.[14] His Honour further held that:

> *For myself, I cannot see why a term should not be implied at both stages; that is, it seems to me relatively obvious that an objective and reasonable outsider to this contract upon reading clause 44.1 would assume without serious question that the principal would have to give reasonable consideration to the question whether the contractor had failed to show cause and then, if the principal had reasonably concluded that the contractor had failed, that reason consideration must be given to whether any power and if any which power should be exercised.*[15]

His Honour held that all the accepted criteria for term 'implied in fact' were clearly satisfied. Priestley J agreed with the findings by the arbitrator that the principal was not entitled to exercise any power under clause 44.1 when the contractor had served the notice to show cause. Therefore, the

[13] Implication by fact, known as implication ad hoc, is an implication by a judge based on the judge's view of the actual intention of the parties drawn from the surrounding circumstances of the particular contract, its language and its purpose as that emerges from the language and in the circumstances. See *BP Refinery (Westernport) Pty Ltd v Hastings Shire Council* (1977) 180 CLR 266, which discusses the rules governing implication in fact. A number of Australian cases treating a duty of good faith as a term 'implied by fact', See, for example, *GSA Group Pty Ltd v Siebe Plc* (1993) 30 NSWLR 573; *News Ltd v Australian Rugby Football League Ltd* (1996) 58 FCR 447, 541; *Hughes Aircraft Systems International v Airservices Australia* (1997) 76 FCR 151; *Advance Fitness Corp Pty Ltd v Bondi Diggers Memorial & Sporting Club Ltd* [1999] NSWSC 264; *Saxby Bridge Mortgages Pty Ltd v Saxby Bridge Pty Ltd* [2000] NSWSC 433 [61]–[62].

[14] Implication by law is based on imputed intention as opposed to actual intention and implies a term as a legal incident of a particular class of contract. For a number of Australian cases treating a duty of good faith as a term 'implied by law', see, for example, *Alcatel Australia v Scarcella* (1998) 44 NSWLR 349, 369; *Garry Rogers Motors Aust Pty Ltd v Subaru (Aust) Pty* Ltd (1999) ¶ ATPR 41-703,43,014; Far *Horizons Pty Ltd v McDonald's Australia Ltd* [2000] VSC 310 (Unreported, Byrne J, 18 August 2000) [120], *Burger King Corporation v Hungry Jack's Pty Ltd* (2001) 69 NSWLR 558, *Apple Communications Ltd v Optus Mobile Pty Ltd* [2001] NSWSC 635 [15]; *Bamco Villa Pty Ltd v Montedeen Pty Ltd* [2001] VSC 192 (Unreported, Mandie J, 20 June 2001) [162]; *Commonwealth Bank of Australia v Renstel Nominees Pty Ltd* [2001] VSC 167 [47]; *Overlook v Foxtel* Aust Contract Reports ¶90-143. 91 972; *Commonwealth Bank of Australia Ltd v Spira* (2002) 174 FLR 274 [140]; *Commonwealth Development Bank of Australia v Cassagrain* [2002] NSWSC 965 [210].

[15] (1992) 26 NSWLR 234, 257.

principal's announcement to the contractor that the contractor was to be excluded from the site and that the remaining work was to be taken over by the principal was undoubtedly repudiatory. In this event, the contractor could bring the contract to an end.

In reaching this conclusion, an analogy was drawn between the incidents judicially attached to various classes of contract and those attached by statute. There are many instances in which Acts of Parliament impose a similar effect in the form of attaching implied conditions to contracts as an incident of law. In both instances, it arrived at the same outcome with the aim of making the contract fairer between the parties. In addition to statutory analogy, His Honour drew support from good faith:

> *Good Faith. The kind of reasonableness I have been discussing seems to me to have much in common with the notions of good faith which are regarded in many civil law systems of Europe and in all States in the United States as necessarily implied in many kinds of contract. Although this implication is not yet been accepted to the same extent in Australia as part of judge-make Australian contract law, there are many indications that the time may be fast approaching when the idea, long recognised as implicit in many of the orthodox techniques of solving contractual disputes, will gain explicit recognition in the same way as it has in Europe and in the United States.*[16]

Priestley J further commented that 'in ordinary English usage there has been a constant association between the word fair and reasonable. Similarly, there is a close association of ideas between the terms unreasonableness and lack of good faith. Although they may not be always co-extensive in their connotations, partly as a result of the varying senses in which each expression is used in different contexts, there can be no doubt that in many of their uses there is a great deal of overlap in their content.'[17]

His Honour also considered that the increased legislative interference with freedom of contract resulted in the fact that:

> *people generally, including judges and other lawyers, from all strands of the community, have grown used to the courts applying standards of fairness to contracts which are wholly consistent with the existence in all contracts of a duty upon the parties of good faith and fair dealing. In my view, this is in these days*

[16] (1992) 26 NSWLR 234, 264.
[17] (1992) 26 NSWLR 234, 265.

> *the expected standard, and anything less is contrary to prevailing community expectations.*[18]

Despite Priestley J's comments concerning the obligation of good faith being regarded as fundamental in the development of the obligation in Australia, it is clear that these comments did not form part of the reasoning upon which his Honour's conclusion was reached. It is interesting to contrast the approaches of Handley JA and Meagher JA with regard to this issue.

4.3.2 Handley JA

His Honour agreed with Priestley J and found that the contractual power must be exercised reasonably but employed different reasoning from Priestley J's decision.[19] As a matter of construction, the contract required the principal to act both honestly and reasonably in forming the opinion that the contractor had failed to show cause and thereafter in deciding whether to take over the work or to cancel the contracts. His Honour concluded that:

> *It seems to me that cl 44.1 should be construed as requiring the principal to act reasonably as well as honestly in forming the opinion that the contractor had failed to show cause to his satisfaction.*[20]

Handley JA held that the principal's decision, although honest, was 'objectively unreasonable and therefore, an invalid exercise of power'.[21]

4.3.3 Meagher JA

Meagher JA disagreed with Priestley J and Handley JA with regard to the requirement of reasonableness implied in clause 44.1. His Honour considered that there was no reason 'why the principal should have regard to any interests except his own'.[22] His Honour agreed that the principal acted 'honestly' where the principal was not corrupted by any pecuniary

[18] (1992) 26 NSWLR 234, 268.
[19] (1992) 26 NSWLR 234, 279.
[20] (1992) 26 NSWLR 234, 280.
[21] (1992) 26 NSWLR 234, 279.
[22] (1992) 26 NSWLR 234, 275.

consideration and the principal believed that he was entitled to act as he did. Meagher JA agreed with Coles J when his Honour rejected the requirement of reasonableness to be implied in clause 44.1 of the contract. His Honour held that:

> *Obviously enough it does not arise as a matter of construction of cl.44.1. It is not referred to expressly in that clause, nor is it to be discerned as a matter arising by necessary implication from the words used. Nor, in my view, is there any room to imply a term ... There is no reason why the principal should have regard to any interests except his own.*[23]

Meagher JA commented that unless that clause was expressly stated or as a matter arising by necessary implication from the words used,[24] his Honour preferred to decide the case on the simple basis that clause 44.1 required the principal to act on accurate information when forming a view on whether the contractor had shown cause.

The *Renard* case is significant in Australia because this case recognised that a duty of good faith could, in some circumstances, be implied into contracts. Although consideration was given to good faith by only one of three members of the NSW Court of Appeal, and only as obiter comments, nevertheless the case has been significant in subsequent cases, which have traced their authority back to *Renard*, including cases in jurisdictions other than NSW.[25]

In 2002, the High Court had the opportunity to discuss the issue of good faith in *Royal Botanic Gardens and Domain Trust v South Sydney CC* [26] but did not discuss the status or definition of the concept, Kirby J stated that:

[23] (1992) 26 NSWLR 234, 275.

[24] (1992) 26 NSWLR 234, 275.

[25] Some of the examples are *Service Station Association Ltd v Berg Bennet & Associates Pty Ltd* (1993) 45 FCR 84, *Vroon BV v Foster's Brewing Group Ltd* [1994] 2 VR 32, *Vodafone Pacific Ltd v Mobile Innovations Ltd* (2004) NSWCA 15 (Unreported, Sheller, Giles and Ipp JJA, 20 February 2004), *Alcatel Australia Ltd v Scarcella* (1998) 44 NSWLR 349, *Gary Rogers Motors (Aust) Pty Ltd v Subaru (Aust) Pty Ltd* (1999) FCA 903, *Burger King Corp v Hungry Jack's Pty Ltd* (2001) 69 NSWLR 558, *Esso Australia Resources Pty Ltd v Southern Pacific Petroleum NL* (2005) VSCA 228 (Unreported, Warren CJ, Buchanan JA and Osborn AJA, 15 September 2005).

[26] (2002) 186 ALR 289.

> *the debate in various Australian authorities concerns the existence and content of an implied obligation or duty of good faith and fair dealing in contractual performance and the exercise of contractual rights and power … The result is that, whilst the issues respecting the existence and scope of a 'good faith' doctrine are important, this is an inappropriate occasion to consider them.*[27]

Although the development of good faith in Australia can be traced to this case, Priestley J nevertheless must have been disappointed since the *Renard* case was discussed almost 20 years ago and yet both the status and meaning of good faith are still unsettled.

4.4 Good Faith in Specific Instances

References to good faith are increasingly found in both common law and legislation. The pervasiveness of the concept of good faith in common law and legislation indicates that good faith behaviour is the commonly expected norm.

4.4.1 Common Law

Common law has developed limited categories in which good faith is a recognised principle in contract law. In the insurance context, good faith is a well-known concept. Apart from insurance, good faith is also recognised in fiduciary and employment relationships, where there is a 'special kind of relationship' established by the contract which carries an implied obligation of good faith via mutual trust and confidence. The duty of good faith in insurance law was introduced almost 250 years ago in *Carter v Boehm*,[28] in which Lord Mansfield commented that:

> *Insurance is a contract of speculation. The special facts upon which the contingent chance is to be computed lie most commonly in the knowledge of the assured only; the underwriter trusts to his representation and proceeds upon confidence that he does not keep back any circumstance in his knowledge to mislead the underwriter into a belief that the circumstances do not exist. The keeping back of such circumstances is fraud, and therefore the policy is void. Although the suppression should happen through mistake, without any fraudulent intention, yet still the underwriter is deceived and the policy is void; because the risqué run*

[27] (2002) 2186 ALR 289, 312.
[28] (1766) 3 Burr 1905.

> *is really different from the risqué understood and intended to be run at the time of the agreement … The policy would be equally void against the underwriter if he concealed … Good faith forbids either party, by concealing what he privately knows to draw the other into a bargain from his ignorance of the fact, and his believing the contrary.*[29]

In a similar case occurring in the US, Stephen J, in *Comunale v Traders & General Insurance Co*, further commented that good faith is an important principle in the insurance contract to ensure the benefits of the agreement is achievable by the insurer and the insured. His Honour stated that:

> *There is an implied covenant of good faith and fair dealing in every contract that neither party will do anything which will injure the right of the other to receive the benefits of the agreement. This principle is applicable to policies of insurance. The rights of the insured 'go deeper' and that implied obligations are imposed 'based upon those principles of fair dealing which enter into every contract'.*[30]

Later, the concept was codified in the *Insurance Contracts Act 1984* (Cth) by requiring the insurer and the insured to exercise utmost good faith before entering into an insurance contract. Section 13 of the *Insurance Contracts Act 1984* (Cth) provides that:

> *A contract of insurance is a contract based on the utmost good faith and there is implied in such a contract a provision requiring each party to it to act towards the other party, in respect of any matter arising under or in relation to it, with the utmost good faith.*

A fiduciary relationship is a relationship in which one party undertakes or agrees to act for or on behalf of, or in the interests of, another person in the exercise of a power or discretion that will affect the interests of that other person in a legal or practical sense.[31] It is a requirement to act in the interests of another as a consequence of a 'special kind of relationship'. In

[29] (1766) 3 Burr 1905, 1910.

[30] 50 Cal.2d 653, 328 P.2d (1958).

[31] It is a kind of relationship of trust and confidence or confidential relationship, viz. trustee and beneficiary, agent and principal, solicitor and agent, employee and employer, director and company and partners.

Hospital Products Limited v United States Surgical Corporation,[32] Mason J noted:

> *The relationship between the parties is, therefore, one which gives the fiduciary a special opportunity to exercise the power or discretion to the detriment of that other person who is accordingly vulnerable to abuse by the fiduciary of his position ... It is partly because the fiduciary's exercise of the power or discretion can adversely affect the interests of the person to whom the duty is owed and because the latter is at the mercy of the former that the fiduciary comes under a duty to exercise his power or discretion in the interests of the person to whom it is owed.*[33]

In this context, the special relationship requires trust and confidence that carries with it an expectation of utmost loyalty and good faith.[34] In the partnership agreement, there is a relationship of trust and mutual confidence, which gives rise to a fiduciary duty of full disclosure on the part of both parties. The partners are bound to exercise the utmost good faith in their dealings with one another. The requirement of trust and mutual confidence was observed in *Helmore v Smith*,[35] where Bacon VC observed that 'their mutual confidence is the life-blood of the concern. It is because they trust one another that they are partners in the first instance; it is because they continue to trust one another that the business goes on.'[36]

In employment, the duty of good faith is implied from the relationship between the employer and employee. It was clearly stated in *Wessex Dairies Limited v Smith* that 'it is a necessary implication which must be engrafted on such a contract (employment) that the servant undertakes to serve his master with good faith and fidelity'.[37] Riley argues that the duty of good faith in the employment context is consistently implied as a duty of 'mutual trust and confidence' where both parties are expected to act in the best interests of maintaining trust in the relationship.[38] This statement is elaborated further in *Eastwood v Magnox Electric Plc*, where Lord Nicholls held that:

[32] (1984) 156 CLR 41.

[33] (1984) 156 CLR 41, 97.

[34] See Roberts S. Adler and Richard A. Mann, 'Good Faith: A New Look at an Old Doctrine' (1995) 28 *Akron Law Review* 31, 34.

[35] (1886) 35 ChD 436.

[36] (1886) 35 Ch D 436, 44.

[37] [1935] 2 KB 80.

[38] See Adler, R. S., & Mann, R. A. (1995). Good Faith: A New Look at an Old Doctrine. *Akron Law Review*, 28, 31–34.

> *[T]he trust and confidence in an implied term means, in short, that an employer must treat his employees fairly. In his conduct of his business and his treatment of his employees, an employer must act responsibly and in good faith.*[39]

4.4.2 *Legislation*

The legislature increasingly relies on good faith as a mechanism to achieve justice. There are more than 154 Federal Acts that mention the term good faith.[40] In legislation, there are two types of expressions to the concept of good faith, which are a) express and b) oblique. Express means a statutory obligation to act in good faith, and oblique means that good faith is a factor that has to be taken into account. An example of express good faith is the *Insurance Contracts Act 1984* (Cth), s 13, in which it is stated that:

> *A contract of insurance is a contract based on the utmost good faith and there is implied in such a contract a provision requiring each party to it to act towards the other party, in respect of any matter arising under or in relation to it, with the utmost good faith.*

By virtue of the above, the requirement of good faith has been interpreted to mean that both parties, namely, the insurer and the insured, must act with fairness and honesty, particularly when disclosing information to each other.[41] Due to its long engagement, the good faith requirement is considered as an important element in the insurance contract to ensure a successful contract.

Another example of good faith in legislation can be found in the *Corporations Act 2001* (Cth), s 181(1), where the requirement of good faith is implied based on the best interests of the corporation as opposed to the mandatory requirement in the insurance contract. That section provides that:

> *A director or other officer of a corporation must exercise their powers and discharge their duties in good faith in the best interests of the corporation and for a proper purpose.*

[39] [2005] 1 AC 503 [11].

[40] *Bropho v Human Rights & Equal Opportunity Commission* [2004] FCAFC 16 [84].

[41] See *Kelly v New Zealand Insurance Co Ltd* (1993) 7 ANZ Insurance Case 61-197 [78, 258].

An example of oblique good faith is found in s 22(1) of the *Australian Consumer Law*, as prescribed in schedule 2 of *Competition and Consumer Act 2010* (Cth). This section provides a list of factors which the court may have to consider for the purpose of determining unconscionable conduct. One factor that needs to be taken into account is the good faith factor which states, 'To the extent to which the supplier and the customer acted in good faith.'

4.5 Implication or Construction

The issue of implying a general term of good faith into contracts has been described as the most important unresolved issue in Australian contract law.[42] As noted earlier, the issue of good faith was raised in the High Court of Australia in *Royal Botanic Gardens and Domain Trust v South Sydney Council*. The Court did not decide whether good faith should be implied but nevertheless acknowledged the importance of the issues in respect to the existence and scope of a good faith doctrine.[43] Kirby J commented that an implied term of good faith would appear to conflict with fundamental notions of *caveat emptor*[44] that are inherent (statute and equitable intervention apart) in common law conceptions of economic freedom.[45] On the other hand, Callinan J noted that a duty of good faith might deny a party an opportunistic or commercial exercise of an otherwise lawful commercial right.[46]

At this stage, the High Court has not decided the method of incorporating good faith either as an 'implication of a term' or based on the 'principle of construction'. Both methods are dissimilar in terms of incorporating good faith. In the context of 'implication of a term', the judge may imply a term into the contract to overcome an oversight on the parties either through inadvertence or poor drafting or may have failed to incorporate terms to cover a particular situation which had they thought about it, they would certainly have made provision for. In such a case, the judge may

[42] See Carter, J. W., & Stewart, A. (2002). Interpretation, Good Faith and the True Meaning of Contracts: The Royal Botanic Decision. *Journal of Contract Law*, 18, 182–190.

[43] (2002) 186 ALR 301 [40].

[44] In English law, there is a well-recognised maxim of 'caveat emptor'. Literally 'caveat emptor' means 'let the buyer beware'. In this context, it means there is no duty on the seller of the goods to point out their defects.

[45] (2002) 186 ALR 301 [88].

[46] (2002) 186 ALR 301 [156].

imply appropriate terms to give 'business efficacy' to the contract in accordance with the presumed intention of the parties. In the context of 'principle of the construction', the judge interprets the meaning of a term in a contract by giving the term a legal effect to give effects to the parties' intention.

In many instances, the duty of good faith is conceived as an implied term.[47] There are two types of implication: term 'implied in law' and term 'implied in fact'. Term 'implied in law' is based on the legal incident of a particular type of contract. Term 'implied in fact' is based on the test of necessity. There has been some debate and some confusion as to whether the implied duty of good faith, if it exists, is an 'implied term in law' or an 'implied term in fact'.

In *Renard*, there is an argument that good faith can be implied in both terms: term 'implied by fact' and term 'implied by law'. However, in practice, there may be some overlap. In *Renard*, Priestley J said:

> *Although the authorities discussed by Hope JA in Castlemaine Tooheys seem to require a sharp distinction to be drawn between implication ad hoc and by law, assigning the former to the fact of particular contract, and the latter to the legal incidents of contracts of different classes, consideration of the contract in the present case shows there may be a good deal of overlap between the two categories.*[48]

On the contrary, Peden argues that the method of incorporating good faith that is usually relied upon, namely the implication of a term, could, in fact, prove a 'hindrance rather than a positive force in the introduction of an obligation of good faith'.[49] Peden argues that construction is the best approach for incorporating good faith in a contract. The rule of construction consists of an interpretation and construction process.[50] Interpretation describes the process whereby courts determine the meaning of words. Construction describes the process of determining their legal effect. The main requirement is to give effect to the parties' intention

[47] Woo, P. Y. (2001). Protecting Parties' Reasonable Expectations: A General Principle of Good Faith. *Oxford University Commonwealth Law Journal*, 1, 195–221.

[48] (1992) 26 NSWLR 234, 260.

[49] Peden. E. (2001). Incorporating Terms of Good Faith in Contract Law in Australia. *Sydney Law Review*, 23, 222.

[50] Peden, E. (2000). Co-operation in English Contract Law—To Construe or Imply. *Journal of Contract Law*, 16, 56.

to construe the contract as a whole and to avoid an unreasonable construction where possible.

The rule of construction was adopted in *Auag Resources Ltd v Waihi Mines Ltd*,[51] where the High Court was asked to determine whether there was a joint venture between the parties. In this case, the parties had signed the joint venture agreement. The issue arose when the defendant sold its interest in the joint venture to another person. The plaintiff, as one of the parties in the joint venture, alleged that there is a breach of the joint venture agreement. The plaintiff claimed, *inter alia*, a breach of fiduciary obligation. The joint venture agreement provided that the parties should be just and faithful in joint venture dealings but are otherwise free to pursue their interests. The joint venture was not a partnership; therefore, there was no fiduciary duty. The defendant claimed that the joint venture agreement covered the parties' legal relationship and applied to strike out the fiduciary course of action. Barker J, referring to the judgement of Mason J in *Hospital Products Ltd v United States Surgical Corporation*,[52] construed the joint venture agreement based on its true construction where the fiduciary relationship cannot be superimposed upon the contract in such a way that it alters the intention of the contract. Therefore, a carefully drawn mining joint venture agreement, such as the one under consideration, is not to be viewed as a partnership.

Peden also emphasised that the principle of construction is based on the theory of cooperation[53] and 'that any other approach can lead to illogical or inappropriate reasoning'.[54] The duty of cooperation has long been part of the law of contract where there is a necessary standard of fairness and cooperation in the performance of contractual obligations.[55] This duty to cooperate is usually traced back to Lord Blackburn's statement in *Mackay v Dick*, where it was held that:

[51] [1994] 3 NZLR 571.

[52] (1984) 156 ALR 417.

[53] Peden, E. (2003). *Good Faith in the Performance of Contract.* LexisNexis Butterworths. ch.6.

[54] Peden, E. (2000). Co-operation in English Contract Law—To Construe or Imply. *Journal of Contract Law*, 16, 56.

[55] See also Rickett, C. E. F. (2001). *Some Reflections on Open-Textured Commercial Contracting.* AMPLA Yearbook, 372-383 Rickett also favoured the duty of cooperation as a principle of construction.

> *As a general rule ... wherein a written contract it appears that both parties have agreed that something shall be done, which cannot effectually be done unless both concur in doing it, the construction of the contract is that each agree to do all that is necessary to be done on his part of the carrying out of that thing, though there may be in express words to that effect.*[56]

It is clear that cooperation is imposed to the extent that it is necessary to make the contract workable and the contract would come to a complete halt if the act in question was not performed.[57] In *Mona Oil Equipment Co v Rhodesia* Railways,[58] Devlin J held that:

> *It is, no doubt, true that every business contract depends for it's smooth working on co-operation, but in the ordinary business contract, and apart, of course, from the express term, the law can enforce co-operation in a limited degree to the extent that is necessary to make the contract workable. For any higher degree of co-operation, the parties must rely on the desire that both of them usually have that the business should be done.*[59]

The courts assume that parties intend their bargain to have legal effect and they would, therefore, intend to cooperate to ensure that this happens unless they express a contrary intention in their contract.[60] Therefore, to imply an obligation of good faith is an unnecessary step where the same result is achieved by considering the parties' intentions in the construction of the contract to ensure cooperation.[61] It is also evident that the duty of cooperation has been established in contract law for over a century, as Griffith CJ said in *Butt v McDonald*:

> *It is a general rule applicable to every contract that each party agrees, by implication, to all such things as are necessary on his part to enable the other party to have the benefit of the contract.*[62]

[56] (1881) 6 App Cas 251, 262.

[57] See Burrows, J. F. (1968). Contractual Cooperation and Implied Terms. *Modern Law Review*, 31, 390.

[58] [1949] 2 All E.R 1014.

[59] [1949] 2 All E.R 1014, 1018.

[60] Peden. E. (2001). Incorporating Terms of Good Faith in Contract Law in Australia. *Sydney Law Review*, 23, 222–230.

[61] Ibid.

[62] (1896) 7 QLJ 68, 70–71.

There is an expectation that one party should cooperate in doing all that is necessary to be done for the performance by the other party of his obligations under the contract. This statement was reaffirmed in the High Court decision in *Secured Income Real Estate (Australia) Ltd v St Martin's Investments Pty Ltd:*

> *But it is common ground that the contract imposed an implied obligation on each party to do all that was reasonably necessary to secure the performance of the contract.*[63]

As mentioned earlier, cooperation is the expected obligation of the parties to ensure the success of the contract. Therefore, cooperation is a term that is not implied from the contract but is a term that arises out of construction. Peden commented that cooperation is the basic rule of construction where she further elaborated by giving an example:

> *it was once thought that contracts contained an implied term about frustrating events. However, today it is accepted as a principle of construction. We do not say it is an implied term in law that frustration will discharge a contract because the doctrine generally applies to all contracts. Once it applies to all contracts the 'term' is a rule of construction, applicable to all contracts. Another example is the 'implication' of a reasonable time for performance. Repudiation could also join the list, since the implied term rationale there has also been rejected, and co-operation could be seen as the basis of the rule of construction that determines whether there is a lack of readiness, willingness and ability to perform.*[64]

It is also argued that as good faith is already inherent in all contracts, when a court implies a term of good faith, it is 'implying a redundant term'.[65] Furthermore, good faith is a universal term, and the status of the implied duty of good faith is clearly that of a universal term, in which 'an obligation implied in all contracts, of whatever kind, along with the duty of cooperation', as described above.[66]

[63] (1979) 144 CLR 596, 607-608 per Mason J.

[64] Peden, E. (2000). Co-operation in English Contract Law—To Construe or Imply. *Journal of Contract Law*, 16, 56–67.

[65] Peden, E., & Carter, J. (2003). Good Faith in Australian Contract Law. *Journal of Contract Law*, 19, 155.

[66] Seddon, N., & Ellinghaus, M. (2002). *Cheshire & Fifoot's Law of Contract* (8th ed.). LexisNexis Butterworths.

4.5.1 *Implication in Fact*

Implication in fact is based on the judge's view of the actual intention of the parties drawn from the surrounding circumstances of the particular contract, its language and its purpose. When a judge is asked to imply a term in a contract, the parties' presumed intention must be determined. The earliest test used to determine this was what came to be called the 'officious bystander' test. The 'officious bystander' test was developed by Mackinnon LJ in *Shirlaw v Southern Foundries*, where Mackinnon LJ said that:

> *For my part, I think that there is a test that may be at least as useful as such generalities. If I may quote from an essay which I wrote some years ago, I then said: 'Prima facie that which in any contract is left to be implied and need not be expressed is something so obvious that it goes without saying; so that, if, while the parties were making their bargain, an officious bystander were to suggest some express provision for it in their agreement, they would testily suppress him with a common "Oh, of course!"'*[67]

The need for terms implied in fact arises out of circumstances not contemplated in the written terms.[68] When the contract has not been reduced to any complete written form, McHugh and Gummow J held in *Byrne v Australian Airlines* that:

> *If the contract has not been reduced to complete written form, the question is whether the implication of the particular term is necessary for the reasonable or effective operation of the contract in the circumstances of the case; only where this can be seen to be true will the term be implied.*[69]

In ascertaining the parties' presumed intentions and in identifying an appropriate term to be implied in a contract, the Privy Council held in *BP Refinery (Westernport) Pty Ltd v Shire of Hastings* that for a term to be implied, the following conditions must be satisfied: (1) it must be reasonable and equitable; (2) it must be necessary to give business efficacy to the contract, so that no term will be implied if the contract is effective without

[67] [1939] 2 KB 206, 227.

[68] Paterson, J. M. (1998). Terms Implied in Fact: The Basis for Implication. *Journal of Contract Law*, 13, 103–106.

[69] (1995) 185 CLR 410, 422.

it; (3) it must be so obvious as to go without saying; (4) it must be capable of clear expression; and (5) it must not contradict any express term.[70]

The leading authority for condition (3) is *The Moorock* case,[71] in which the defendant had agreed to allow the plaintiff to load his vessel at the defendant's wharf on the River Thames. However, the plaintiff's vessel suffered damage when resting at the defendant's jetty during low tide. The damage to the vessel had been due to a ridge of hard ground beneath the mud, and the plaintiff claimed compensation. The English Court of Appeal said that a term had to be implied into the contract imposing an obligation of the defendant to see that the bottom of the river was reasonably fit or to exercise reasonable care in finding out its condition and to advise the plaintiff of its condition. Bowen LJ held that:

> *In business transaction such as this, what the law desires to effect by the implication is to give such business efficacy to the transaction as must have been intended at all events by both parties who are businessmen; not to impose on one side all the perils of the transaction, or to emancipate one side from all the chances of failure, but to make each party promise in law as much, at all events, as it must have been in contemplation of both parties that he should be responsible for in respect of those perils or chances.*[72]

It is clear that the parties are expected to know that the vessel will rest on the bottom at low tide, and therefore the contract cannot be performed unless the ground is safe for the vessel. In this case, the plaintiff was able to recover damages for breach of contract. In *Narni Pty Ltd v National Australia Bank*, Tadgell JA commented that:

> *[T]he remark of the 'officious bystander' postulated by Mackinnon LJ, from which the condition number (3) evidently draws inspiration, is not always helpful or useful; and that 'it seems no longer the exclusive means of approaching the question'. The five conditions, although evidently expressed to operate cumulatively, may nevertheless overlap; and in some cases, I think this is one of them; a more simplified approach may be appropriate and permissible.*[73]

[70] (1977) 180 CLR 266, 282–283.
[71] (1889) 14 PD 64.
[72] (1889) 14 PD 64, 68.
[73] [2001] VSCA 31 [16].

In *Shipping (London) Ltd v Polish Steamship Co (The Manifest Lipkowy)*, May LJ remarked that:

> *For my part, I think that reference to the officious bystander frequently does not assist in deciding whether or not a term is to be implied. Officious bystanders may well take different views depending on which side they happen to be standing. In my opinion, it is quite clear from such cases as Liverpool City Council v Irwin [1997] AC 239 that the real basis upon which a term can be implied in contracts such as this is that they are necessary in order to make the contract work.*[74]

The following cases illustrate the term 'implied in fact', which is based on the requirement of the *BP Refinery* test. One of the requirements in the *BP Refinery* test holds that to be an 'implied term in fact', a term must be capable of being expressed in a clear or precise manner. This is illustrated in *Ansett Transport Industries v Commonwealth.*[75] This case between Commonwealth and Ansett refers to the implementation of the 'two airlines' policy by the Commonwealth. Ansett complained that there was a breach of an implied term in its agreement with the Commonwealth upon granting permits to rival companies which allows the Commonwealth to compete with Ansett in interstate air freight services. The argument of breach of an implied term in its agreement was rejected by the High Court. One of the reasons given by Gibbs J was that:

> *If a term were to be implied it would be to the effect that the Commonwealth would do whatever it might lawfully do to maintain the position (which has already been secured) that there are two and more than two operators of trunk route airline services in Australia, or put negatively, that it would not do anything which would destroy or undermine that position. The width and lack of precision of such a condition is an argument against implying it.*[76]

On the other hand, the *BP Refinery* test also discussed the requirement of obviousness in ascertaining the parties' presumed intention. This is illustrated in *Codelfa Construction Pty Ltd v State Rail Authority of New South Wales.*[77] In this case, Codelfa was hired to do work for the State Rail

[74] (1989) 2 Lloyd's Rep 138, 142.
[75] (1977) 139 CLR 54.
[76] (1977) 139 CLR 54, 62.
[77] (1982) 149 CLR 337.

Authority. The contract required Codelfa to complete work by certain dates and to complete all work within 130 weeks. Codelfa commenced work three shifts a day and seven days a week. Because of the noise, dirt and disruption, local residents obtained an injunction preventing work from being carried out on Sundays between the hours of 10 pm and 6 am. This injunction was granted and had caused Codelfa to reduce their working days to six days a week, which meant no work on Sundays and only to work two shifts a day. At the time of contracting, there was a common assumption of the parties that the work was subject to s 11 of the *City and Suburban Electric Railways (Amendment) Act 1967* (NSW), which protected Codelfa from injunctions due to nuisance. Therefore, Codelfa argued that a term has to be implied into the contract to give business efficacy to it due to their inability to work three shifts a day. However, the claim by Codelfa was denied by the High Court. Mason J commented that the inability of Codelfa to work three shifts a day could not be implied because it was unclear what form it would have taken. In this regard, a term can only be implied if it is 'necessary to do so' and if it is so obvious that it 'goes without saying', as stated in the *BP Refinery* test.

Implication, in fact, gives little scope for good faith. Only in rare situations is a contract ineffective without it. Recently, courts have moved away from implying terms of good faith in fact to implying them in law.[78] This is partly because of the difficulty in satisfying the legal test for implication in fact. It is also argued that the express intention of the parties at the time of the making of the contract is less easily identified than an established term implied in law, which encompasses standard terms implied in all contracts of a particular class.[79] In addition, when the express intention is difficult to deduce, there can be no other conclusion than that it is the court that is imposing its own views of what was intended, which is contrary to the parties' intention.[80]

[78] See Peden, E. (2003). Construction Distinguished from Implication in Fact. In Peden, E. *Good Faith in the Performance of Contract*. LexisNexis Butterworths.

[79] Paterson, J. M. (1998). Terms Implied in Fact: The Basis for Implication. *Journal of Contract Law*, 13, 103–106.

[80] Burrows, J. F. (1968). Contractual Cooperation and Implied Terms. *Modern Law Review*, 31, 390.

4.5.2 *Implication in Law*

Implication in law is the implication of a term into a contract as a necessary incident of a specific type of contract, with reference to the circumstances of the case and for which the particular implied term has sufficient policy justifications. In *Simonius Vischer & Co v Holt & Thompson*, Samuels JA commented that 'the imposition of terms as a matter of law amounts to no more than the imposition of legal duties in cases where the law thinks that policy requires it'.[81] Terms 'implied in law' are obligations that arise within the contract irrespective of the intentions of the parties. In *Australis Media Holdings Pty Ltd v Telstra Corporation Ltd*, Mason P, Beazley JA and Stein JA held that 'At the end of the day, it is to be remembered that terms implied at law do not depend upon the intention of the parties'.[82] The court is reluctant to imply new terms in law. This is partly because legislation covers many important areas and probably partly because courts are wary of creating new obligations that will catch a vast number of contracts.[83]

An example of the kind of contracts in which terms are implied is relational contracts such as distributorship, partnership, franchise arrangements and joint ventures. A relational contract is a type of contract, often a long-term contract, where there is a need to maintain the relationship because these types of contracts are often exposed to uncertainty and unforeseen factors that cannot readily be provided for in advance due to the long engagement. In *Bobux Marketing Ltd v Raynor Marketing Ltd*, Thomas J commented that:

> *The norms of the ongoing relationship, of necessity, tend to supplement the express contractual obligations. Good faith is required to ensure that the requisite communication, cooperation and predictable performance occur for the advantage of both parties.*[84]

The test of necessity was introduced in the decision of *Liverpool City Council v Irwin*,[85] in which the landlord and tenant disputed an obligation with respect to the common areas of the stairs and lift. The express term

[81] [1979] 2 NSWLR 322, 348.
[82] (1998) 43 NSWLR 104, 123.
[83] Peden. E. (2001). Incorporating Terms of Good Faith in Contract Law in Australia. *Sydney Law Review*, 23, 222–229.
[84] [2002] 1 NZLR 506.
[85] [1977] AC 239, 254.

of the contract between the parties contained a list of obligations owed by the tenant, however none by the landlord. The House of Lords held that the landlord was under an implied obligation to take reasonable care of the common area. The House of Lords was prepared to imply the term in law in the class of contract in question, namely tenancies in high-rise apartment blocks. Lord Wilberforce held that:

> *In my opinion, such an obligation should be read into the contract as the nature of the contract itself implicitly requires, no more, no less: a test, in other words, of necessity. The relationship accepted by the corporation is that of landlord and tenant: the tenant accepts obligations accordingly, in relation to the stairs, the lifts and the chutes. All these are not just facilities, or conveniences provided at discretion; they are essentials of the tenancy without which life in the dwellings, as a tenant, is not possible. To leave the landlord free of contractual obligation as regards these matters, and subject only to administrative or political pressure, is, in my opinion, inconsistent totally with the nature of this relationship. The subject matter of the lease (high rise blocks) and the relationship created by the tenancy demand, of their nature, some contractual obligation on the landlord.*[86]

The underlying concern of the above case revealed that the test for an implied term at law is not whether it is necessary for the existence of the contract but whether it is necessary to the fair functioning of the agreement. In *Bryne v Australia Airlines Ltd*,[87] McHugh and Gummow JJ determined the meaning of 'necessity' and held that:

> *Many of the terms now said to be implied by law in various categories of cases reflect the concerns of the court that unless such a term be implied, the enjoyment of the rights conferred by the contract would or could be rendered nugatory, worthless, or perhaps being seriously undermined. Hence the reference in the decisions to 'necessity' … This notion of 'necessity' has been crucial in the modern cases in which the courts have implied for the first to a new term as a matter of law.*[88]

Finn J, a proponent of good faith, writing extrajudicially, commented that:

[86] [1977] AC 239,254, 255.
[87] (1995) 131 ALR 422, 450.
[88] (1995) 185 CLR 410, 450.

While it is true in the South Sydney case I indicated ... that our law has not yet committed itself unqualified to the proposition that every contract imposes on each party a duty of good faith and fair dealing (and I believe that was then an accurate summary of the law), the implication when it is made should in my view be an implication of law.[89]

A number of cases treat a duty of good faith as a term implied in law as follows: In *Burger King Corporation v Hungry Jack's Pty Ltd*, the New South Wales Court of Appeal stated that:

There also appears to be increasing acceptance ... that if terms of good faith and reasonableness are to be implied, they are to be implied as a matter of law. We consider that to be correct.[90]

Similarly, in *Hughes Aircraft v Airservices Australia*, a universal duty of good faith was suggested. Finn J held that:

I should add that, unlike Gummow J [in Service Station Association v Berg Bennet (1993) 45 FCT 84][91] *I consider a virtue of the implied duty to be that it expresses in a generalisation of universal application the standard of conduct to which all contracting parties are to be expected to adhere throughout the lives of the contract.*[92]

Some cases treat an implied term of good faith as a legal incident of every contract. In *Overlook v Foxtel*, Barrett J held that:

An additional term implied by law into commercial contracts is a term requiring the exercise of good faith in the performance of contracts. This is now in this State a legal incident of every such contract.[93]

In *Alcatel Australia Ltd v Scarcella & Ors*,[94] the lessee was under an agreement to keep the premises in 'substantially good repair or in

[89] Finn, P. (2001). Equity and Commercial Contracts: A Comment. *AMPLA Yearbook*, 414–418.

[90] [2001] NSWCA 187.

[91] In this case, Gummow J stated that 'no authority which binds this Court supports the implication by law of a term of such a width [as the duty of good faith]'.

[92] (1997) 146 ALR 1, 37.

[93] [2002] Aust Contract Reports ¶90-143. 91 972.

[94] (1998) 44 NSWLR 349.

reasonable repair'. When the council issued a fire safety order, it was unusual because it was on the request of the lessor. Twenty-four items were subsequently found not to comply with building regulations, including the stairway. The lessee failed to comply with a subsequent fire safety order. The lessee argued that there is an implied term of good faith in the lessors' performance of their lease obligations, which bound them to cooperate in a reasonable way to ensure that the lessee was not subjected to the expense and impact of an unreasonable fire order. On the facts, the lessee's action failed because it could not be said that a property owner acted unconscionably or in breach of an implied term of good faith in a lease of the property by taking steps to ensure that the requirements for fire safety advised by an expert fire engineer should be put in place. However, it was held by Sheller JA (with whom Powell and Beazley JJA agreed) that the decisions in *Renard* and *Hughes Bros* mean that in New South Wales, a duty of good faith in performing obligations and exercising rights may by implication be imposed upon parties as part of their contract.[95] In this context, there is an obvious reason why the duty of good faith can be implied in a commercial lease between the lessor and the lessee.

The same position is found in *Gary Rogers Motors (Aust) Pty Ltd v Subaru (Aust) Pty Ltd*,[96] where Subaru terminated the plaintiff's dealership with 13 months' notice, ostensibly because the plaintiff was not prepared to abide by a new '6 star revitalisation program' that Subaru wanted implemented in all dealerships. The provision concerned with termination was to be found in clause 11.1, which provided that:

> *Notwithstanding anything contained in the Letter of Appointment and the Terms and Conditions, either party may terminate this arrangement by giving to the other notice in writing*

The plaintiff claimed that there was a breach of, *inter alia*, an implied term not to exercise any power conferred by the agreement, including the power of termination otherwise than in good faith. Finskelstein J affirmed *Renard*, *Hughes* and *Alcatel* and held that the recent cases accepted that inappropriate contracts, perhaps even in all commercial contracts, such a term will ordinarily be implied, not as implication in fact (based on the presumed intention of the parties) but as a legal incident of the relationship. Finskelstein J held that:

[95] (1998) 44 NSWLR 349, 368.
[96] (1999) ATPR ¶ 41-703.

> *A term of a contract that requires a party to act in good faith and fairly, imposes an obligation upon that party not to act capriciously. It would not operate so as to restrict actions designed to promote the legitimate interests of that party. In addition, provided the party exercising the power acts reasonably in all the circumstances, the duty to act fairly and in good faith will ordinarily be satisfied.*[97]

Many cases have shown support for implied good faith by way of implied 'term in law'.[98] It is easier to identify good faith from the term 'implied by law' based on the legal incident of a particular class of contract, for example in the relational contract. To satisfy the requirement of term 'implied by law' is less contentious because it is not what the parties intended but what the court or legislature thinks is necessary for the fair functioning of the contract.

4.6 The Developing Australian Position

As noted above, the decision of *Renard* opened up the possibility for the development of the doctrine of good faith in Australian jurisprudence.[99] However, to date, the position of the concept of good faith in contractual performance is still unclear.

Most Australian cases rely on the duty of good faith in contractual performance where the duty of good faith is implied in various types of commercial contracts such as tenders,[100] commercial leases,[101] licence agreements,[102] building contracts, contracts between football clubs and

[97] (1999) ATPR ¶ 41-703, 43, 014.

[98] Carlin, T. M. The Rise (and Fall) of Implied Duties of Good Faith in Contractual Performance in Australia (2005) 25 *University of New South Wales Law Journal*, 99, 123.

[99] *Renard* was affirmed in *Hughes Bros Pty Ltd v Trustees of the Roman Catholic Church* (1993) 31 NSWLR 91 [93], Kirby P noting that: 'I am therefore bound by what was decided by the Court in *Renard* [good faith]. I must therefore apply *Renard* in the present appeal. To do so is part of my judicial duty'. There is a strong support received in *Alcatel Australia Ltd v Scarcella* (1998) 44 NSWLR 349, 368, where Shellar JA held that 'the decision in *Renard* and *Hughes Bros* means that in New South Wales a duty of good faith, both in performing obligations and exercising rights, may by implication be imposed upon parties as part of the contract'.

[100] See *Hughes Aircraft Systems International v Airservices Australia* (1997) 76 FCR 151, *Dalcon Constructions Pty Ltd v State Housing Commission* (1998) 14 BCL 477.

[101] See *Alcatel Australia Ltd v Scarcella* (1998) 44 NSWLR 349; *Advance Fitness v Bondi Diggers Memorial and Sporting Club Ltd* (NSW Supreme Court, Austin J, 30 March 1999).

[102] See *Asia Television Ltd v Yau's Entertainment Pty Ltd* [2000] FCA 254.

leagues,[103] contracts between business consultants and their subcontractors,[104] dealership agreements,[105] contracts for supply of materials and labour,[106] and transportation.[107] What is interesting about these cases is the state of confusion about the definition and attitude of the judges in expressing the concept of good faith.

In the development of the concept on the context of Australia, much debate has centred on its meaning,[108] with many believing that good faith takes on different meanings depending on its context.[109] Einstein J in *Aiton Australia Pty Ltd v Transfield Pty Ltd* held that 'the concept of good faith acquires substance from the particular events that take place … the standard must be fact-intensive and it is best determined on a case by case basis'.[110]

Peden suggested that the most appropriate meaning of good faith is a requirement 'to have regard to the interests of the other party including the obligation of loyalty to the contract and honesty'.[111] The requirement 'to have regard to the interests of the other party including the obligation of loyalty to the contract and honesty' does not require the parties to behave with 'unreasonableness' or 'unconscionability'.[112] Peden's proposed definition of good faith was given strong support in *Overlook v Foxtel*,[113] where Barratt J stated that:

> *It must be accepted that the party subject to the obligation is not required to subordinate the party's own interests, so long as the pursuit of those interests does not entail unreasonable interference with the enjoyment of a benefit conferred by the express contractual terms so that the enjoyment becomes (or could*

[103] See *News Ltd v Australian Rugby Football League Ltd* (1996) 135 ALR 33; *South Sydney District Rugby League Football Club Ltd v News Ltd* (2000) 177 ALR 611 [695–696, 701].

[104] See *Saxby Bridge Mortgages Pty Ltd v Saxby Bridge Pty Ltd* [2000] NSWSC 187.

[105] See *Gary Rogers Motors (Aust) Pty Ltd v Subaru (Aust) Pty Ltd* (1999) [21] ATPR ¶ 43,008, 41–703.

[106] See *Howtrac Rentals Pty Ltd v Thiess Contractors (NZ) Limited* (Victorian Supreme Court, Gillard J, 21 December 2000).

[107] See *K & S Freighters Pty Ltd v Linfox Transport (Aust) Pty Ltd* (2006) FCA 219.

[108] See Chap. 8 for further discussion on the problem of defining good faith.

[109] See Hird, N. J., Howells, G. G., Brownsword, R. (Eds). (1999). *Good Faith in Contract, Concept and Context.* Ashgate.

[110] (1999) 153 FLR 236, 263.

[111] Peden, E. (2002). The Meaning of Contractual Good Faith. *Australian Bar Review,* 22, 235–247.

[112] Ibid.

[113] [2002] NSWSC 17.

> *become) ... 'nugatory, worthless or, perhaps, seriously undermined' ... the implied obligation of good faith underwrites the spirit of the contract and support the integrity of its character. A party is precluded from cynical resort to the black letter. But no party is fixed with the duty to subordinate self-interest entirely which is the lot of the fiduciary ... The duty is not a duty to prefer the interests of the other contracting party. It is rather, a duty to recognise and to have due regard to the legitimate interests of both the parties in the enjoyment of the fruits of the contract as delineated by its terms.*[114]

The proposed definition is in line with the proposition of Sir Anthony Mason, who suggested that good faith embraces three notions: an obligation on the parties to cooperate in achieving the contractual objects (loyalty to the promise itself), compliance with honest standards of conduct and compliance with standards of conduct that are reasonable, having regard to the interests of the parties.[115] Honesty is a moral value that is the most common expression of good faith. Cooperation is the expected requirement of the parties to a contract. In *Butt v McDonald*, cooperation is regarded as 'a general rule applicable to every contract that each party agrees, by implication, to all such things as are necessary on his part to enable the other party to have the benefit of the contract'.[116] Having regard to the other person's interests is an important element to reflect the common intention of both parties.

In an attempt to define the meaning of good faith, two theories were developed based on two general groups: the 'contractual approach' and the 'generalised moral standards'.[117] The 'contractual approach to good faith' is based on the intention or expectation of the parties. In this context, the approach is in line with the term 'implied in fact' to give business efficacy to a contract. Meanwhile, when the definition of good faith is based on 'generalised moral standards of conduct approach', it seems the definition is based on desirable behaviour in a contractual relationship. For example, by virtue of the *Uniform Commercial Code* s 2-103(1)(b), in contracts for the sale of goods where the party subject to the duty is a merchant, good faith means 'honesty in fact' and the observance of

[114] [2002] NSWSC 17 [65], [67].

[115] Mason, A. (2000). Contract, Good Faith and Equitable Standards in Fair Dealing. *Law Quarterly Review*, 116, 66–69.

[116] (1896) 7 QLJ 68, 70–71.

[117] Paterson, J. M. (2000). Duty of Good Faith Does It Have a Place in Contract Law? *Law Institute Journal*, p. 48.

reasonable commercial standards of fair dealing in trade. In Australia, these types of morally based theories find some support in the approach of Priestley J, where his Honour suggested that a certain standard of 'fairness' in contract performance may be demanded by prevailing community expectations.[118]

The uncertainty surrounding the concept left judges without a guide in their interpretation of the concept as reflected in their decisions. It is unclear as to which approach judges refer, that is whether a judge refers to the common law traditional approach or adopts the civil law tradition where good faith is part of the statutory provision. There are two types of judges in dealing with the concept of good faith: 'timorous souls' and 'bold spirits'. The 'timorous souls' judges may argue that an implied obligation of good faith will add to uncertainty to the contract. In *Bilgola Enterprises Ltd v Dymocks Franchise Systems (NSW) Pty Ltd*, Henry J commented that 'the significance of the need for certainty, particularly where parties to an arm's length commercial transaction have carefully set out the details of their relationship, must be an important factor in any particular case'.[119]

On the other hand, 'bold spirits' judges, like Priestley J, propose the idea of good faith in *Renard.* His Honour also referred to other jurisdictions which have a clear understanding and foundation of the concept of good faith such as in the US, where good faith is a well-established principle in the *Uniform Commercial Code* and the *Restatement (Second) of Contracts.* Similarly, Meagher JA also supports the idea of good faith in *Renard*[120] and *Hughes Bros Pty Ltd v Trustee of the Roman Catholic Church for the Archdiocese of Sydney.*[121] In addition to that, Finn J supported the concept of good faith in *Hughes Aircraft Systems International v Air Services Australia*, in which his Honour stated that 'I consider a virtue of the implied duty [good faith] to be that it expresses in a generalization of universal application, the standard of conduct to which all contracting parties are to be expected to adhere'.[122]

In contrast, Roger CJ is clearly a more 'timorous soul' in this debate. His Honour raised concerns that parties are able to secure their own

[118] (1992) 26 NSWLR 234, 268.
[119] (2000) 3 NZLR 169, 180.
[120] (1992) 26 NSWLR 234.
[121] (1993) 31 NSWLR 91.
[122] (1997) 146 ALR 1, 37.

interests in the contract, in contradiction to the concept of good faith. This can be illustrated in *GSA Group Pty Ltd v Siebe Plc*, in which Roger CJ held that:

> *Against a trend towards a general obligation of good faith, fairness, or reasonableness, there have been judicial comments to the effect that the courts should be slow to intrude the commercial dealings of parties who are quite able to look after their own interests. The courts should not be too eager to interfere in the commercial conduct of the parties, especially where the parties are all wealthy, experienced, commercial entities able to attend to their own interests.*[123]

A step towards dispelling this confusion is apparent in the context of franchising, whereby the previous Australian government made a major step towards legislating an obligation of good faith but hardly a major step to the definition. The Australian government accepted the recommendation made by Wein to introduce an express obligation of good faith for both the franchisor and the franchisee to regulate the unethical conduct of the franchisor towards the franchisee by taking advantage of any imbalance of the bargaining power between the two of them. The Wein review recommended the incorporation of the common law duty of good faith rather than devising some new and different definition of good faith. This was decided based on the premise that the concept will not be defined but understood through 'non-discretionary reference criteria', namely in a manner similar to the unconscionable conduct prohibition set out in s 22 of the *Australian Consumer Law*.[124]

Nonetheless, some scholars have suggested that the explicit recognition of such a duty would be beneficial and its development possible. Other scholars, however, suggest that the development of a duty of good faith should be approached with considerable caution and care,[125] while others reject it outright.[126] These competing views from the scholars are central to the understanding of the development of good faith in Australia.

[123] (1993) 30 NSWLR 573, 579.

[124] Australian Government, *Commonwealth Government Response to the Review of the Federal Franchising Code of Conduct* - Forward Looking Franchising Regulation (2013) 13.

[125] Paterson, J. M. (2000). Duty of Good Faith Does It Have a Place in Contract Law? *Law Institute Journal*, p. 48.

[126] Peden, E. (2003). Good Faith in the Performance of Contract Law. Law *Journal Society*, p. 64.

4.7 Conclusion

It is interesting to trace the emergence of an obligation to act in good faith since Priestley J first raised the concept of good faith in *Renard*. To date, the High Court has yet to pronounce its application, status and definition of good faith and there is a lack of consistency in the decisions of Federal and state courts. Despite its unclear position, references to good faith are increasingly found both in common law and in legislation. The issue of implying a general term of good faith is still a dilemma in Australian contract law. Despite that, good faith is increasingly recognised as a term 'implied by law', not as a term 'implied by fact'. It is easier to identify good faith from the term 'implied by law' based on the legal incidents of a particular class of contract compared to the test set by the *BP Refinery* case to determine the term 'implied by law'. Its status remains vague despite good faith being implied in various types of commercial contracts.

The recent approach to the concept of good faith in the franchising context provides a context to develop a definition of good faith. This is a positive development. Although the debate is ongoing in Australia, there is nevertheless a trend towards recognising that a duty to act in good faith is important in determining the direction of good faith in contractual performance in the future.

CHAPTER 5

Good Faith: An Empirical Study of Australian Cases

5.1 Overview

The doctrinal discussion of good faith in the context of a developing concept in Australian contract law was discussed in the earlier chapter. However, the doctrinal discussion offered only a limited view of the concept of good faith in Australian contract law. For this purpose, an empirical overview of good faith is provided in this and the following chapters to supplement the doctrinal discussion of good faith. A more detailed review of the 'landscape' of decided cases on the issue of good faith in contractual performance during the period of review is presented, with tables and graphs to aid in the understanding of the discussion.

5.2 Introduction

As mentioned in Chap. 4, good faith was put onto the judicial agenda in Australia through *obiter* comments by Priestley J in the landmark case of *Renard* in 1992.[1] Priestley J was clearly of the opinion that the appropriate course was towards the development of a general principle of good faith in Australia. The issue of good faith nevertheless continues to be debated, with its status and meaning still uncertain in the absence of an authoritative High Court judgement. In these circumstances, there is benefit in examining the line of development of good faith in contract law cases in

[1] (1992) 26 NSWLR 234.

N. Abdullah, *Good Faith in Contractual Performance in Australia*,
https://doi.org/10.1007/978-981-15-6078-1_5

Australia in an attempt to extract the general principles of the concept, the growth of the concept, its extension and its development.[2]

Good faith was identified as an issue in 104 cases in Australia. In 74 of these, the source of good faith was from implication.[3] There are 64 cases where the court implied good faith as 'implied in law' and 10 cases where the court implied it as a term 'implied in fact'. From these 74 cases of implication, 32 cases were found to have breached the implied term of good faith. The cases are divided into three phases: 'Introduction Phase from 1992 to 1998', 'Development Phase from 1999 to 2003' and 'Consolidation Phase from 2004 to 2009'. This allows the evolution of the concept to be monitored over time.

It is the aim of this chapter to analyse and evaluate the reception and acceptance of the concept of good faith in Australia by using empirical data categorised by years (1992–2009) and jurisdiction. The remainder of the chapter proceeds as follows. Section 5.3 analyses cases in which good faith is raised as an issue. Section 5.4 explains the cases in which the court recognised an implied term of good faith. The discussion encompasses the total implication rate by year and jurisdiction and the term 'implied in law' and the term 'implied in fact'. Section 5.5 discusses findings of a breach of the implied term of good faith.

5.3 Good Faith as an Issue in Australian Contract Law

5.3.1 Cases Raising Good Faith as an Issue (Per Year)

One means of analysing the good faith phenomenon in Australia is to measure the number of instances in which the issue of good faith was raised as a material issue. Figure 5.1 shows, by year, that there were 104 identified good faith cases in Australia during the 1992–2009 period.

Introduction Phase

During the 'Introduction Phase' from 1992–1998, only eight cases were identified. In 1992, 1994, 1995, 1996 and 1998, one case was identified

[2] Fitzgerald. P. J. (1970). Are Statutes Fit for Academic Treatment. *Journal of Society of Public Teachers of Law*, 142–144.

[3] The sources of good faith of the remaining 30 cases were from express term of the contract.

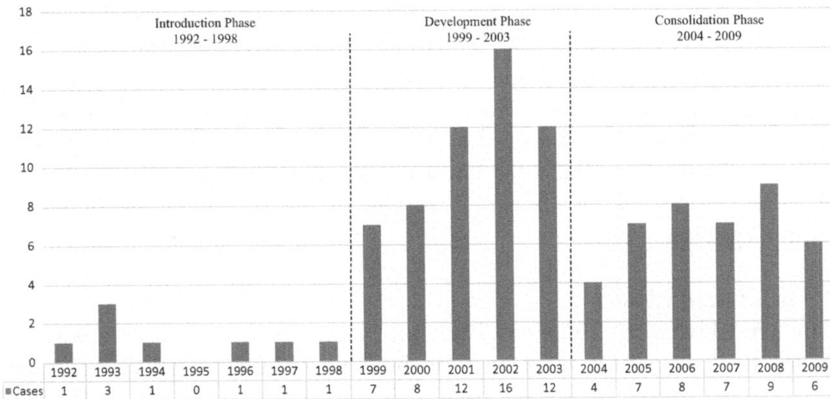

Fig. 5.1 Cases that raised good faith as an issue (per year)

for each year. However, in 1993, three cases were identified. During this phase, there appears to have been a degree of confusion about the issue of good faith, with only eight cases being identified. One interpretation of this may be that plaintiffs and judges were not well versed in the concept and as such lacked confidence to discuss the issue of good faith in their cases. The discussion of the concept of good faith in *Renard* was only *obiter* comments and as such did not constitute a binding precedent for other courts. The acceptance and recognition of the concept of good faith may take time because good faith is still a new concept without a clear meaning. A good example is the duty of cooperation which has a long-standing acceptance and recognition in contract law. In *Mackay v Dick*,[4] the duty of cooperation has been recognised as part of the underlying concept of contract law as early as 1881. Since then, the duty of cooperation has developed to the extent that it has become the expected standard that the parties in the contract are required to secure the expected benefit of the contract. The longer period of time has provided ample opportunity for a duty of cooperation to be well established in contract law.

Development Phase

During the 'Development Phase' between 1999 and 2003, there was an increasing number of identified reported good faith cases compared to the

[4] (1881) 6 App Cas 251.

Introduction Phase. The number of identified good faith cases by year is as follows: 1999 (7), 2000 (8), 2001 (12), 2002 (16) and 2003 (12). This shows a dramatic increase in identified good faith cases. Of the 104 cases in the entire study period, 55 occurred during the development phase (1999 to 2003). The figure also shows that the majority of good faith cases were raised in 2002 (16) and the least in 1999 (7). One conclusion that can be drawn from this is that the issue of good faith had become part of the legal landscape.

Consolidation Phase

The period between 2004 and 2009 constitutes the consolidation phase in which there is greater acceptance of the issue of good faith. The number of identified good faith cases by year is as follows: 2004 (4), 2005 (7), 2006 (8), 2007 (7), 2008 (9) and 2009 (6). Forty-one cases were identified from a total sample of 104 cases. This phrase suggests that the judges are ready to hear pleadings put forward by the plaintiff on the basis of the concept of good faith. One conclusion that could be drawn from this phase is that the issue of good faith has become more recognised.

Overall, the data suggests that the development of good faith in Australian case law from 1992 to 2009 is inconsistent due to the inconsistent distribution of cases that raised good faith as an issue, as illustrated in Fig. 5.1. The development of good faith as a new concept has undergone a development similar to the experience of any new principle of law. A good example is s 52 (misleading or deceptive conduct) of the *Trade Practices Act 1974* (Cth),[5] which received little attention before becoming an accepted provision. French J observed in *Trade Practices Act 1974* (Cth) that 'judicial exploration of the scope of s 52 (misleading or deceptive conduct) has, in the 14 years since its enactment, generated a considerable body of case law'.[6] His Honour's statement is supported by the increasing number of decisions involving the section reported in the *Australian Trade Practices Reports*:

> *In the first years to 1979, there were 19. In the next five years to 1984, there were 131. In the three years and eight months to August 1988, there have been a*

[5] See *Trade Practices Act 1974* (Cth), which was enacted as schedule 2 of the *Competition and Consumer Act* 2010(Cth), which came into effect on 1 January 2011.

[6] French, R. S. (1989). A Lawyer's Guide to Misleading or Deceptive Conduct. *Australian Law Journal*, 63, 250.

further 236 cases reported or digested in that service. In the two years since August 1988, there have been a further 166 cases reported or digested.[7]

At present, s 52 is currently referring to s 18 of the *Australian Consumer Law*, which is commonly used, but only after the concepts of the section underwent a lengthy development process. Similarly, it is also expected that the concept of good faith must also undergo a similar process before it becomes more widely accepted.

Figure 5.2 provides an overview of the identified good faith cases raised in Australia by jurisdiction. Table 5.1 illustrates the quantity and percentage of identified cases by jurisdiction.

Figure 5.2 suggests an unbalanced distribution of the issue of good faith in Australia. The number of identified good faith cases by jurisdiction is as follows: New South Wales (NSW) (47), Queensland (QLD) (2), Tasmania (TAS) (3), Victoria (21), Australian Capital Territory (ACT) (1), Western Australia (WA) (7) and Federal (23) identified good faith cases. No cases were identified in South Australia and the Northern Territory. A small number of cases of good faith were identified from Queensland, Tasmania, ACT and Western Australia. These states are grouped together and classified as 'Other States'. The figure is interpreted cautiously because it is influenced by an uneven population distribution. For example, New South Wales (NSW) has the highest population, with approximately 7,247,700 people, followed by Victoria, with approximately 5,574,500 people, while the Northern Territory has the least, which constitutes approximately 232,400 people.[8]

It is apparent from Table 5.1 that the majority (47) of identified cases are decisions of NSW courts, which is not surprising as it has the largest population. The number of reported cases amounts to 45 percent of all identified cases. Victoria has the second most number of reported cases with 21 percent, again most likely because it is the second most populated area. This percentage amounts to 20 percent of the total cases. The Federal Courts reported 23 cases, amounting to 22 percent of the total. 'Other States' reported 13 cases out of the total of 104 identified cases (Western

[7] See Healey, D., & Terry. A. (1995). *Misleading or Deceptive Conduct* (pp. 19–20). Australia: CCH Australia Limited.

[8] Australian Bureau of Statistics, Dec. 2011. http://www.abs.gov.au/ausstats/abs@.nsf/mf/3101.0/.

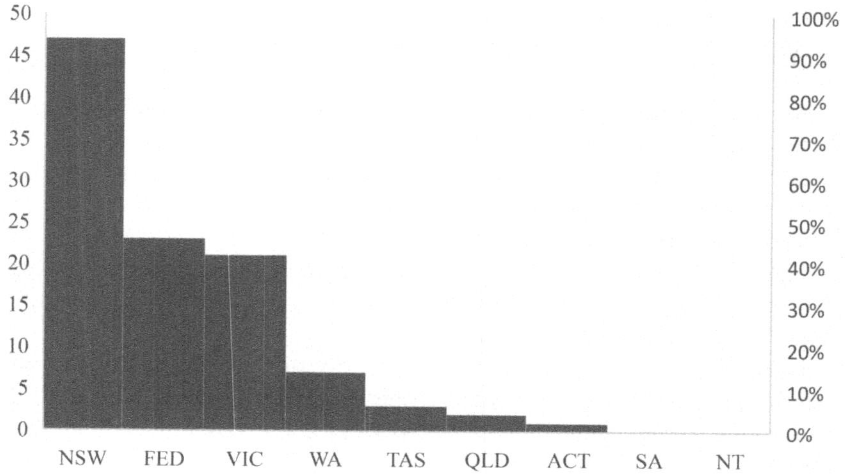

Fig. 5.2 Cases in which good faith was raised as an issue (by jurisdiction)

Table 5.1 Percentage of cases in which good faith was raised as an issue (by jurisdiction)

	NSW	*QLD*	*TAS*	*VIC*	*ACT*	*WA*	*FED*	*SA*	*NT*
Cases	47	2	3	21	1	7	23	0	0
%	45%	2%	3%	20%	1%	7%	22%	0	0

Australia 7, Queensland 2, ACT 1 and Tasmania 3), amounting to 13 percent of the total percentage.

One conclusion that can be drawn from this is that the issue of good faith is influenced by jurisdiction. The fact that the *Renard* case was first decided in NSW undoubtedly influenced many cases in NSW to follow suit. The data also reveals that good faith is a well-known issue in NSW and that there is strong judicial support for the term compared to the other states.

Analysis of the influence of good faith in each Australian jurisdiction provides a more comprehensive view of the growing awareness of the good faith issue. Figure 5.3 identifies cases in which good faith is raised as an issue by year and jurisdiction.

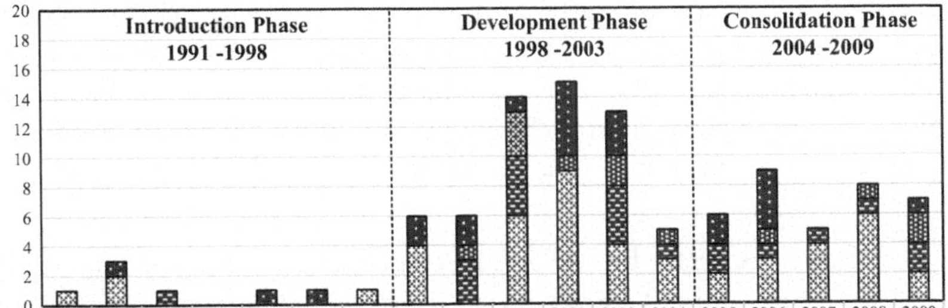

	1992	1993	1994	1995	1996	1997	1998	1999	2000	2001	2002	2003	2004	2005	2006	2007	2008	2009
FED	0	1	0	0	1	1	0	2	2	1	5	3	0	2	4	0	0	1
OTHERS	0	0	0	0	0	0	0	0	1	3	1	2	1	0	1	0	1	2
VIC	0	0	1	0	0	0	0	0	3	4	0	4	1	2	1	1	1	2
NSW	1	2	0	0	0	0	1	4	0	6	9	4	3	2	3	4	6	2

Fig. 5.3 Cases in which good faith is raised as an issue by year and jurisdiction. (Note: 'Others' comprises the jurisdictions of WA, QLD, TAS and ACT)

Introduction Phase

During the 'Introduction Phase' from 1992 to 1998, four cases relying on an argument of good faith were identified in NSW, three in Federal Courts and one in Victoria with no identified cases in the other states. During this stage, it is undeniable that the issue of good faith was still in its infancy.

Development Phase

During the 'Development Phase' from 1999 to 2003, there was a growing number of identified cases relying on good faith as an issue when compared to the 'Introduction Phase'. The number of identified good faith cases by jurisdiction is as follows: NSW (23), Victoria (11), Federal Courts (13) and other states (8). The highest number of identified cases is in NSW (23), followed by Federal Courts (13), Victoria (11) and other states (8). This suggests a growing awareness of, and interest in, the issue of good faith. It may be considered that the opinion of Priestley J had convinced litigants in NSW to plead the issue of good faith.

Consolidation Phase

In the 'Consolidation Phase' from 2004 to 2009, the distribution of identified cases arguing good faith as an issue across jurisdictions is stable. The number of identified good faith cases by jurisdiction is as follows: NSW (20), Victoria (9), Federal Courts (5) and other states (7). The number of reported cases during the period of the review showed a consistent distribution of cases compared to the 'Development Phase'. One interpretation that can be inferred here is that good faith is beginning to receive a warm welcome in NSW. This may be because the concept has become more widely recognised and the judges are more willing to consider the concept as a result of it having been introduced in NSW.

5.4 Good Faith Identified as an Implied Term in Australian Contract Cases

Section 5.3 addressed the total sample of cases which raised good faith as a substantial issue. This section examines the sample to determine the cases in which the court upheld an argument that an obligation of good faith was implied in the contract. As mentioned in Chap. 4, the issue of the implication of a good faith term has yet to be decided upon by the High Court.

Good faith can be implied as a term of the contract in two ways: term 'implied in law' and term 'implied in fact'. A term 'implied in law' is based on the legal incident of a particular class of contract.[9] A term 'implied in fact' is based on the intention of the parties.[10] This section examines the data pertaining to the number of instances in which a term requiring good faith performance was implied compared to the total number of cases in which good faith was raised by year (1992–2009).

Figure 5.4 illustrates the cases by year in which the court recognised implication of a term requiring good faith in contractual performance. Table 5.2 depicts the total number of cases and the quantity and percentage of implied cases during the period of review.

5.4.1 Introduction Phase

In the 'Introduction Phase', from 1992 to 1998, only five cases were found to have been implied from the eight identified cases. The number of identified cases of implied term recognised by year is as follows: 1996 (1), 1997 (2) and 1998 (2). This shows that the implication rate and the identified cases are almost equal with an exception in 1993, where there is no implied term recognised from three identified cases. It shows that the court has not yet established a direction to take in deciding to imply a term of good faith in contracts.

[9] See Chap. 4 for further discussion.
[10] See Chap. 4 for further discussion.

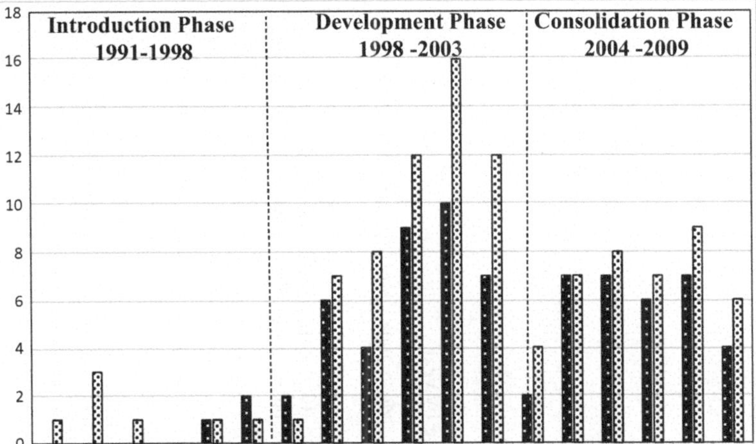

	1992	1993	1994	1995	1996	1997	1998	1999	2000	2001	2002	2003	2004	2005	2006	2007	2008	2009
Implied	0	0	0	0	1	2	2	6	4	9	10	7	2	7	7	6	7	4
cases	1	3	1	0	1	1	1	7	8	12	16	12	4	7	8	7	9	6

Fig. 5.4 Implied term recognised by year

5.4.2 *Development Phase*

In the second phase of 1999 to 2003, the implication rate is higher. Thirty-six cases were found to have been recognised as an implied term of good faith from the 55 identified cases. The number of identified cases of implied term recognised by year is as follows: 1999 (6), 2000 (4), 2001 (8), 2002 (10) and 2003 (7). The average implication rate is more than 50 percent, with the year 1999 having the highest implication rate wherein six cases were found to imply a term from seven identified cases or 86 percent. At this stage, it can be said that there is an emerging trend in implying a term of good faith.

5.4.3 *Consolidation Phase*

In the 'Consolidation Phase', from 2004 to 2009, 33 cases were found to have been recognised as an implied term of good faith from 41 identified cases. The number of identified cases of implied term recognised by year is as follows: 2004 (2), 2005 (7), 2006 (7), 2007 (6), 2008 (7) and 2009 (4). The implication rate is greater than 50 percent, showing a growing recognition for the concept. In 2005, all seven identified cases are also

Table 5.2 Total number of cases, the quantity and percentage of implied case by year

	1992	*1993*	*1994*	*1995*	*1996*	*1997*	*1998*	*1999*	*2000*	*2001*	*2002*	*2003*	*2004*	*2005*	*2006*	*2007*	*2008*	*2009*
Implied	0	0	0	0	1	2	2	6	4	9	10	7	2	7	7	6	7	4
Cases	1	3	1	0	1	1	1	7	8	12	16	12	4	7	8	7	9	6
% Implied	0%	0%	0%	0%	100%	220%	220%	86%	50%	75%	63%	58%	50%	100%	88%	86%	78%	67%

found to be implied terms. This indicates that in 2005, the court was willing to accept implication of a good faith term in seven identified cases.

One conclusion that could be drawn from this is that the implication of a term is increasingly accepted over the study period.

As discussed in Sect. 5.5, there are two types of implications recognised by the court. The court has approached good faith as a term which may be either term 'implied in fact' or term 'implied in law'. Figure 5.5 illustrates the instances of the term 'implied in fact' and the term 'implied in law' by year in Australia.

5.4.4 *Introduction Phase*

In the first phase from 1992 to 1998, there are two identified cases in which the term 'implied in fact' was found, namely, in 1996 (1) and 1997 (1), and three cases in which the term 'implied in law' was found, in 1997 (1) and 1998 (2). During this stage, there remains no binding authority to decide which concept is preferable.

5.4.5 *Development Phase*

Interestingly, in the second phase, from 1999 to 2004, there was only one case in which the term 'implied in fact' was found, in 1999, and 35 cases in which the term 'implied in law' was found, in 1999 (5), 2000 (4), 2001 (9), 2002 (10) and 2003 (7). This empirical data clearly suggests that there is an increasing acceptance of the term good faith as a term 'implied in law'.[11]

5.4.6 *Consolidation Phase*

There are seven cases where the court decided to imply a term 'implied in fact' as found in 2004 (1), 2005 (1), 2006 (2), 2008 (2), and 2009 (1). No such case was found in 2007. There are 26 cases where the court decided to imply a term 'implied in law' as found in 2004 (1), 2005 (6), 2006 (5), 2007 (6), 2008 (5) and 2009(3). Overall, there are more cases identified using the term 'implied in law'. This finding clearly supports the

[11] See *Burger King Corporation v Hungry Jack's Pty Ltd* (2001) 69 NSWLR 558, 569.

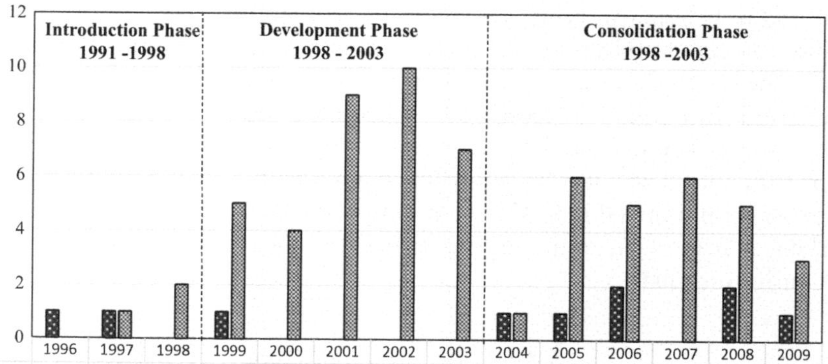

	1996	1997	1998	1999	2000	2001	2002	2003	2004	2005	2006	2007	2008	2009
Fact	1	1	0	1	0	0	0	0	1	1	2	0	2	1
Law	0	1	2	5	4	9	10	7	1	6	5	6	5	3

Fig. 5.5 By year: term implied in fact v term implied in law

comments of the NSW Court of Appeal that this term (implied in law) is preferred to imply a good faith obligation.[12]

Figure 5.6 depicts the cases by jurisdiction during the period of review. Table 5.3 explains the quantity and percentage of term implied based on the number of cases from each of the jurisdictions. These rates contrast significantly with the observed implication for cases by year, as illustrated in Fig. 5.6.

5.4.7 NSW

NSW has the most cases identified, 36 out of 47 cases, where the terms are implied. This amounts to 77 percent from the total percentage of cases where the terms are implied. There has been strong judicial support for the implication of term of good faith in NSW.[13]

[12] See *Service Station Association Limited v Berg Bennett & Associates Pty Limited* (1993) 45 FCR 84.

[13] See *Overlook v Foxtel* [2002] Aust Contract Reports 90–143, 91 972.

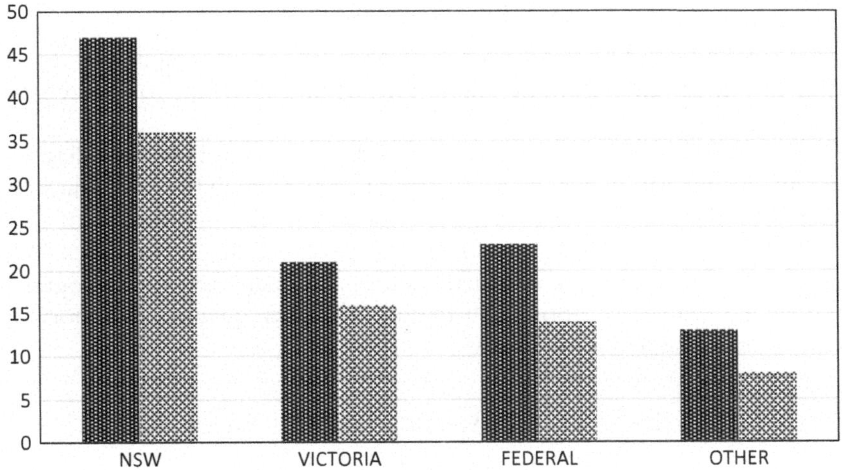

Fig. 5.6 Cases where term implied by jurisdiction. (Note: 'Others' comprises the jurisdictions of WA, QLD, TAS and ACT)

Table 5.3 Percentage of cases where term implied by jurisdiction

	NSW	*Victoria*	*Federal*	*Other*
No.of cases	47	21	23	13
Tenn implied	36	16	14	8
% of term implied	77%	76%	61%	62%

5.4.8 Victoria

In Victoria, the frequency of cases where the term is implied is also significant with 16 out of 21 cases identified where the term is implied. This amounts to 76 percent from the total percentage of term implied.

5.4.9 Other States

It is reported that in other states, there was a small number of cases reported where the term is implied, that is eight cases where the court decided to imply a term from 13 identified cases. This amounts to 62 percent of the total percentage of term implied.

5.4.10 Federal Courts

In Federal Courts, the number of cases where the term is implied by jurisdiction was 14 out of 23. This amounts to 61 percent of the total percentage of term implied.

Overall, the implication of good faith demonstrated that NSW has an acceptance rate of 79 percent and Victoria 76 percent. This data indicates that Victoria and NSW showed most interest in the implication of the concept. The rate of Federal Courts (61 percent) and other states (62 percent) shows that these jurisdictions take an equal interest in recognising an implication of good faith despite a smaller quantity of reported cases during the period of review.

5.5 Breaches of Implied Term of Good Faith in Australian Contract Cases

The previous discussion in Sect. 5.4 addresses the issue of the number of cases in the total sample in which the court found an implied term of good faith. Section 5.5 examines cases in which breaches of implied term of good faith was found.

5.5.1 Recognised Implication Cases and Breach Cases

Figure 5.7 depicts the number of cases where the court recognised breaches that implied term of good faith. Table 5.4 shows the number of total cases, number and percentage of implication cases and the number of implication and breach cases during the period of review.

Seventy-four out of 104 cases are implication cases, amounting to 71 percent. Thirty-two out of 74 cases are implication and breach cases, amounting to 43 percent. Thirty-two out of 104 cases are the total number of implication and breach cases from the total sample of cases, amounting to 31 percent of the total cases.

Figure 5.7 and Table 5.4 illustrate two important figures for the study. Firstly, it shows the total implication cases in which 74 cases are identified from the total identified cases and, secondly, the total implication and breach cases, that is, 32 of 74 total implication cases. The data suggests that at least 70 percent of the total cases recognised implication rates compared to the smaller number of cases recognising implication and at the same time recognising breach of implication, that is, 43 percent. From the

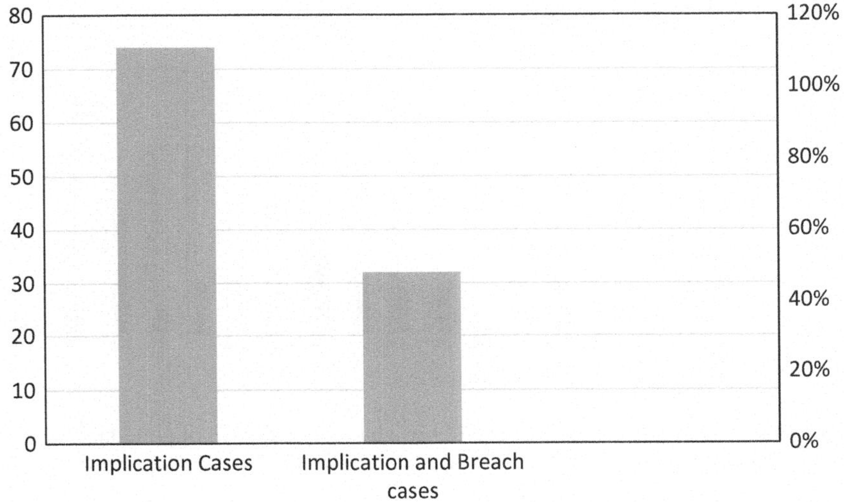

Fig. 5.7 Recognised implication and breach cases

Table 5.4 Percentage of recognised implications and breach cases

	Total cases	*Implication cases*	*Implication and breach cases*
Quantity	106	74	32
%	100	70%	30%
% Total sample	0	0	31%

total cases, only 31 percent are implication and breach cases. This data suggests a gap between the capacity to convince a court of the existence of an implied term and the capacity to demonstrate that such a term had in fact been breached.

5.5.2 *Cases Where the Court Found Breach of Implied Term of Good Faith from Implied Term Cases*

The tendency of the court to find a breach of implied term of good faith from implication cases also varied by year. Figure 5.8 depicts the number of cases where breaches of implied term of good faith from implication cases were recognised during the period of review.

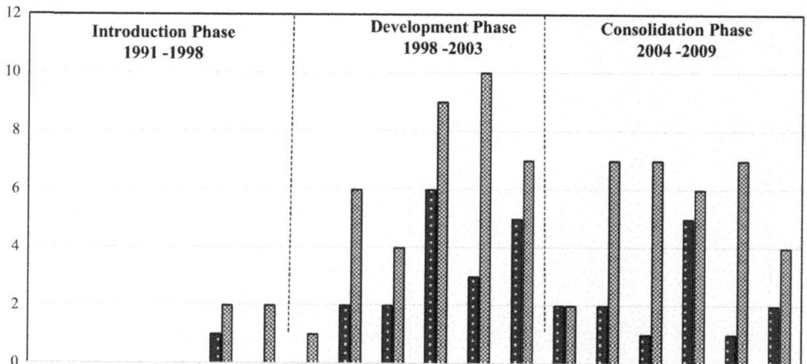

	1992	1993	1994	1995	1996	1997	1998	1999	2000	2001	2002	2003	2004	2005	2006	2007	2008	2009
Term Breached	0	0	0	0	1	0	0	2	2	6	3	5	2	2	1	5	1	2
Term Implied	0	0	0	0	2	2	1	6	4	9	10	7	2	7	7	6	7	4

Fig. 5.8 Cases where the court found breach of implied term of good faith from implied term cases

Introduction Phase

During the 'Introduction Phase' from 1992 to 1998, a small number of cases were found to be in breach of the implied term of good faith. In 1996, two cases were found to be implied term cases. One out of the two cases found breach of implied term of good faith from an implication case. In 1997, two cases were found to be implication cases, but no cases were found to be in breach of an implied term of good faith. In 1998, one case was found to be an implication case but no case was found to be in breach of an implied term of good faith. The data suggests that when there is an implication issue, it is not necessarily a breach of an implied term of good faith issue. This indicates that the court is still unclear about dealing with the issue of breach of an implied term of good faith.

Development Phase

In the 'Development Phase' from 1999 to 2003, there is an upsurge of interest in the number of cases found to be in breach of the implied term of good faith, in which 18 cases were reported to have breached an implied term of good faith from 36 implication cases. In 1999, there were six implication cases. In two of the six cases, there was found to be a breach of an implied term of good faith. In 2000, there were four implication cases of which two were found to have breached an implied term of good faith. In 2001, there were nine implication cases. Six out of the nine cases were found to be breaches of an implied term of good faith. In 2002, there were ten implication cases. Three out of the ten cases were found to have breached an implied term of good faith. In 2003, there were seven implication cases. Five out of seven were found to have breached an implied term of good faith. The data suggests that both instances reflect the increasing recognition of the plaintiff and judges of the issue as compared to the introduction phase.

Consolidation Phase
During the 'Consolidation Phase' from 2004 to 2009, the distribution of breach of an implied term of good faith and implication cases was not stable. In this phase, there are 13 cases where the court found a breach of an implied term of good faith from 33 cases of implication. In 2004, there were two implication cases. The two cases were found to have breached an implied term of good faith. In 2005, there were seven implication cases of which two were found to have breached an implied term of good faith. In 2006, there were seven implication cases of which one was found to have breached an implied term of good faith. In 2007, there were six implication cases of which five were found to have breached an implied term of good faith. In 2009, there were four implication cases of which two were found to have breached an implied term of good faith. This shows that the court had not accepted an implication issue where there was a small possibility that there was a breach of implied term of good faith. Nevertheless, in 2007, the court found five cases of breach of an implied term of good faith from six implication cases. The data in 2007 indicates that there was a higher chance than in any other year that when there was an implication, the case was likely to be found as a breach of an implied term of good faith.

Overall, the data suggests that when the parties plead breach of an implied term of good faith in implication cases, there is a low chance of the court accepting its plea. One conclusion that can be drawn from this is that pleading for a breach of an implied term of good faith is a fairly new course of action.

Figure 5.9 illustrates the trend pertaining to breaches of implied term of good faith by year. Table 5.5 shows the number of breaches and the percentage of breaches based on the number of cases during the period of review in Australia.

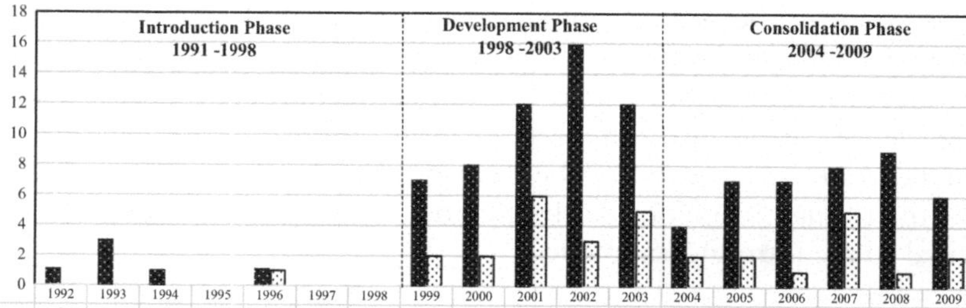

	1992	1993	1994	1995	1996	1997	1998	1999	2000	2001	2002	2003	2004	2005	2006	2007	2008	2009
■ Cases	1	3	1	0	1	1	1	7	8	12	16	12	4	7	7	8	9	6
□ Breaches	0	0	0	0	1	0	0	2	2	6	3	5	2	2	1	5	1	2

Fig. 5.9 Breaches of implied term of good faith

Introduction Phase

The first phase is the 'Introduction Phase' from 1992 to 1998, in which there was only one identified case in 1996 that recognised a breach of an implied term of good faith. In this phase, the issue of a breach of an implied term of good faith was newly pleaded and considered to be in the 'embryonic' stage after *Renard* in 1992. This was also the case in Fig. 5.5, where the implication rate in the 'Introduction Phase' was also in its infancy.

Development Phase

During the 'Development Phase' from 1999 to 2003, there was an upsurge of interest in the issue compared to the 'Introduction Phase'. In 1999, two out of seven cases recognised a breach of an implied term of good faith, equating to 29 percent of the total cases. In 2000, two out of eight cases recognised a breach of an implied term of good faith, which equates to 25 percent. In 2001, six out of 12 cases recognised a breach of an implied term of good faith, which equates to 50 percent. In 2002, three out of 16 cases recognised breach of implied term of good faith, which equates to 19 percent. In 2003, five out of 12 cases recognised a breach of an implied term of good faith, which equates to 42 percent.

The data showed that the level of recognition was increasing, for example, six out of 12 cases, or 50 percent, were identified in 2001 to have breached an implied term of good faith in contractual performance. However, the data showed that the percentage of breaches is less than 50 percent, which indicated that the level of recognition of the breach of an implied term of good faith remained low.

Table 5.5 Breaches of implied term of good faith

	1992	*1993*	*1994*	*1995*	*1996*	*1997*	*1998*	*1999*	*2000*	*2001*	*2002*	*2003*	*2004*	*2005*	*2006*	*2007*	*2008*	*2009*
Breaches	0	0	0	0	1	0	0	2	2	6	3	5	2	2	1	5	1	2
Cases	1	3	1	0	1	1	1	7	8	12	16	12	4	7	7	8	9	6
% Breaches	0%	0%	0%	0%	100%	0%	0%	29%	25%	50%	19%	42%	50%	29%	14%	63%	11%	33%

Consolidation Phase

In the third phase from 2004 to 2009, the acceptance of breaches of an implied term of good faith in contractual performance was steadier when compared to the 'Development Phase'. In 2004, two out of four cases recognised a breach of an implied term of good faith, which equates to 50 percent. In 2005, two out of seven cases recognised a breach of an implied term of good faith, which equates to 29 percent. In 2006, one of seven cases recognised a breach of an implied term of good faith, which equates to 14 percent. In 2007, five out of eight cases recognised a breach of an implied term of good faith, which equates to 63 percent. In 2008, one out of eight cases recognised a breach of an implied term of good faith, which equates to 11 percent. In 2009, two out of six cases recognised a breach of an implied term of good faith, which equates to 33 percent.

There are two instances where there are higher rates of acceptance of breaches which were evident, in 2004 and 2007, where two out of the four identified cases were breach cases, which equates to 50 percent. In 2007, five out of eight cases were breach cases, equating to 63 percent. The remaining years were reported to be less than 50 percent. The data demonstrated that the recognition of breaches as an implied term of good faith was still low.

Overall, the data demonstrated that the argument of breach of an implied term of good faith was not able to convince the court. One conclusion that could be drawn from this data was that the claim of breach of an implied term of good faith was a new course of action. There was also the possibility that the claim of breach was misguided, given that there were no clear guidelines for interpreting the concept of good faith.

Figure 5.10 illustrates the number of breach rates as a proportion of the total sample and the sub-sample of cases in which a good faith obligation term was implied respectively. Table 5.6 shows the number of cases and percentage of breach rates by year. It shows that throughout the period of review, the breach rate where term implied by year was less than 20 percent compared to the breach of implied term of good faith cases, as illustrated in Fig. 5.9. Both Figs. 5.9 and 5.10 demonstrate a high degree of inconsistency between breaches of implied term of good faith and breaches of term implied by year. One interpretation of this inconsistency is that the nature of good faith is still not clear in Australian contract law.

The data is now analysed by jurisdiction in order to evaluate the overall legal construct opinion. Figure 5.11 illustrates the cases where the court found breaches of an implied term of good faith by jurisdiction. Table 5.7

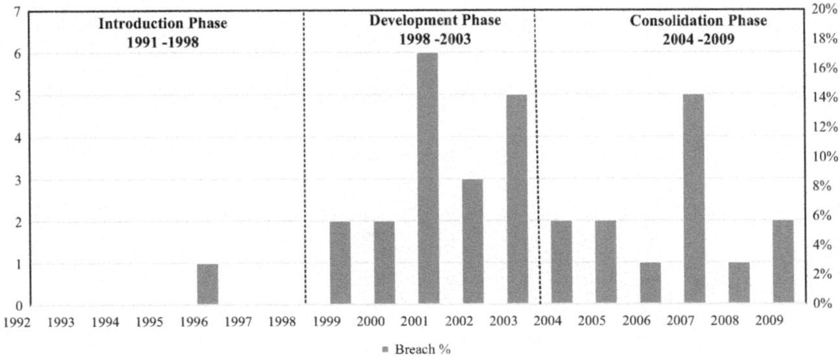

Fig. 5.10 Breach rate where term implied by year

depicts the quantity and percentage of breach rates and the quantity and percentage of implied term of good faith based on the total number of cases from each jurisdiction.

NSW

Forty-seven cases of good faith were identified, which equates to 45 percent of good faith cases. The number of implication cases was 36, which equates to 77 percent of implication cases. The breach cases are 13, which equates to 28 percent of breach cases.

Victoria

There are 21 identified good faith cases, which equates to 20 percent of good faith cases. The implication cases are 16, which equates to 76 percent of implication cases. The breach cases are six, which equates to 29 percent of breach cases.

Federal

There are 23 identified good faith cases, which equates to 22 percent of good faith cases. The implication cases are 14, which equates to 61 percent of implication cases. The breach cases are seven, which equates to 30 percent of breach cases.

Table 5.6 Breach rate where term implied by year

	1992	*1993*	*1994*	*1995*	*1996*	*1997*	*1998*	*1999*	*2000*	*2001*	*2002*	*2003*	*2004*	*2005*	*2006*	*2007*	*2008*	*2009*
Breach	0	0	0	0	1	0	0	2	2	6	3	5	2	2	1	5	1	2
%	0%	0%	0%	0%	3%	0%	0%	6%	6%	18%	9%	15%	6%	6%	3%	15%	3%	6%

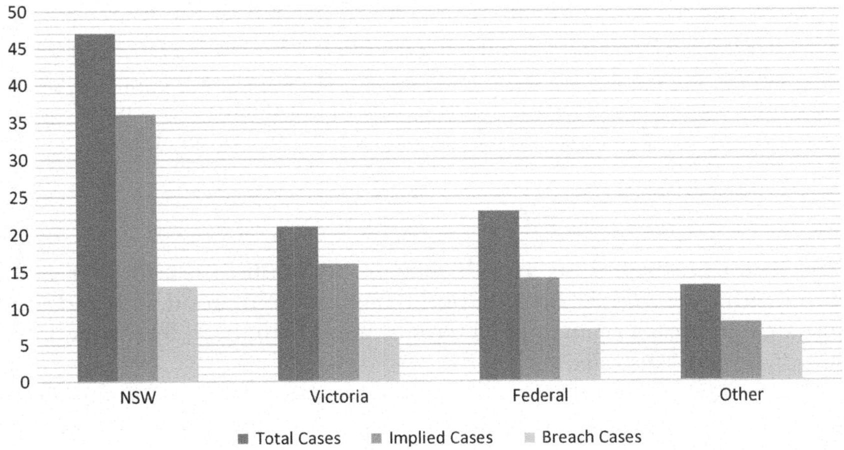

Fig. 5.11 Cases where the court found a breach and implied term of good faith by jurisdiction. (Note: 'Others' comprises the jurisdictions of WA, QLD, TAS and ACT)

Table 5.7 Cases where court found a breach and implied term of good faith by jurisdiction

	NSW	*Victoria*	*Federal*	*Other*
Total	47	21	23	13
% Total	45%	20%	22%	13%
Implied	36	16	14	8
% Implied	77%	76%	61%	62%
Breach	13	6	7	6
% Breach	28%	29%	30%	46%

Note: 'Other' comprises the jurisdictions of ACT, WA, Queensland, Tasmania

Other States

There are 13 identified good faith cases, which equates to 13 percent of good faith cases. The implication cases are eight, which equates to 62 percent of implication cases. The breach cases are six, which equates to 46 percent of breach cases.

Overall, the empirical evidence suggests that NSW has the highest number of cases from the total case sample: 47 of 104 cases, which equates to 45 percent of the total case sample. The implication rate is higher. Out of 36 of the 47 cases, which equates to 77 percent of the total cases, a good faith term was implied. The breach rate is also higher across samples; 13 of 36 of implication cases, or 28 percent, came from NSW. This empirical data is significant to prove that the issue of good faith is receiving more attention in NSW compared to Victoria, Federal and other states.

5.6 Conclusion

The data described above reveals material variation in the incidence of good faith cases raised, the issue of the implication of good faith and the instances of breach of an implied term of good faith, both by year and by jurisdiction, in Australia.

It is noteworthy to discover that there had been 104 cases from 1992 to 2009 which discussed an implied term of good faith in Australia since it was first put onto the judicial agenda in 1992 in the case of *Renard*. The number of issues concerning good faith is growing over the period of review, as illustrated by the three phases: Introduction Phase (1992–1998), Development Phase (1999–2003) and Consolidation Phase (2004–2009). NSW had the most identified cases pleading an implied term of good faith both by year and jurisdiction, with 47 cases, which equates to 45 percent. Victoria followed with 21 cases, which equates to 20 percent; Federal Court cases numbered 23 cases, which equates to 22 percent; and other states reported 13 cases, which equates to 13 percent, as illustrated in Fig. 5.2 and Table 5.1 above.

The empirical data shows that the implication rate is higher. There are 74 cases of implication from the 104 identified cases which equates to 77 percent, as illustrated by Fig. 5.7. The empirical data demonstrates that when courts imply a term, they prefer to imply the term 'implied in law' as a legal necessity. The empirical data demonstrates that there are 64 cases identified to have implied a term 'implied in law' and 10 cases identified to have implied a term 'implied in fact'. The empirical data also reported that NSW had the most implication cases, 36 cases of implication from 47 identified cases, which is equivalent to 79 percent. It was followed by Victoria, 16 cases of implication from 21 identified cases, which is equivalent to 76 percent. Commonwealth courts and other states had 14 cases of implication from 23 identified cases, which is equivalent to 61 percent, and eight cases of implication from 13 identified cases, which is equivalent to 62 percent, respectively, as illustrated in Fig. 5.6 and Table 5.3.

The courts recognised breach of an implied term of good faith based on implication in the form of either term 'implied in law' or term 'implied in fact'. Forty-three percent are cases found to be breach of an implied term of good faith. This data suggests that less than half of all cases accepted pleading for a breach of an implied term of good faith, as illustrated in Fig. 5.7 and Table 5.4 above. The number of cases argued for a breach of an implied term of good faith is low. There is also the possibility that the claim of term breach was misguided in the absence of specific and precise meaning of good faith. This indicates that the argument of breach of an implied term of good faith was not able to convince the court, as illustrated in Fig. 5.9. Therefore, when the party pleads a breach of an implied term of good faith based on implication, the rate is low as the court is not convinced.

The NSW data suggests that litigants in NSW were able to convince a court that a breach of an implied good faith term had transpired during the period of review. Figure 5.11 suggests that there is a popular reception of good faith in NSW, in terms of the total number of cases, implied cases and breach cases compared to other jurisdictions. In NSW, the implication cases are 36, which equates to 77 percent, and the breach of an implied good faith term is 13 cases, which equates to 28 percent, as illustrated in Table 5.7.

Three key propositions may be derived from this exercise. Firstly, the instability in the incidence of good faith from the three phases (Introduction Phase 1992–1998, Development Phase 1999–2003 and Consolidation Phase 2004–2009) suggests that the law relating to the concept of good faith is still fractured along jurisdictional lines. NSW was still the dominant state in dealing with the issue of good faith. Secondly, volatility remains in the incidence of good faith litigation, implication rates and breach, suggesting considerable tension and inconsistency in the judiciary. Finally, while there was a growth of recognition from when it was first introduced in 1992, the empirical data indicates that the growth of the recognition was inconsistent across the three phases.

It should also be noted, however, that the observed incidence, term implication rates and breach rates represent only a partial view of the data. To gain further insight into good faith in Australia, the role played by the judges concerning the legal acceptance of good faith needs to be examined. This is endeavoured in the following chapter.

CHAPTER 6

Defining Good Faith

6.1 Introduction

This chapter explores the numerous meanings of good faith in contract law. The wide range of meanings attributable to good faith supports the argument made in this book that essentially the concept of good faith has no specific or precise meaning. Most of the meanings identified in this study are complex, contradictory and unclear. The apparent lack of a single authoritative definition of good faith has resulted in an ongoing and diverse conceptualisation of the concept in addition to a constant reinterpretation of existing definitions. As a concept, good faith remains widely debated with each new meaning subjected to criticism. This chapter not only seeks to demonstrate the lack of consensus among judges and scholars as to the meaning of good faith but also proposes a workable meaning of good faith.

It is the aim of this chapter to address the meaning and content of good faith in contract law. Analyses of the meaning of good faith advocated by judges and scholars will be descriptively catalogued by grouping the various meanings into families of meaning in order to propose a taxonomic solution. The significance of this exercise is to develop a workable meaning of good faith. This chapter proceeds as follows. Section 6.2 outlines the problem of defining good faith. Section 6.3 demonstrates that there are numerous meanings of good faith available in the relevant legal literature and in the 104 cases that represent the sample for this study. Many of the meanings collected were grouped together based on similarities.

N. Abdullah, *Good Faith in Contractual Performance in Australia*,
https://doi.org/10.1007/978-981-15-6078-1_6

Section 6.4 demonstrates that the numerous meanings of good faith can be simplified by proposing a taxonomic solution. A definition of good faith is finally proposed in Sect. 6.5.

6.2 Overview

In specific legal contracts such as insurance contracts and fiduciary and employment relationships, the meaning of good faith is established. Outside of these categories, however, its meaning remains vague due to a lack of an established definition. Many legal experts have expressed concern over the ambiguity in the meaning of good faith. Steyn J has argued that 'a definition of good faith and fair dealing is impossible'.[1] Goode laments that 'we do not know quite what it means',[2] while White and Summers have warned that 'we caution anyone who is confident about the meaning of good faith to reconsider'.[3] Similarly, Lucke observed that 'good faith has not just one but many meanings, as well as an unusual capacity to acquire expanded and altogether new meanings'.[4] Reiter commented that despite many meanings of good faith, 'no one meaning will suffice universally'.[5] All the above comments indicate that those legal experts were sceptical of the concept of good faith due to the inherent difficulty of establishing a specific or precise meaning of good faith. In *Council of the City of Sydney v Goldspar Australia Pty Ltd*, Gyles J referred to 'the "variety of opinions" in both the authorities and commentaries as "bewildering" and noted that approaches vary from the "cautious" to the "adventurous"'.[6]

The above comments suggest a mood of dissatisfaction among legal experts concerning the meaning of good faith. This is because good faith is a concept for which it is difficult to attach a specific and precise meaning. Despite the current lack of consensus regarding its meaning, legal scholars

[1] van Zyl Steyn, J. (1991). The Role of Good Faith and Fair Dealing in Contract Law: A Hair-Shirt Philosophy? *Denning Law Journal*, 6, 131–140.

[2] Goode, R. (1992). *The Concept of Good Faith in English Law*. Paper presented at the Centro di Studi e Ricerche di Diritto Comparato e Straniero, Rome, 3.

[3] *Uniform Commercial Code*, Vol 1 (4th ed) 5, 187.

[4] See Lucke, H. K. (1987). Good Faith and Contractual Performance. In Finn, P. (Ed). *Essays on Contract*. The Law Book Co.

[5] Reiter, B. (1983). Good Faith in Contracts. *Valparaiso University Law Review*, 17, 705–707.

[6] (2006) 230 ALR 437, 498–499.

remain interested in the concept of good faith and continue to invest time and effort in the subject. To date, much has been written by scholars from various countries about the meaning and definition of good faith in the context of contract law, yet no consensus has been reached concerning the fundamental step of its definition. It is agreed that good faith is a term often used but rarely defined or analysed with care.[7] Many believe that good faith has different meanings depending on its context.[8]

6.3 The Problem of Defining Good Faith

As noted earlier, one of the main problems with the concept of good faith is its definition. As a concept, good faith has several problems associated with its diverse interpretation, the difficulty of defining the meaning and content of good faith in a factual vacuum, and the different perspectives of the term based on the experience of other jurisdictions such as the US.[9] These issues are discussed below.

6.3.1 A Concept in Search of a Definition

The main reason for the lack of a commonly agreed upon or specific definition of good faith in contract law is that good faith has many meanings. Most identified meanings of good faith are complex, contradictory and unclear. In his attempt to define good faith, Davis claimed that:

> *The more that I have sought to give some meaning to the phrase, the more I have realised that any possible meaning would need to be so qualified, or so general, as to be of no real assistance at all.*[10]

[7] Hunter, O. H. (1992). Book Reviews: Good Faith in English Law. [Review of the book *Good faith in English Law*]. *Journal of Contract Law*, 5, 172.

[8] See *Aiton Australia Pty Ltd v Transfield Pty Ltd* (2000) 16 BCL 70,156 per Einstein J; R. Brownsword, N. J. Hird and G. Howells (eds), *Good Faith in Contract, Concept and Context* (Ashgate, 1999) 3.

[9] US is a common law country like Australia.

[10] Davis, J. L. R. (1993). *Good Faith in Building Contracts and Construction*. Paper presented at the Construction Law Committee's Construction Law Seminar.

He further commented that:

> *Let me hasten to say that I am by no means alone in this inability to provide a meaning, or even a working description, of good faith. Everyone intuitively knows what it is, and would recognise good faith, or bad faith, if confronted with an example, but that does not aid the process of meaning.*[11]

The most contentious aspect of the concept of good faith is the variety and generality of possible meanings, which lead to confusion, frustration and difficulty in its application. The competing meanings of the concept are a direct result of different frames of reference. The most prominent of these definitions frame good faith as a moral concept. However, ambiguity surrounds certain key moral values such as honesty. The inclusion of such moral values as part of the meaning of the concept gives it a definite orientation, yet leaves unavoidable room for flexibility. Another approach has been to frame good faith based on the interpretation of the intention of the contracting parties. This can be expressed in terms of ensuring a workable contract such that the benefit of the contract is achievable. Both approaches, namely a moral framing in terms of honesty and the expected intent of the parties, involved both concrete and malleable aspects. For example, although the general meaning of honesty is easily understood, its specific meaning within a specific religious or cultural framework is by no means uniform. Similarly, intention can be rather difficult to determine. In other words, the general meaning of good faith is to honour the contract and to exercise moral standards. However, moral standards vary and are therefore malleable. It is the subjectivity of ethical standards that renders the concept of good faith difficult to define. It is ultimately this aspect that injects a significant degree of complexity to the task of attributing to the concept of good faith a single definite and authoritative meaning.

6.3.2 *Diverse Interpretations of Good Faith*

In attempting to define the meaning of good faith, Paterson explained that many commentators divided the problem of interpreting the context of good faith into two groups: the contractual approach to good faith and the generalised moral standard of the conduct approach.[12]

[11] Ibid.

[12] Paterson, J. M. (2000). Duty of Good Faith Does It Have a Place in Contract Law? *Law Institute Journal*, p. 48.

The first group, the contractual approach to good faith, attempts to give good faith a meaning consistent with existing contractual doctrines by treating it as an implied term based on the parties' probable intention or expectation.[13] This is consistent with the traditional contractual approach to the implication of terms to give business efficacy to the contract.

The second approach grounds the duty of good faith in generalised moral standards of conduct. This measure of good faith is based on desirable behaviour in a contractual relationship not determined by reference to the parties. This is demonstrated in s 2-103(b) of the *Uniform Commercial Code,* which states that:

> *'Good faith' in the case of a merchant means honesty in fact and the observance of reasonable commercial standards of fair dealing in the trade.*

In this context, good faith is based on the moral standard of honesty. In commercial practice, good faith is the expected commercial practice. This 'moral standards' approach gained support in the case of *Renard*, where Priestley J suggested that certain standards of 'fairness' in contract performance may be demanded by prevailing community expectations.

From the above, it can be seen that there are two approaches to interpret good faith, namely by means of intention and moral standard. Given the complexities of both approaches, interpretations can vary significantly, leading to uncertainty. One is left confused as to whether the benefit of the contract has been achieved.

6.3.3 *Difficulty of Defining the Meaning and Content of Good Faith in a Vacuum*

One reason for the difficulty in defining the meaning of good faith is that it cannot be expressed in a vacuum.[14] In *Asia Pacific Resources Pty Ltd v Forestry Tasmania*, Wright J commented that:

[13] Burton, S. J., & Andersen, E. G. (1990). The World in Contract. *Iowa Law Review*, 75, 861.

[14] See Davies, J. (2002). Why a Common Law Duty of Contractual Good Faith Is Not Required. *Canterbury Law Review*, 8, 529–530.

> *'Good faith' is incapable of abstract definition and can only be assessed as being present or absent if the relevant facts are known or are capable of being known.*[15]

Holmes argued that 'there is a problem in describing the content of good faith where the language and even philosophy are vague'.[16] In contrast with the duty of cooperation whereby the content of the duty is clearly established,[17] it is argued that good faith is only able to be determined in the context of the agreement. In *Thiess Contractors Pty Ltd v Placer (Granny Smith) Pty Ltd*, Templeman J held that:

> *In reaching my conclusion as to the proper construction of the term 'good faith' in this contract, I have had regard to a number of authorities and articles which I have been referred to. In particular, I have considered the decision of Gummow Judge in Service Stations Association Ltd v Berg Bennett & Associates Pty Ltd (1993) 45 FCR 84 which contains a helpful analysis of many of these materials. But in the end, the term must be construed in the context of the agreement in which it appears.*[18]

In *Hudson Resources Limited v Australian Diatomite Mining Pty Limited & Anor*, Einstein J likewise held that good faith is determined based on the context and circumstances of the agreement. His Honour stated that:

> *The proper construction of the agreement requires to be determined in the light of the context provided by the agreement as a whole and the circumstances in which the agreement was made.*[19]

Good faith is a broad concept, and its meaning is changeable in nature. It is ultimately difficult to determine good faith without a context. This is because without knowledge of the context of a specific agreement, good faith is meaningless. For example, if good faith is based on the context of an agreement during the negotiation process, surrounding factors not related to the negotiation process in the agreement should be ignored.

[15] Unreported, Supreme Court of Tasmania, 4 September 1997. See also, *Aiton Australia Pty Ltd v Transfield Pty Limited* (1999) 153 FLR 236, 260 (Einstein J).

[16] See Holmes, E. M. (1977). A Contextual Study of Commercial Good Faith: Good Faith Disclosure in Contract Formation. *University of Pittsburgh Law Review*, 39, 381–408.

[17] See Chap. 2 for further discussion.

[18] [1999] WASC 1046.

[19] [2002] NSWSC 314 [127].

This is to ensure that the expected benefit of the contract is achievable without the interruption of other factors that will hinder the success of the contract.

6.3.4 The Experience of One Other Jurisdiction

The US is the only common law country that has legislated a general obligation of good faith, in the *Uniform Commercial Code*[20] and the *Restatement (Second) of Contracts.* Article 1 (General Provisions) of the *Uniform Commercial Code* clearly mentions the role of good faith in the contract. This is clearly illustrated in s 1-203 of the *Uniform Commercial Code*, which provides that 'Every contract or duty within this Act imposes an obligation of good faith in its performance or enforcement'. Section 1-201(19) (General Definitions and Principles of Interpretation) defines 'good faith' as 'honesty in fact in the conduct or transaction concerned'. A special definition of good faith concerning merchants is provided in Article 2 (Sales), s 2-103(1)(b) of the *Uniform Commercial Code*, which provides that '… good faith in the case of merchant means honesty in fact and the observance of reasonable commercial standards of fair dealing in the trade'. Section 205 of the *Restatement (Second) of Contracts* provides that 'Every contract imposes upon each party a duty of good faith and fair dealing in its performance and its enforcement'.

In the *Uniform Commercial Code*, good faith has two different meanings depending on the status of the contracting parties. The status of the contracting parties is divided into merchant and non-merchant. A merchant is one who regularly trades in goods. A person who sells his car through an advertisement in the classifieds is not considered a merchant. However, if that person sells a car every week through the classifieds, for the purpose of the *Uniform Commercial Code*, he or she is considered a merchant because he or she regularly deals in goods of a particular kind. Under the *Uniform Commercial Code*, any store that sells merchandise is considered a merchant.

Article 1 (General Provisions) of the *Uniform Commercial Code* refers to non-merchants. Under the 'honesty in fact' definition, good faith is determined based on the intent or state of mind of the party. According to

[20] The *Uniform Commercial Code* is divided into 11 substantive articles. For the purpose of this discussion, the content of this chapter almost exclusively deals with Article 1 (General Provisions) and Article 2 (Sales), which discussed good faith.

Robert Braucher, this is called the 'pure heart empty head' approach, which solely considers the actual belief of the party and not the reasonableness of that belief.[21] Article 2 (Sales) of the *Uniform Commercial Code* refers specifically to merchants. Under the broader definition, an objective standard applies which includes the actual belief of the party along with the reasonableness of the belief and conduct.

Although good faith is clearly mentioned in the codes, there is no specific or precise definition of good faith. One of the main problems is the difficulty of a specific or precise definition of good faith due to the uncertainty of the concept. In *Watseka First International Bank v Ruda*, the Illinois Supreme Court held that:

> *… what the term [good faith] means … remains somewhat of a mystery. It's meaning moreover may change, depending upon the context in which it is used.*[22]

The Illinois Supreme Court described good faith as a 'mystery' because the meaning of good faith is based on the circumstances of the case. Although it was clearly legislated, there are comments from the legal scholars in the US who did not agree with the definition of good faith as stated in the Code and Restatement. Farnsworth commented that the definition of good faith in Article 1 (General Provisions) of the *Uniform Commercial Code* is 'too restrictive' because the conduct of the contracting parties is based solely on honesty. In contrast to Article 2 (Sales) of the *Uniform Commercial Code*, in the case of merchants, the requirement of good faith includes honesty and reasonableness.[23] Farnsworth commented that 'limiting good faith to an inquiry into actual honesty would frustrate this use'.[24] Farnsworth based his critique on the 'rationale for a court to imply contract terms [good faith] is necessary to secure the expected benefits of the contract to a party or to protect reasonable expectations'.[25]

Summers, one of the early legal commentators on good faith, agreed with the critique by Farnsworth. Summers commented that 'if an obligation of good faith is to do its job, it must be open-ended rather than sealed

[21] Braucher, R. (1958). The Legislative History of the Uniform Commercial Code. *Columbia Law Review*. 798–812.

[22] 135 3d 140 (III, 1990).

[23] Dubroff, H. (2006). The Implied Covenant of Good Faith in Contract Interpretation and Gap-Filling: Reviving a Revered Relic. *St. John's Law Review*, 80, 559–587.

[24] Ibid.

[25] Ibid.

off in a definition'.[26] He claimed that good faith should be conceptualised as an 'excluder'.[27] In this context, good faith as an 'excluder' is defined as a 'phrase without general meaning (or meanings) of its own and serves to exclude a wide range of heterogeneous forms of bad faith'.[28] Summers asserted that it is important to define bad faith because the outcome of the cases depends on how the doctrine is conceptualised.

Summers' analysis of the term 'excluder' had an influence on Robert Braucher, the section's principal drafter,[29] who did not attempt to define good faith, opting instead to use the 'excluder' approach. In Comment (a) to s 205 of the *Restatement (Second) of Contracts*, Robert Braucher acknowledged that:

> *[T]he phrase 'good faith' is used in a variety of contexts, and its meaning varies somewhat with the context. Good faith performance or enforcement of a contract … excludes a variety of types of conduct characterised as involving 'bad faith' because they violate community standards of decency, fairness and reasonableness.*[30]

Comment (d) to s 205 of the *Restatement (Second) of Contracts* proceeded to define good faith by providing an example of bad faith, which includes 'evasion of the spirit of the bargain, lack of diligence and slacking off, willful rendering of imperfect performance, abuse of a power to specify terms, and interference with or failure to cooperate in the other party's performance'.

In short, as outlined above, the conflicting interpretations of good faith show that American jurisprudence has yet to develop a coherent theory of good faith. Lucke pointed out that there is an overwhelming variety of meanings and 'observed that the very fact of there being such an array of interpretations shows that American jurisprudence has not yet developed

[26] Summers, R. (1968). Good Faith in General Contract Law and the Sales Provision of the Uniform Commercial Code. *Virginia Law Review*, 54, 195–196.

[27] Dubroff, above n.23, 592.

[28] Summers, R. (1968). Good Faith in General Contract Law and the Sales Provision of the Uniform Commercial Code. *Virginia Law Review*, 54, 195–198.

[29] Summers, R. S. (1982). The General Duty of Good Faith—Its Recognition and Conceptualization. Cornell Law Review, 67, 810–819.

[30] Summers, R. (1968). Good Faith in General Contract Law and the Sales Provision of the Uniform Commercial Code. *Virginia Law Review*, 54, 195–196.

a coherent theory of good faith'.[31] Despite various attempts to define good faith, American jurisprudence has not yet managed to define the term.

Despite these criticisms and problems pertaining to the definition of good faith, some judges and scholars are endeavouring to determine the meaning and actual content of good faith as discussed in Sect. 6.3 by means of a taxonomy of the 'families of meaning' of good faith. The database from which this taxonomy is drawn derives from a survey of all the attempts thus far made to define the meaning of the concept.

6.4 Good Faith Families

The definitions or meanings of good faith examined in this study were collected from a variety of books and articles supported by a review of the database comprising of 104 cases. Figure 6.1 illustrates the cases that define good faith by year. The years are divided into three phases, 'Introduction Phase 1992–1998', 'Development Phase 1999–2003' and 'Consolidation Phase 2004–2009', with the aim to detect the evolution of the cases which defined good faith. Out of 104 cases, 19 defined good faith, as illustrated in Fig. 6.1:

Introduction Phase

During the 'Introduction Phase', from 1992 to 1998, there were two instances in which good faith was defined as illustrated in 1992 and 1997. From 1993 to 1996 and in 1998, there were no cases in which good faith was defined. This means that two out of the eight identified cases in which good faith was mentioned sought to define good faith.[32] One interpretation that can be drawn from this is that Australian judges lacked confidence in regard to defining the meaning of good faith as it was a fairly new concept in Australia.

Development Phase

In the 'Development Phase', namely from 1999 to 2003, it is surprising to note that there is a sudden interest in the concept of good faith, as shown

[31] See Lucke, H. K. (1987). Good Faith and Contractual Performance. In Finn, P. (Ed). *Essays on Contract*. The Law Book Co.

[32] See Figure 6.1: Cases Which Raised Good Faith as an Issue (Per Year), 138.

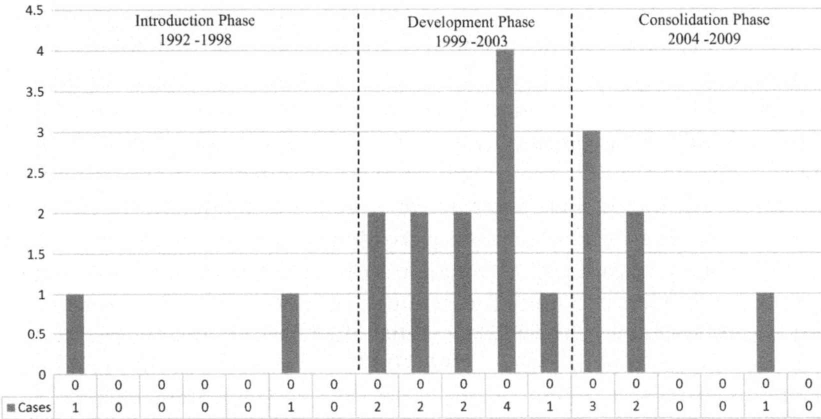

Fig. 6.1 Overall cases which define good faith

by the number of cases that attempted to define its meaning. Eleven out of the 55 identified cases[33] that raised good faith attempted its definition. The distribution of the cases by year include two cases in 1999, two cases in 2000, two cases in 2001, four cases in 2002 and one case in 2003 in which these cases attempted to define its meaning. The highest number of identified cases determining the meaning of good faith is in 2002, wherein four cases were identified. This situation resonates with the highest number of cases reported in the same year, wherein 16 cases raised the issue of good faith. This suggests that the level of confidence in applying the concept of good faith increased. It seems that with the turn of the twenty-first century, Australian judges have become more open to the concept of good faith, as indicated in 2002. This is a positive indication of the development of the meaning of good faith during this period.

Consolidation Phase

It was expected that in the 'Consolidation Phase', that is from 2004 to 2009, there would be an increase in the acceptance and recognition of the term 'good faith' and its meaning. However, the empirical data shows a different pattern. During this period, there were fewer attempts to define

[33] See Figure 6.1: Cases Which Raised Good Faith as an Issue (Per Year), 138.

the concept, with only 6 out of 41 identified cases[34] attempting a definition of its meaning. The distribution of the cases by year that attempted to define its meaning is as follows: three cases in 2004, two cases in 2005 and one case in 2008. No attempts were made to define the term in 2006, 2007 and 2009. One presumption that could be drawn from this is that in 2006, 2007 and 2009, the judges showed no interest in attempting its definition. Although there were active attempts at its definition between 2004 and 2005, whereby five cases were identified with one case identified in 2008, the significant gap between 2006 and 2009 shows that the judges were becoming less certain of the definition of good faith. One conclusion that could be drawn from this data is that after having once supported the idea (i.e. 'Development Phase 1999–2003'), its translation into real practice highlighted the difficulties of defining the concept of good faith.

Figure 6.2 identifies good faith defined by jurisdiction during the review period. It aims to identify support by jurisdiction in Australia. By jurisdiction, the states were divided into New South Wales (NSW), Victoria, Federal and other states. For the purpose of this study, 'other states' refers to Western Australia (WA).[35]

There are ten cases in NSW, two cases in Victoria, one Federal case and five cases in other states which have attempted to determine the meaning of good faith. It is interesting to note that the identified cases that have attempted to determine the meaning of good faith have mostly come from NSW, comprising 10 out of 18 cases. In Western Australia, five out of 18 cases attempted definitions of good faith. In Victoria, two out of 18 cases attempted definitions, one of which was in the Federal Court. There are two presumptions that could be drawn from the data: firstly, judges in NSW actively support the idea that the concept of good faith should be defined, and secondly, the many attempts by judges in NSW to define the concept of good faith is a sign of its ambiguity due to its limited practice and acceptance.

The next section discusses the several families of meaning for good faith that emerged from the analysis of prior literature and as supported by the above database of 104 cases. The collected definitions or meanings of good faith were analysed, and similar expressions or terminologies were

[34] See Figure 6.1: Cases Which Raised Good Faith as an Issue (Per Year).

[35] During the review of the cases, no empirical data was detected from ACT, Western Australia, Tasmania and Queensland.

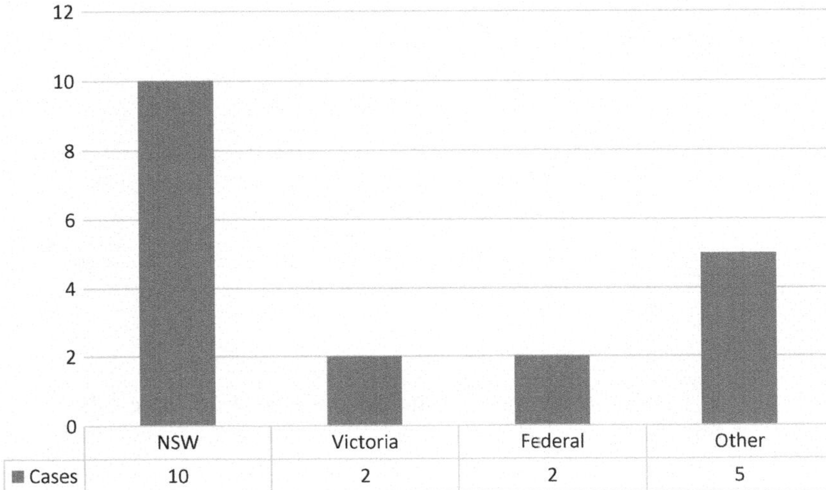

Fig. 6.2 Good faith defined by jurisdiction. Note: 'Others' comprises the jurisdictions of WA

grouped together as a 'family' based on their similarity. Definitions were categorised into 'single' and 'multi-category' groupings. In the 'single' category, only one element expresses the meaning of good faith, while instances in the 'multi-category' involve a combination of more than one element in the expression of the meaning of good faith.

The objective of this chapter is to analyse prior literature and commentary on the concept of good faith to develop a robust synthesis or taxonomy comprising a limited number of cohesive 'families of meaning'. Based on this analysis, a list of nine categories of good faith definitions were identified, as illustrated in Table 6.1.

The next section discusses the several families of meaning for good faith that emerged from an analysis of prior literature and as supported by the database of 104 cases.

6.4.1 Labels of the Meaning of Good Faith

There are many expressions for the concept of good faith proposed by judges and scholars. This is because of the nature of the concept of good faith, which is susceptible to changes in meaning, which in turn makes it

Table 6.1 Summary of the labels of meaning of good faith identified as **follows**

Label	*Theme*
Label 1	Honesty
Label 2	Reasonableness
Label 3	Fairness
Label 4	The standard of appropriate behaviour
Label 5	Parties' reasonable expectation
Label 6	Cooperation
Label 7	Loyalty
Label 8	Having regard to other's interest
Label 9	Excluder

difficult to determine its specific and precise meaning. The labels are derived from the cases and are supported by literature. The labels are expressed as a 'single category'. In a 'single category', good faith is expressed by one element. However, in some cases, the definition of good faith consists of more than one element. Such definitions are classified as 'multi-category'. The above nine labels are supported by empirical data classified by year and jurisdiction to detect the frequency of the definition of good faith defined. By year, the review period is divided into three phases, namely 'Introduction Phase 1992–1998', 'Development Phase 1999–2003' and 'Consolidation Phase 2004–2009', with the aim to trace the evolution of the concept of good faith. By jurisdiction, the states are divided into NSW, Victoria, Federal and other states. For the purpose of this study, 'other states' refers to Western Australia.[36]

Good faith finds expression in the following nine main labels.

Label One: Honesty

The first category identifies good faith as honesty. Honesty is a moral concept. The essence of honesty is 'truth and moral rectitude'.[37] In any commercial contract, honesty is a vital requirement for the contracting parties to ensure the success of the contract. Paterson claimed that it is generally agreed among legal scholars that the minimum content of the duty of

[36] During the review of the cases, no empirical data was detected from ACT, Western Australia, Tasmania and Queensland.

[37] Allsop, J. (2011). Good Faith and Australian Contract Law: A Practical Issue and a Question of Theory and Principle. *Australian Law Journal*, 85, 342–344.

good faith requires honesty from contracting parties.[38] Beyond honesty, there is no generally accepted explanation of the meaning that should be attributed to the duty of good faith performance as found in common law.[39]

Among the cases that support the meaning of honesty in good faith is *Thiess Contractors Pty Ltd v Placer (Granny Smith) Pty Ltd*, in which Templeman J held that:

> *In addition, I think that the obligation of good faith requires the parties to deal honestly with each other.*[40]

In *Linfox v Ellul & Ors*, Studdert J held that:

> *The exercise of good faith necessarily imports the requirement of adherence to a standard of honest behaviour by a contractor in the discharge of his contractual obligations.*[41]

The above cases interpret good faith as honesty. Although honesty falls under the 'single category', in certain occasions, a 'single category' like honesty can be combined with another 'single category' like reasonableness to constitute 'multi-categories'. Therefore, no issue arises when good faith is expressed by way of 'multi-categories'. This is clearly demonstrated in *Tomlin v Ford Credit Australia*, in which McDougall J claimed that:

> *The content of an implied duty to perform obligations and exercise contractual rights in good faith could be said to consist of an obligation to act honestly and reasonably.*[42]

Figure 6.3 illustrates good faith defined as honesty by year, while Fig. 6.4 illustrates good faith defined as honesty by jurisdiction.

Introduction Phase
No data was found from 1992 until 1998.

[38] Paterson, J. M. (2000). Duty of Good Faith Does It Have a Place in Contract Law? *Law Institute Journal*, p. 48.
[39] Ibid.
[40] [1999] 16 WASCA 1046.
[41] [2004] NSWSC 276 [55].
[42] [2005] NSWSC 540, 540.

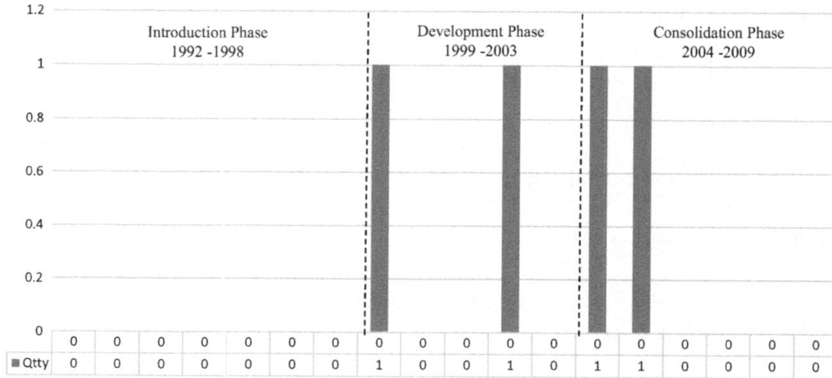

Fig. 6.3 Good faith defined as honesty by year

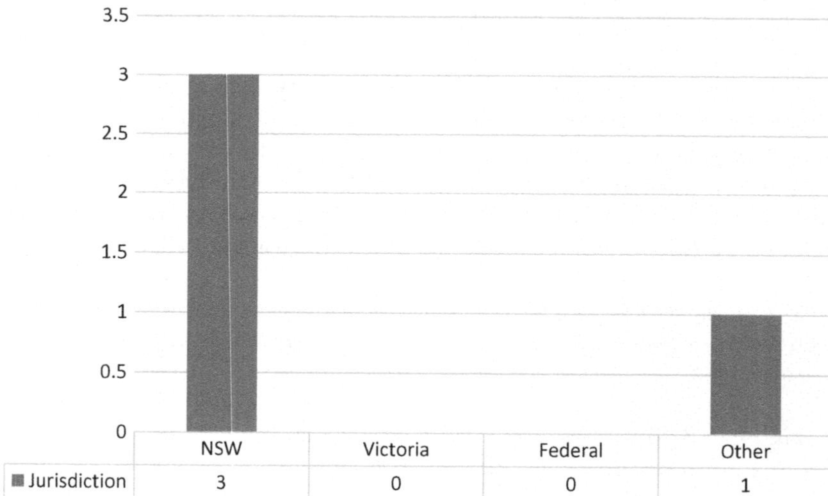

Fig. 6.4 Good faith defined as honesty by jurisdiction

Development Phase

There are two instances in which good faith is defined as honesty as demonstrated in 1999 and 2002. No such data were found in 2000, 2001 and 2003.

Consolidation Phase
During this phase, there are two instances in which good faith is defined as honesty as illustrated in 2004 and 2005. No such data was found in 2006, 2007, 2008 and 2009.

Overall, the empirical data shows that between 1992 until 2009, good faith was defined as honesty on four occasions.

There are three cases from NSW and one case from other states, as illustrated in Fig. 6.4. No such cases were found in Victoria and at the Federal level. This means that good faith defined as honesty received support from NSW. Much of the literature and the empirical data, as illustrated in Figs. 6.3 and 6.4, claim that honesty is a concept associated with good faith. Sometimes the terms good faith and reasonableness are used interchangeably. Therefore, it is argued that the least controversial aspect of good faith is that it requires the parties to act with honesty.[43]

Label Two: Reasonableness
Priestley J in *Renard* discussed the commonality of meanings between the terms fairness and reasonableness. His Honour commented that:

> *In ordinary English usage, there has been constant association between the words fair and reasonable. Similarity, there is a close association of ideas between the terms unreasonableness, lack of good faith, and unconscionably.*[44]

Among the cases that support good faith as reasonableness is *Burger King Corporation v Hungry Jack's Pty Ltd*, in which Sheller JA, Beazley JA and Stein JA held that:

> *It is worth noting that the Australian cases make no distinction of substance between the implied term of reasonableness and that of good faith.*[45]

In *Alcatel Australia Ltd v Scarcella*, Giles JA supported the proposition that:

[43] Terry, A., & Cary. D. L. (2009). Franchising and the Quest for the Holy Grail: Good Faith or Good Intentions. *Melbourne University Law Review*, 33, 542–554.

[44] (1992) 26 NSWLR 234, 268.

[45] [2001] NSWCA 187[169].

> *An obligation of good faith and reasonableness in the performance of a contractual obligation or the exercise of a contractual power may be implied as a matter of law as a legal incident of a commercial contract'.*[46]

This type of expression of good faith was supported by Homes, who explained that the key to understanding good faith lies in the word 'reasonableness'. He further stated that:

> *The requirement of good faith invokes notions of unselfishness and impartiality … Bad faith refers to unreasonable conduct wrongfully depriving the other party of the benefits of the agreement … The good faith standard requires a party to seek a fair mean, to try to strike an equitable balance when a conflict of interests appears.*[47]

Cole argued that attempts to define reasonableness will naturally meet with difficulties due to the complexities inherent in defining its meaning and determining the standard of expectation by various parties.[48] In *Armstrong v State of Victoria (No.2)*, Taylor J commented:

> *But reasonableness, alone, is an abstract concept and does not by itself provide a test for determining what charges may or may not be made; it is a useful guide if, and only if, we are aware of the various matters which must be considered when the necessity arises of determining whether particular charges are or are not reasonable.*[49]

Despite the difficulties inherent in the definition of the concept of reasonableness, the court has recognised its existence and importance in the law of contract. In *Biotechnology Australia Pty Ltd v Pace*, Hope JA commented:

> *The law has filled innumerable lacunae in the contractual arrangements of parties by applying a doctrine of reasonableness.*[50]

[46] (1998) 44 NSWLR 349, 368.

[47] Holmes, E. M. (1980). Is There Life After Gilmore's Death of Contract – Inductions from a Study of Commercial Good Faith in First-Party Insurance Contract. *Cornell Law Review*, 65, 330–377.

[48] Cole, T. R. H. (1994). The Concept of Reasonableness in Construction Contracts. *Building and Construction Law Journal*, 10, 7–12.

[49] (1957) 99 CLR 28, 88–89.

[50] (1988) 15 NSWLR 130, 145.

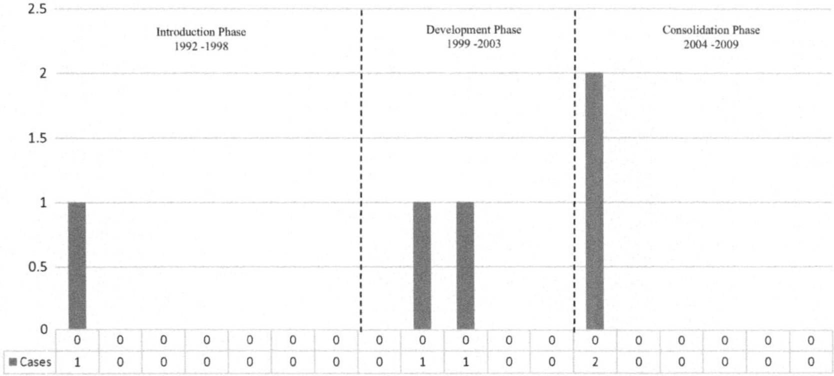

Fig. 6.5 Good faith as reasonableness by year

Figure 6.5 illustrates how good faith has been defined as reasonableness by year, while Fig. 6.6 illustrates attempts to define it as reasonableness by jurisdiction.

Introduction Phase
In 1992, one case defined good faith as reasonableness. No such cases were found in 1993, 1994, 1995, 1996, 1997 and 1998.

Development Phase
Two instances of good faith defined as reasonableness were found in 2000 and 2001. No such data was found in 1999, 2002 and 2003.

Consolidation Phase
During this phase, two cases defined good faith as reasonableness, both from 2004. No such data was found in 2005, 2006, 2007, 2008 and 2009.

Overall, the empirical data shows that from 1992 until 2009, there was a total of five (5) attempts to define good faith as reasonableness.

Four attempts to define good faith as reasonableness were reported in cases from NSW and one attempt from a case in Victoria, as illustrated in

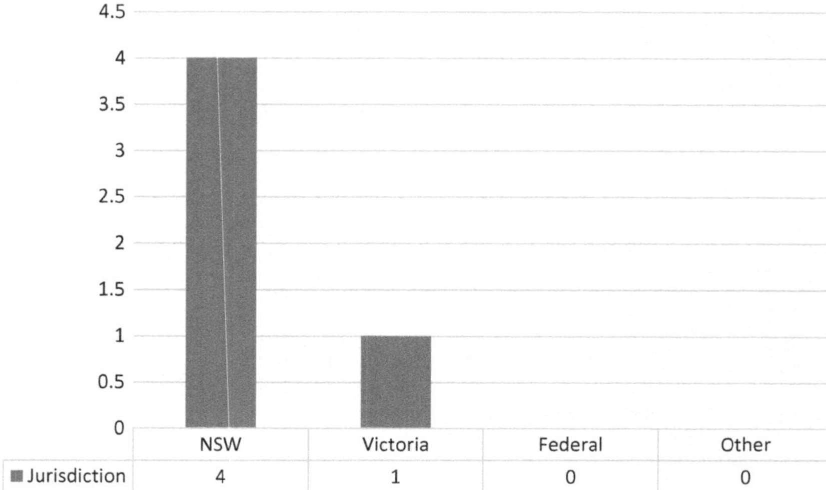

Fig. 6.6 Good faith as reasonableness by jurisdiction

Fig. 6.6. No other cases were found attempting this definition in Federal and other states. This means that good faith defined as reasonableness received support from NSW.

The concept of good faith as reasonableness also received support from the literature and the empirical data, as illustrated in Figs. 6.5 and 6.6. The empirical data illustrated that five (5) attempts were made to define good faith as reasonableness, which indicates strong support. However, it is argued here that as a concept, reasonableness cannot stand alone; it must be associated with other concepts to ensure the clarity of its meaning. In explaining the concept of reasonableness, 'the courts have sought to explain the concept by reference to other concepts, equally uncertain such as fairness, good faith or absence of unconscionable conduct'.[51]

Label Three: Fairness

The notion of fairness is based on the nature of the agreement, along with the duty of cooperation to ensure the performance of the contract. The notion of fairness was mentioned in the landmark case of *Interfoto Picture Library v Stiletto Visual Programmes Ltd*, where Bingham L J stated:

[51] Cole, above n. 48, 10.

> *Acting in good faith does not simply mean that [parties] should not deceive each other ... its effect is perhaps most aptly conveyed ... as 'playing fair', 'coming clean' or 'putting one's cards face upwards on the table'. It is, in essence, a principle of fair and open dealing.*[52]

Among the cases that support the meaning of good faith as fairness is *Commonwealth Bank of Australia v Spira*, where Gzell J held that:

> *The obligation of good faith requires a party to exercise rights and obligations under the contract fairly and, it would seem, reasonably. It does not require anything else.*[53]

In 'multi-categories', it is also found that the expression of good faith as fairness combines with the expression of 'not to act capriciously', as illustrated in *Garry Rogers Motors (Aust) Pty Ltd v Subaru (Aust) Pty Ltd*, where Finkelstein J held that:

> *In my view, a term of a contract that requires a party to act in good faith imposes an obligation upon that party not to act capriciously. It would not operate so as to restrict actions designed to promote the legitimate interests of that party. That is to say, provided the party exercising the power acts reasonably in all the circumstances, the duty to act fairly and in good faith will ordinarily be satisfied.*[54]

Hillman claims that the concept of good faith takes on many different meanings in different contexts because, at the base, it is nothing more than a requirement of fairness.[55] Farnsworth[56] offers some general remarks on the concept of good faith in *Restatement* 208. He suggests that:

[52] [1989] QB 433, 439.

[53] [2002] NSWSC 905 [176].

[54] (1999) ATPR 41-703, 43 014.

[55] Hillman, R. A. (1979). Policing Contract Modifications Under Uniform Commercial Contract: Good Faith and the Doctrine of Economic Duress. Iowa Law Review, 64, 849–877.

[56] Professor E. Allan Farnsworth in 1963 wrote the first major article on good faith under the *Uniform Commercial Code*. See Farnsworth, E. A. (1963). Good Faith Performance and Commercial Reasonableness Under the Uniform Commercial Code. *University of Chicago Law Review*, 30, 666–667.

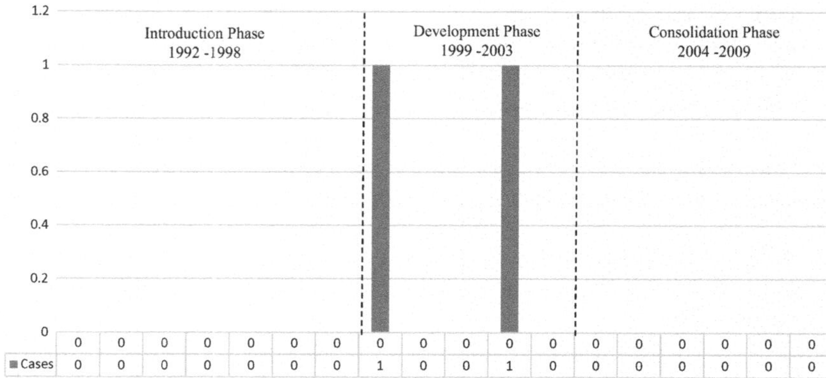

Fig. 6.7 Good faith as fairness by year

> *This duty is based on fundamental notions of fairness, and its scope necessarily varies according to the nature of the agreement. Some conduct such as subterfuge and evasion clearly violate the duty. However, the duty may not only proscribe undesirable conduct but may require affirmative action as well. A party may be under a duty not only to refrain from hindering or preventing the occurrence of conditions of the party's own duty or performance of the other party's duty but also to take some affirmative steps to co-operate in achieving these goals.*[57]

Figure 6.7 illustrates attempts to define good faith as fairness by year, while Fig. 6.8 illustrates good faith defined as fairness by jurisdiction.

Introduction Phase
No attempts were made to define good faith as fairness from 1992 to 1997.

Development Phase
There are two cases in which good faith is defined as fairness in 1999 and 2002, respectively. No such data was found in 2000, 2001 and 2003.

Consolidation Phase
No such data was found from 2004 to 2009.

[57] Farnsworth. E. A. (2004). *Farnsworth on Contracts* (3rd ed.). Aspen Publishers. p. 311.

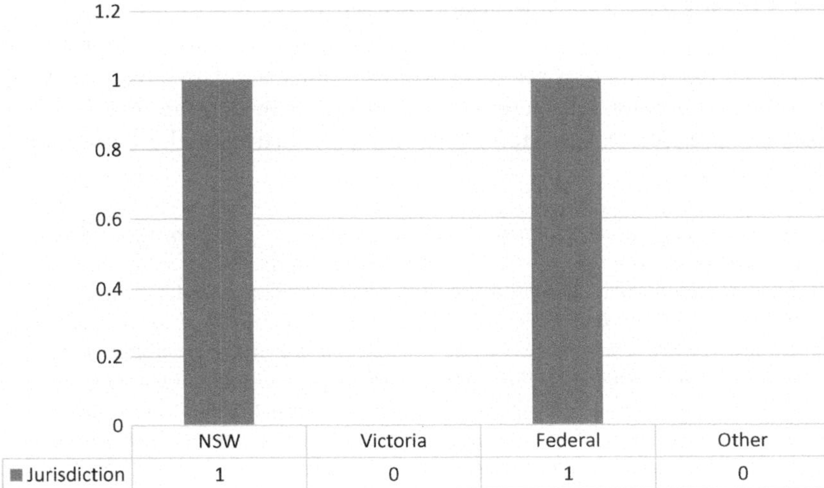

Fig. 6.8 Good faith as fairness by jurisdiction

Overall, the empirical data depicts that there are two (2) instances in which good faith is defined as fairness from 1992 to 2009.

In NSW, there was one reported instance in which good faith was defined as fairness and one such case in the Federal Court, as illustrated in Fig. 6.8. No such cases were found in Victoria and the other states. This means that good faith defined as fairness received support from NSW.

Good faith as fairness is a fundamental expression, as illustrated by the above literature. The empirical data shows that there are two cases that defined good faith as fairness, indicating little support. It is argued that fairness is too abstract and poses a problem to the expression of good faith as fairness. It is difficult to determine what is fair. Fairness varies in different contexts and cannot possibly be viewed consistently. Fairness is often associated with justice. Justice is subjective depending on the context. Given the ambiguity of the term, there is potential for unreasonable opinions based predominantly on an individual's values and beliefs.[58]

[58] Hillman, above n 55, 877.

Label Four: Standard of Appropriate Behaviour

Label Four defines the meaning of good faith as a standard of appropriate behaviour determined by reference to community standards. Reiter argued that the best approach to determine good faith is by determining the standard of appropriate behaviour from the perspective of the community. Reiter argued:

> *When I speak of good faith here, I refer to standards of appropriate behaviour relevant in the community … The good faith I consider is not necessarily the relevant community's view of what the most moral and other-regarding contractor would do, though this is certainly a part of good faith more broadly defined. Rather, what interests me here is that community's view of what range of conduct is appropriate. The 'appropriate' range will include the 'very best' behaviour, but will also incorporate less virtuous conduct. It is a circumstances-bound concept that will, in many cases be reducible to the notion of fairness and reasonableness in the circumstances.*[59]

Reiter based his statement on the notion that social groups practise a certain standard of behaviour that corresponds to the views and practices widely shared by the same community.[60] For example, in leasing transactions, good faith is defined as going beyond a mere state of mind on the part of the lessee and requires an inquiry into what type of business conduct conforms with community standards of fairness, decency and reasonableness in performance and enforcement.[61] Hutchison stated that:

> *What emerges quite clearly from recent academic writings and from some of the leading cases, is that good faith may be regarded as an ethical value or controlling principle, based on community standards of decency and fairness, that underlies and informs the substantive law of contract. It finds expression in various technical rules and doctrines, defines their form, content and field of application and provides them with a moral and theoretical foundation. Good faith thus has a creative, a controlling and a legitimating or explanatory function.*[62]

[59] Reiter, above n. 5, 706.

[60] Ibid.

[61] Thigpen, R. (1981). Good Faith Performance Under Percentage Leases. Mississippi Law Journal, 315–320.

[62] Hutchinson, D. (1999). Good Faith in the South African Law of Contract. In Brownsword, R., Hind, N. J., Howells, G. (Eds). *Good Faith in Contract, Concept and Context* (p. 215): Ashgate.

Furthermore, Hutchinson commented that good faith operates in conjunction with individual autonomy and responsibility but not dominating the outline of the contract law. The most important issue commented on by Lubbe and Murray was:

> *It will ensure just results only if judges are alert to their task of testing existing doctrines and the operation of particular transactions against the constantly changing mix of values and policies of which bona fides is an expression.*[63]

O'Connor claimed that good faith has to conform to currently acceptable behaviour in the community. It is important to identify which community is to determine the best behaviour. This is described through the provisional meaning adopted:

> *The principle of good faith in English Law is a fundamental principle derived from the rule of pacta sunt servanda (agreements are to be kept) and other legal rules, distinctively and directly related to honesty, fairness and reasonableness prevailing in the community which are considered appropriate for formulation in new or revised legal rules.*[64]

It is argued here that as the standard of appropriate behaviour, good faith is meaningless. It is difficult to establish the standard of appropriate behaviour in the community. The appropriate behaviour of one group may differ from another based on their understanding, beliefs, customs or mutual agreement. It is claimed that there is no judicial support from this concept from the case law databases.

Label Five: Parties' Reasonable Expectations

Paterson, Robertson and Heffey proposed that good faith can be measured based on the parties' reasonable expectations.[65] The parties' reasonable expectation approach focuses on how the contractual parties themselves may have expected their contract to be performed based on the probable intentions at the time the contract was made.[66] A commercial

[63] Ibid.

[64] O'Connor, J. F. (1990). *Good Faith in English Law*. Darmouth Publishing Company.

[65] Paterson, J., Robertson, A., Heffey, P. (2005). *Principles of Contract Law* (2nd ed.). Law Book Co. p. 304.

[66] See also Paterson, J. M. (2001). Good Faith in Commercial Contracts? A Franchising Case Study. *Australian Business Law Review*, 29, 270–291.

contract is designed for a specific purpose and with a clear objective. It is expected that the parties to the contract understood the terms of the contract as the contract was drafted by the parties themselves.

A contract commonly contains contractual provisions, including express or implied contractual provisions. For example, there may be an express exclusion clause designed to protect a particular contractual party from the risk of harmful implied contractual terms. In such a case, the court will give priority to the express terms of the contract or the parties' reasonable expectations as produced by the contractual relationship.[67]

There is one case that supports the notion that good faith should be based on the reasonable expectations of the contracting parties. In *Hughes Aircraft Systems International v Airservices Australia*, Finn J, a proponent of the duty of good faith, commented:

> *It may well be that, on analysis, [good faith] would be found to advance little the standard that presently may be extracted from contracting parties by other means.*[68]

Figure 6.9 illustrates the attempts made to define good faith as parties' reasonable expectations by year, while Fig. 6.10 illustrates such attempts by jurisdiction.

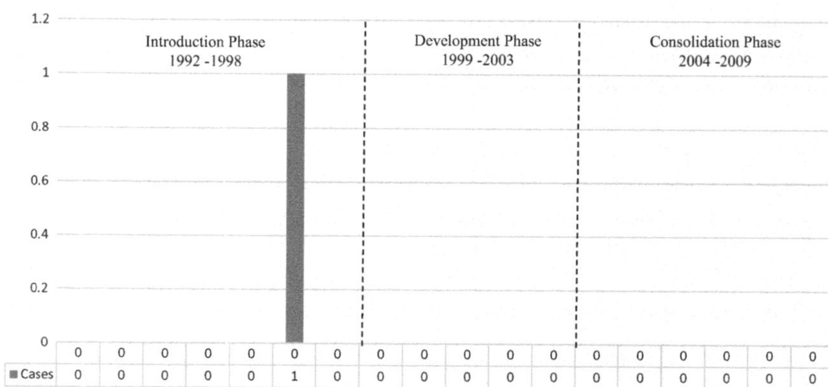

Fig. 6.9 Good faith defined as parties' reasonable expectations

[67] See Dixon, B. (2007). Can the Common Law Obligation of Good Faith Be Contractually Excluded? *Australian Business Law Review*, 35, 110–113.

[68] (1997) 146 ALR 1, 37.

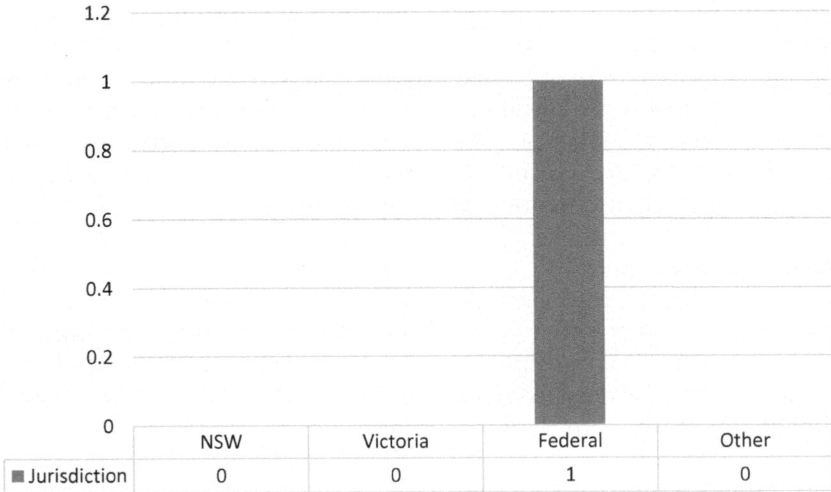

Fig. 6.10 Good faith defined as parties' reasonable expectations by jurisdiction

Introduction Phase
In 1997, one case attempted to define good faith as parties' reasonable expectations.

Development Phase
No such data was found from 1999 to 2003.

Consolidation Phase
No such data was found from 2004 to 2009.

Overall, the empirical data shows that only one (1) attempt was made to define good faith as parties' reasonable expectations.

There is only one reported case from the Federal Court defining good faith as the parties' reasonable expectations. No such cases were found in NSW, Victoria and the other states. This means that good faith defined as parties' reasonable expectations received support only from the Federal Court.

The empirical data illustrated in Figs. 6.9 and 6.10 shows that only one case supported good faith as parties' reasonable expectations. It is argued here that good faith as parties' reasonable expectations is logical because the expectation of the contract is determined by the parties themselves.

For example, two business operators running a similar kind of business are measured by standard business measures of a similar group of business operators to establish reasonable expectations. On the other hand, it is argued here that it is difficult to ascertain the reasonable expectations of the parties and how they are to be determined. The expectations of the parties themselves are difficult to ascertain because, in some contracts, the intention of the parties is not properly spelt out.

Label Six: Cooperation

Good faith defined as cooperation means that both parties are required to cooperate to secure the expected benefit of the contract. The duty of cooperation has been accepted as part of the law as early as 1881. In *Mackay v Dick*, the duty to cooperate was found to be part of the obligation of good faith. Lord Blackburn stated:

> *Where in a written contract it appears that both parties have agreed that something shall be done, which cannot effectually be done unless both concur in doing it, the construction of the contract is that each agrees to do all that is necessary to be done on his part for the carrying out of that thing, though there may be no express words to that effect. What is the part of each must depend on circumstances.*[69]

A duty of cooperation is imposed to the extent that it is necessary to make the contract workable for both parties. This definition received support in *Thiess Contractors Pty Ltd v Placer (Granny Smith) Pty Ltd*, wherein the court in Western Australia was faced with a dispute over a mining contract that contained a clause which stated that:

> *The successful operation of this contract requires that both parties agree to act in good faith in all matters relating both to carrying out the works, derivation of rates and interpretation of this document.*[70]

In this case, the Full Court of Western Australia interpreted the above clause as to mean that there is an obligation of good faith where:

> *The parties were obliged to agree on rates in advance of work done and they were required to co-operate in the establishment of rates based as far as reasonably possible on actual costs.*[71]

[69] (1881) 6 App Case 251, 263.
[70] [2000] WASCA 102 [22].
[71] [2000] WASCA 102 [33].

Farnsworth claimed that good faith performance has always required the cooperation of one party where it was necessary so that the other might secure the expected benefit of the contract.[72] The standard for determining what cooperation was required has always been an objective standard based on decency, fairness and reasonableness in the business community and not on the individual's own belief as to what might be decent, fair or reasonable. Both common sense and tradition dictate an objective standard for good faith performance. Peden also claimed that 'often co-operation is seen as equivalent to good faith'.[73] She argued that cooperation is analogous to good faith:

> *'Cooperation' is sometimes seen as equivalent to 'good faith', and this seems appropriate. The effect of requiring cooperation often overlaps with what is trying to be achieved by the newly created obligation of 'good faith'. Cooperation (or good faith if that term is preferred) basically must embrace a duty to act honestly and a duty to have regard to the legitimate interests of the other party.*[74]

It is unnecessary to imply an obligation of good faith where the same result is achieved by considering the parties' intentions via the duty of cooperation, as illustrated by Griffith CJ in *Butt v McDonald*:

> *It is a general rule applicable to every contract that each party agrees, by implication, to all such things as are necessary on his part to enable the other party to have the benefit of the contract.*[75]

This statement was reaffirmed in the High Court decision in *Secured Income Real Estate (Australia) Ltd v St Martin's Investments Pty Ltd*, which held that:

> *But it is common ground that the contract imposed an implied obligation on each party to do all that was reasonably necessary to secure performance of the contract.*[76]

[72] Farnsworth, above n. 56, 672.
[73] Peden, E. (2003). Good Faith in the Performance of Contract Law. *Law Journal Society*, p. 170.
[74] Ibid.
[75] (1896) 7 QLJ 68, 70–71.
[76] (1979) 144 CLR 596, 607–608 per Mason J.

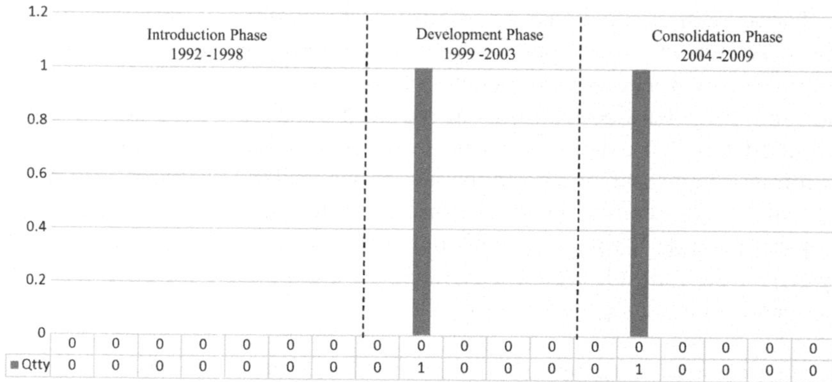

Fig. 6.11 Good faith defined as cooperation by year

Moreover, when Sir Anthony Mason formulated the definition of good faith, his Honour defined good faith from three notions: honesty, regards to the interests of the parties and cooperation/loyalty (that is loyalty to the contract where the contract is treated as a promise).[77] This definition affirms Peden's view that good faith is analogous to the duty to cooperate.[78]

Figure 6.11 illustrates good faith defined as cooperation by year, while Fig. 6.12 illustrates good faith defined as cooperation by jurisdiction.

Introduction Phase

No data was found from 1992 to 1997 concerning good faith defined as cooperation.

Development Phase

In 2000, one case defined good faith as cooperation. No such cases were found in 1999, 2001, 2002 and 2003.

Consolidation Phase

In 2005, one case defined good faith as cooperation. No such cases were found in 2004, 2006, 2007, 2008 and 2009.

[77] Mason, A. (2000). Contract, Good Faith and Equitable Standards in Fair Dealing. *Law Quarterly Review*, 116, 66–69.

[78] Peden, E., & Carter, J. W. (2003). Good Faith in Australian Contract Law. *Journal of Contract Law*, 19, 155–162.

Fig. 6.12 Good faith defined as cooperation by jurisdiction

Overall, the empirical data shows that there were two attempts to define good faith as cooperation.

There are two cases in which good faith was defined as cooperation, both of which were found in other states, as illustrated in Fig. 6.12. No such cases were found in NSW, Victoria and the Federal Court. This means that good faith defined as cooperation received support from other states.

The empirical data, as illustrated in Figs. 6.11 and 6.12, shows that two cases supported good faith as the duty to cooperate. This indicates low support. The duty to cooperate is a general duty expected by both parties to the contract in which the expected benefit should be reaped. It is argued here that the duty to cooperate has a similar task to good faith. Therefore, it is claimed that there is no need to associate good faith with the duty to cooperate as it is sufficiently comprehensive to ensure a workable contract. Although vague, it is well established in common law and establishes a clear foundation when compared to good faith.

Label Seven: Loyalty

Lucke claimed that good faith is defined as loyalty. When good faith is defined as loyalty, there is an expectation that both parties in the contract have to be loyal to each other to secure the benefit of the contract.

According to him, good faith as loyalty is a useful definition because good faith serves as an implied term to ensure an effective contract. He states that the expression good faith itself means loyalty, which is the expected expectation from the contracting parties. He further explained:

> *Many rules of our existing contract law can quite plausibly be seen as manifestations of good faith as loyalty. Example are those rules of construction, and those rules providing for the implication of terms and for the severance of ineffective terms, which serve to give business efficacy to contracts. Good faith as loyalty finds an even simpler and more fundamental expression in the recognition of a legal duty to perform contractual undertakings; pacta sunt servanda. Furthermore, reading loyalty into good faith amounts to a generous, even an expansive interpretation, but it does not seem forced or artificial from a linguistic point of view. 'Faith', according to the Oxford English Dictionary, means inter alia, 'loyalty' or 'fidelity'. There is no linguistic reason why we should not regard this as the core meaning of the whole phrase.*[79]

It is argued here that good faith as loyalty is a fundamental expression. Loyalty is the expected standard of behaviour of the contracting party to ensure an effective contract. However, no judicial support was received due to the expansiveness of the interpretation of good faith.

Label Eight: Having Regard to Other's Interests

Among the cases that support good faith as having regard to other's interests is *Automasters Australia Pty Ltd v Bruness Pty Ltd & Anor*, in which his Honour claimed:

> *The term 'good faith' imports a duty to have due regard to the legitimate interests of both parties in the enjoyment of the fruits of the contract.*[80]

In 'multi-categories', the element of having regard to other's interests combines with the elements of cooperation and honesty. This definition was given recognition in *Central Exchange Ltd v Anaconda Nickel Ltd*, where Parker J held that:

> *It is submitted for the applicants that the implication of a term of good faith requires, at least, that the parties be bound to 'the spirit of the bargain' and not*

[79] Lucke, above n. 31, 162.
[80] [2002] WASC 286 [388].

> *to render illusory contractual entitlements … [which reflects the discussion of the three notions of good faith as explained below by Mason]. On the assumption for the purposes of this decision, that an obligation of good faith is to be implied into this Deed and that by virtue of this the defendant may not render illusory the contractual entitlements of the plaintiff, and is to co-operate with the plaintiff in achieving the contractual objects, and is to act honestly and reasonably having regard to the respective interests of the parties.*[81]

Mason J argued that good faith embraces three notions: an obligation on the parties to cooperate in achieving the contractual objects (loyalty to the promise itself), compliance with honest standards of conduct and compliance with standards of conduct which are reasonable, having regard to the interests of the parties.[82] Peden also suggested that the true meaning of good faith must be a requirement to have regard to the interests of the other party, which includes loyalty to the contract and subjective honesty.[83] This definition has recently been given strong support by Barrat J in *Overlook v Foxtel*, where his Honour stated:

> *It must be accepted that the party subject to the obligation is not required to subordinate the party's own interests, so long as pursuit of those interests does not entail unreasonable interference with the enjoyment of a benefit conferred by the express contractual terms so that the enjoyment becomes (or could become) nugatory, worthless or, perhaps, seriously undermined' … the implied obligation of good faith underwrites the spirit of the contract and supports the integrity of its character. A party is precluded from cynical resort to the black letter. But no party is fixed with the duty to subordinate self-interest entirely which is the lot of the fiduciary … The duty is not a duty to prefer the interests of the other contracting party. It is, rather, a duty to recognise and to have due regard to the legitimate interests of both the parties in the enjoyment of the fruits of the contract as delineated by its terms.*[84]

[81] [2001] WASC 128 [24][28].

[82] Mason, above n. 77, 69.

[83] Peden, E. (2002). The Meaning of Contractual Good Faith. *Australian Bar Review*, 22, 235–247. Peden agreed with two of the definitions proposed by Sir Anthony Mason, which are cooperation or loyalty and honesty.

[84] (2002) ATPT (Digest) 46–219: Aust Contract R 90–143 [67]. See also Einstein J's 'essential or core content' of the obligation to mediate or negotiate in good faith in *Aiton Australia Pty Ltd v Transfield Pty Ltd* (1999) 153 FLR 236, 262:

1. to undertake to subject oneself to the process of negotiation or mediation (which must be sufficiently precisely defined by the agreement to be certain and hence enforceable)

Figure 6.13 illustrates good faith defined as having regard to other's interests by year, while Fig. 6.14 illustrates the same data by jurisdiction.

Introduction Phase
No cases defined good faith as having regard to other's interests from 1992 to 1998.

Development Phase
There is one case in 2001 and three cases in 2002 where good faith is defined as having regard to other's interests. No such cases were found in 1999, 2000 and 2003.

Consolidation Phase
No such data was found from 2004 to 2009.

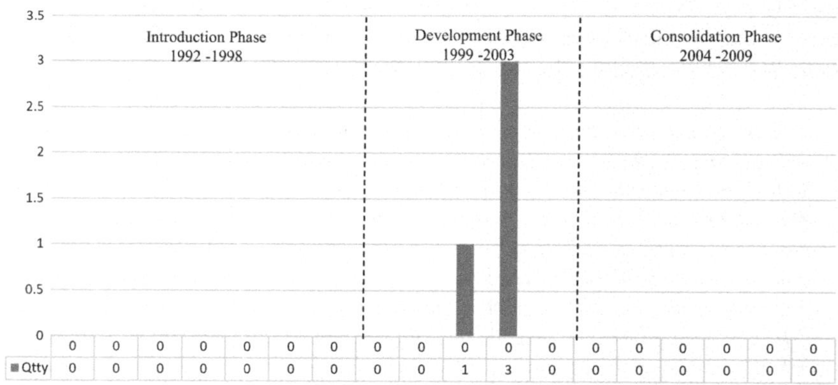

Fig. 6.13 Good faith defined as having regard to other's interests by year

2. to undertake and subjecting oneself to that process, to have an open mind in the sense of:

(a) a willingness to consider such options for the resolution of the dispute as may be propounded by the opposing party or by the mediator, as appropriate
(b) a willingness to give consideration to putting forward options for the resolution of the dispute

He specifically excluded from this any requirement: (a) to act for or on behalf or in the interests of the other party; (b) to act otherwise than by having regard to self-interest.

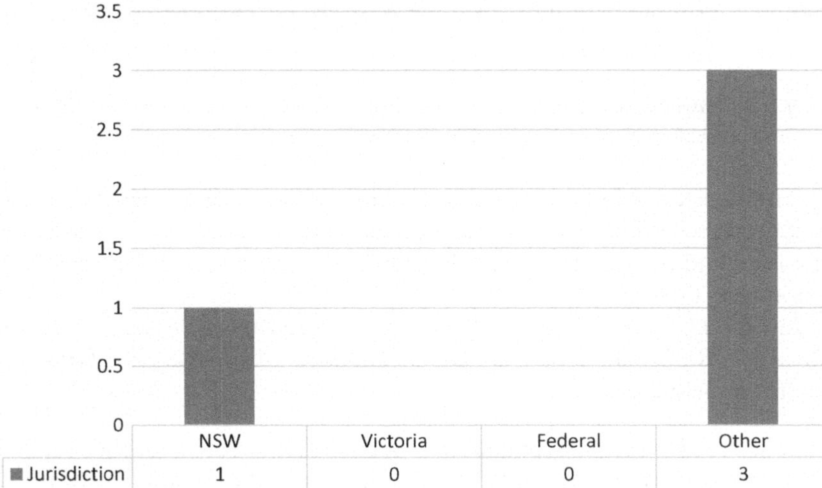

Fig. 6.14 Good faith defined as having regard to other's interests by jurisdiction

Overall, the empirical data shows that there are four (4) attempts to define good faith as having regard to other's interests.

There is one case from NSW and three cases from other states where good faith is defined as having regard to other's interests, as illustrated in Fig. 6.14. No such cases were found in Victoria and Federal Courts. This means that good faith defined as having regard to other's interests received the most support from other states.

The empirical data, as illustrated in Figs. 6.13 and 6.14, shows that there were four attempts to define good faith as having regard to other's interests, which shows strong support. It is argued here that good faith as having regard to other's interests enjoys a broader scope than other definitions by means of the following three elements: cooperation, honesty and having regard to other's interests. Undeniably, the expressions of cooperation and honesty are the most common expression of good faith, as explained above.

Label Nine: Excludes Any Form of Bad Faith or 'Excluder'

Label Nine defines good faith from a negative perspective, that is, where it excludes any form of bad faith. This is known as the 'excluder' approach.

Summers proposed the idea of good faith as an 'excluder' of bad faith behaviour[85] and claimed that:

> *It is a phrase which has no general meaning or meanings of its own, but which serves to exclude many heterogeneous forms of bad faith.*[86]

Summers identified four broad categories of bad faith, namely bad faith in contract negotiation and formation, bad faith in performance, bad faith in raising and resolving contract disputes and bad faith in taking remedial action (see Table 6.2).[87]

In *PRP Diagnostic Imaging Pty Limited (in its capacity as trustee for the Pittwater Radiology Trust) & Ors v Pittwater Radiology Pty Limited*, Einstein J held that:

> In many ways, the implied obligation of good faith is best regarded as an obligation to eschew bad faith. This is borne out by the following succinct statement by Lord Scott of Foscote in Manifest Shipping Co Ltd v Uni-Polaris Shipping Co Ltd [2001] 2 WLR 170, a case concerning the duty of good faith in the insurance context:
>
> Unless the assured has acted in bad faith, he cannot, in my opinion, be in breach of a duty of good faith, utmost or otherwise.[88]

In *Tymshare Inc v Covell*, Scalia J held that:

> *The doctrine of good faith performance is a means of finding within a contract an implied obligation not to engage in the particular form of conduct which, in the case at hand, constitutes 'bad faith'.*[89]

Understood as an excluder, good faith has received much criticism. Atiyah explained that good faith is difficult to define or even summarise, although it is often easy to recognise examples of bad faith.[90] In Summers' view, good faith as an excluder could be used flexibly by judges so as to do

[85] Summers, R. (1968). Good Faith in General Contract Law and the Sales Provision of the Uniform Commercial Code. *Virginia Law Review*, 54, 195–196.

[86] Ibid.

[87] See Dubroff, H. (2006). The Implied Covenant of Good Faith in Contract Interpretation and Gap-Filling: Reviving a Revered Relic. *St. John's Law Review*, 80, 559–587.

[88] [2008] NSWSC 701 [68].

[89] 727 F2d 1148 (1984).

[90] See Atiyah, P. S. (2005). Atiyah's Introduction to the Law of Contract. Oxford University Press.

Table 6.2 Good faith and bad faith according to Summers

Form of bad faith conduct	*Meaning of good faith*
Seller concealing a defect in what he is selling	Fully disclosing material facts
Builder willfully failing to perform in full, through otherwise substantially performing	Substantially performing without knowingly deviating from specifications
Contractor openly abusing bargaining power to coerce an increase in the contract price	Refraining from abuse of bargaining power
Hiring a broker and then deliberately preventing him from consummating the deal	Acting cooperatively
Conscious lack of diligence in mitigating the other parts' damages	Acting diligently
Arbitrarily and capriciously exercising a power to terminate the contract	Acting with some reason
Adopting an overreaching interpretation of contract language	Interpreting contract language fairly
Harassing the other party for repeated assurances of performance	Accepting adequate assurances

justice and do it according to law.[91] Priestley J agreed with the explanation of Summers when he said:

> *The typical judge who uses this phrase is primarily concerned with ruling out specific conduct and only secondarily, or not at all, with the formulation of the positive content of a standard.*[92]

However, this approach fails to provide a clear idea of what observance of the standard of good faith is actually required. Bridge commented that:

> *[I]t seem tantamount to saying that the good faith duty is breached whenever a judge decides that it has been breached … [which] hardly advances the cause of intellectual inquiry and provides absolutely no guide as to the disposition of future cases except to the extent that they may be on all fours with a decided case.*[93]

Figure 6.15 illustrates good faith defined as an 'excluder' by year, while Fig. 6.16 illustrates the same data by jurisdiction.

[91] Summers, above n. 85, 196.

[92] Ibid., 202.

[93] Bridge, M. (1984). Does Anglo-Canadian Contract Law Need a Doctrine of Good Faith? *Canadian Business Law Journal*. 9, 385–413.

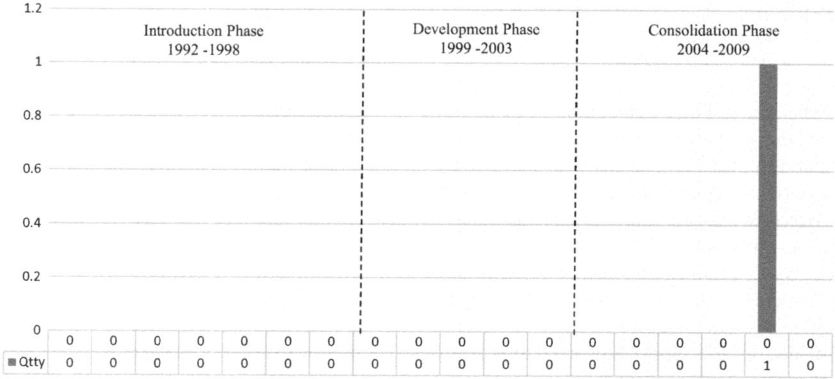

Fig. 6.15 Good faith defined as an 'excluder' by year

Introduction Phase
No cases were identified from 1992 to 1998 that define good faith as an 'excluder'.

Development Phase
No such data was found from 1999 to 2003.

Consolidation Phase
In 2008, only one case defined good faith as an 'excluder'.

Overall, the empirical data shows that there was one attempt to define good faith as an 'excluder'.

NSW is the only jurisdiction to have attempted a definition of good faith as an 'excluder'. No such cases were found in Victoria, Federal and other states. This means that good faith defined as an 'excluder' only received support from NSW.

The empirical data, as illustrated in Figs. 6.15 and 6.16, shows that there was only one case in which good faith was defined as an 'excluder', thus indicating low support. It is argued here that this meaning completely differs from the other meanings included in this chapter because it stands alone. It is a loose interpretation containing a phrase which has no

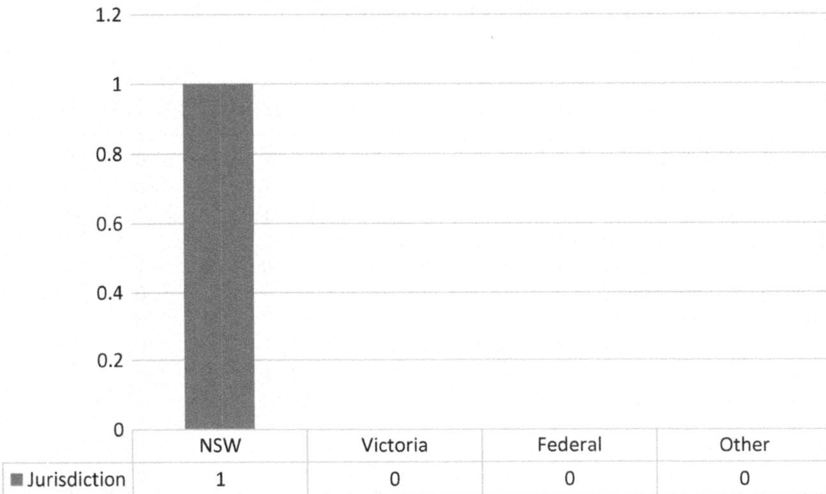

Fig. 6.16 Good faith defined as an 'excluder' by jurisdiction

meaning of its own, that is, any behaviour which is bad faith is by definition not good faith and thus leads to an undesirable lack of certainty in a contract.

6.5 The Proposed Taxonomic Solution

Based on the analysis in Sect. 6.3, a list of nine categories of good faith definitions was identified, as illustrated in Table 6.3. Table 6.3 summarises the labels based on the above empirical data according to frequency and jurisdiction.

The frequency of the distribution of the labels is as follows: Label 1: Honesty (4), Label 2: Reasonableness (5), Label 3: Fairness (2), Label 5: Parties' reasonable expectations (1), Label 6: Cooperation (2), Label 8: Having regard to other's interests (4) and Label 9: Excluder (1). No frequency was detected for Label 4: Standard of appropriate behaviour and Label 7: Loyalty. The above empirical data reveals that the most frequent labels detected are honesty (4), reasonableness (5) and having regard to other's interests (4). These three labels received the most support from jurisdictions, as illustrated in Table 6.3. The attempt made by

Table 6.3 Summary of labels, including frequency and jurisdiction

Labels	*Theme*	*Times*	*Jurisdiction*			
			NSW	*VIC*	*FED*	*Others*
Label 1	Honesty	4	3	0	0	1
Label 2	Reasonableness	5	4	1	0	0
Label 3	Fairness	2	1	0	1	0
Label 4	Standard of appropriate behaviour	0	0	0	0	0
Label 5	Parties' reasonable expectation	1	0	0	1	0
Label 6	Cooperation	2	0	0	0	2
Label 7	Loyalty	0	0	0	0	0
Label 8	Having regard to other's interests	4	1	0	0	3
Label 9	Excluder	1	1	0	0	0
	Total	19	10	1	2	6

Table 6.4 Seven general groupings of good faith from the identified label

Group	*Theme*	*Label*
1	Moral values	Label 1: Honesty, Label 6: Cooperation and Level 7: Loyalty
2	Reasonableness	Label 2: Reasonableness
3	Having regard to other's interests	Label 8: Having regard to other's interests
4	Fairness	Label 3: Fairness
5	Standard of appropriate behaviour	Label 4: Standard of appropriate behaviour
6	Parties' reasonable expectations	Label 5: Parties' reasonable expectations
7	Excluder	Label 9: Excluder

each of the jurisdictions to define good faith indicates that good faith is, in fact, capable of being defined.

This section proposes a solution to the current problematic approaches to the meaning of good faith. Table 6.4 reveals that some of the expressions have a similar scope of expression and could together form a meaningful definition. Most of the expressions are stand-alone because they do not belong to any specific group. This is because good faith is a concept 'protean' in nature; therefore, it has many ways of expressing its meaning. Sometimes the expression is based on the context or circumstances which lead to difficulties in attaching a meaning or definition to it. These nine categories are reorganised into seven main types or forms of definitions of good faith.

6.5.1 Group 1: Honesty, Loyalty and Cooperation and Group 2: Reasonableness

Group 1 consists of honesty, loyalty and cooperation. These are considered moral values. Group 2 consists of reasonableness. From the empirical study, the label most commonly used in relation to good faith is 'honesty and reasonableness'. Between the two expressions, 'honesty' is the least controversial concept to define good faith. In *Aiton Australia Pty Ltd v Transfield Pty Ltd*, Einstein J stated that:

> *Parties are subject to a universal duty to act honestly in any case'.*[94] *This statement gained recognition in Insight Oceania Pty Ltd v Philips Electronics Australia Ltd, where Bergin J held that 'The duty to act in good faith seems to me to subsume the obligation to act honestly.*[95]

While 'honesty' is universally recognised, 'reasonableness' is a more difficult concept where a reasonable expectation approach seems to be broad enough to include references to norms of the relationship as designated by the contract. In *The Mogul Steamship Co Ltd v McGregor, Gow & Co*, Bowen L J commented on the concept of reasonable standards for commercial contracting. His Lordship held that:

> *I myself should deem it to be a misfortune if we were to attempt to ... adopt some standard of judicial 'reasonableness' ... to which commercial adventurers, otherwise innocent, were bound to conform.*[96]

Peden, however, observed that equating good faith with reasonableness is more 'confusing than instructive' and commented that:

> *There is no precise meaning given, but rather a repetition of well-worn phrase and quotes, without explanation of how and why they fit together. There is fur-*

[94] (1999) 153 FLR 236, 262.
[95] [2008] NSWSC 710 (Unreported, Bergin J, 23 July 2008) [178].
[96] (1889) 23 QBD 598, 620.

thermore, no explanation of why 'reasonableness' is a justified inclusion in the meaning of good faith, and why it is considered identical to 'good faith.[97]

In *Garry Rogers Motors (Aust) Pty Ltd v Subaru (Aust)*, Finkelstein J commented that acting reasonably was seen as central to acting fairly and in good faith. His Honour stated that:

... provided the party exercising the power acts reasonably in all the circumstances, the duty to act fairly and in good faith will ordinarily be satisfied.[98]

Both expressions are stand-alone definitions,[99] but this does not preclude them from being used in combination. For example, both expressions are found in *Tomlin v Ford Credit Australia*, where McDougall J claimed that 'The content of an implied duty to perform obligations and exercise contractual rights in good faith could be said to consist of an obligation to act honestly and reasonably'.[100]

6.5.2 Group 3: Having Regard to Other's Interests

Group 3 consists of the label 'Having regard to other's interests'. It is also another common expression in relation to good faith where the interests of the contracting parties are given due consideration. This kind of expression has received judicial recognition. In *Central Exchange Ltd v Anaconda Nickel Ltd*, Parker J held that:

It is submitted for the applicants that the implication of a term of good faith requires, at least, that the parties be bound to 'the spirit of the bargain' and not to render illusory contractual entitlement ... On the assumption for the purposes of this decision, that an obligation of good faith is to be implied into this Deed and that by virtue of this the defendant may not render illusory the contractual entitlements of the plaintiff, and is to cooperate with the plaintiff in achieving the contractual objects, and is to act honestly and reasonably having regard to the respective interests of the parties.[101]

[97] Peden, above n. 73, 176.
[98] [1999] FCA 903 [37].
[99] See Sect. 6.3 above.
[100] [2005] NSWSC 540 [116].
[101] [2001] WASC 128 [24]–[28].

The duty is not to prefer the interests of the other contracting party but rather a duty to recognise and to have due regard to the legitimate interests of both parties.[102] In *Overlook v Foxtel*, Barrett J further commented that the obligation does not require subordinating the party's own interests. His Honour further stated that the paramount consideration is that:

> *... so long as pursuit of those interests does not entail unreasonable interference with the enjoyment of a benefit conferred by the express contractual terms so that the enjoyment becomes (or could become) nugatory, worthless or, perhaps, seriously undermined' ... the implied obligation of good faith underwrites the spirit of the contract and supports the integrity of its character.*[103]

In the context of a franchise, the duty of good faith must have regard to the legitimate interests of both franchisor and franchisee to ensure a successful relationship of the business. This is supported in *JF Keir Pty Ltd v Priority Management Systems Pty Ltd (administrators appointed)*, where it was held that:

A franchisor is required to act reasonably and honestly (to an objective standard), not to act for an ulterior motive, to recognize and have regard to the legitimate interest of both parties in the enjoyment of the fruits of the contract, and to avoid rendering the franchisee's interest under the agreement nugatory or worthless or seriously undermining it.[104]

Hence, it is illustrated that the requirement of 'Having regard to other's interests' is important to ensure the successful relationship between the parties where the legitimate interests of the parties are recognised, with the duty not to subordinate one's own interests.

6.5.3 Group 4: Fairness

Fairness is an abstract concept. It is difficult to define fairness because different individuals perceive it differently. Fairness is often associated with justice. In this context, it is difficult to define what justice is when fairness itself is difficult to determine and is susceptible to an individual's perspective of justice.

[102] See *Automasters Australia Pty Ltd v Bruness Pty Ltd & Anor* [2002] WASC 286 (Unreported, Hasluck J, 4 December 2002) [388].

[103] [2002] NSWSC 17 [65–67].

[104] (2007) NSWSC 789 [27].

6.5.4 Group 5: The Standard of Appropriate Behaviour

The standard of appropriate behaviour of an individual or a community is difficult to determine. The perspective of the standard of appropriate behaviour is inconsistent. The standard of appropriate behaviour may be influenced by understandings, beliefs, customs or mutual agreement among the group. Hence, it is meaningless in expressing the definition of good faith.

6.5.5 Group 6: Parties' Reasonable Expectations

It is challenging to ascertain the parties' reasonable expectations and how they are to be determined in a contract. This is because, in some contracts, the expectations of the parties are not properly spelt out or are different from those that are stated in a contract.

6.5.6 Group 7: Excluder

'Excluder' is a vague expression of good faith because it is defined by means of what is not, that is, bad faith. It is an expression that lacks a definite meaning.

Figure 6.17 shows the three labels which have the potential to serve as the definition or meaning of good faith.

Overall, the literature and empirical observations suggest that the three labels above are best suited to serve as the definition or meaning of good faith.

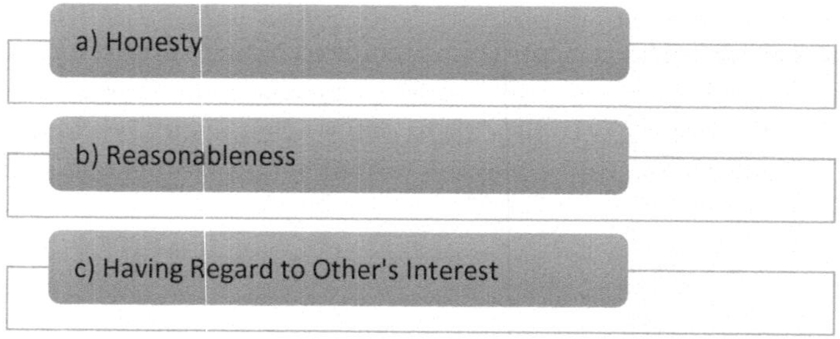

Fig. 6.17 The three labels which have the potential to serve as the definition or meaning of good faith

6.6 A Proposed Definition of Good Faith

Formulating a new definition of good faith is a difficult task. It is the biggest impediment to the acceptance of the concept. To propose a definition is obviously ambitious, however, it is the intention of this study to propose a workable definition. The discussion in Sect. 6.4 suggests that there are three labels that serve as potential definitions or meanings of good faith, as illustrated in Fig. 6.17. These are (a) honesty, (b) reasonableness and (c) having regard to other's interests. They are commonly used in reference to the concept of good faith as discussed in Sect. 6.4.

The findings of this discussion are also supported by the empirical data as illustrated in Table 6.5, which demonstrates the summary of labels, including frequency and percentage from the case law databases.

The frequency and percentage of the distribution of the labels are as follows: Label 1: Honesty (4), which is equivalent to 21 percent; Label 2: Reasonableness (5), which is equivalent to 26 percent; Label 3: Fairness (2), which is equivalent to 11 percent; Label 6: Cooperation (2), which is equivalent to 11 percent; Label 8: Having regard to other's interests (4), which is equivalent to 21 percent; and Label 9: Excluder (1), which is equivalent to 5 percent. Hence, the empirical data demonstrated that Label 1: Honesty (4), which is equivalent to 21 percent; Label 2: Reasonableness (5), which is equivalent to 26 percent; and Label 8: Having regard to other's interests (4), which is equivalent to 21 percent, received the most support from the rest of the identified labels, which amount to 68 percent of the total percentage. This data suggests strong support for the three labels, which received more than half of the total support.

The above findings are consistent with the definition of good faith proposed by the *Competitive Foods Australia Pty Ltd* in its submission to a Parliamentary Joint Committee on Corporations and Financial Services, *Inquiry into Franchising Code of Conduct*, in September 2008,[105] which proposed a 'multi-categories' definition:

> *Good faith in relation to conduct by a franchisor or a franchisee means that the party has acted:*

[105] A draft model amendment was included in Competitive Foods Australia, Submission No.22 to Parliamentary Joint Committee on Corporations and Financial Services, *Inquiry into Franchising Code of Conduct*, 2008.

Table 6.5 Frequency and percentage of the good faith labels

Theme	*Label 1: Honesty*	*Label 2: Reasonableness*	*Label 3: Fairness*	*Label 5: Parties' Reasonable expectation*	*Label 6: Cooperation*	*Label 8: Having regard to others interest*	*Label 9: Excluder*	*Total*
Frequency	4	5	2	1	2	4	1	19
Percentage	21%	26%	11%	5%	11%	21%	5%	100%

(a) *honestly and reasonably; and*
(b) *with regard to the interests of the other parties to the franchise.*

This definition was supported by a list of six factors which may be taken into account by a court in determining whether or not conduct by a franchisee or franchisor has been in good faith. The factors are as follows:

(c) *the commercial and business objects of the franchise;*
(d) *the legitimate business interests of each of the parties, and what is reasonably necessary for the protection of those interests;*
(e) *the respective financial and non-financial contributions made by each of the parties to the establishment and conduct of the franchised business;*
(f) *the risks taken by each of the parties in the establishment and conduct of the franchised business;*
(g) *the alternative courses of action available to the parties in respect of the matter under consideration; and*
(h) *the usual practices in the industry to which the franchise relates.*

From the proposed definition of good faith, 'honesty' is an obvious example that is commonly associated with good faith.[106] In *Aiton Australia Pty Ltd v Transfield Pty Ltd*, Einstein J stated that 'Parties are subject to a universal duty to act honestly in any case'.[107] Even though honesty falls under the 'single category', it can be combined with another 'single category' to constitute a 'multi-categories' definition. Therefore, combining two or more 'single category' definitions is not a problem. The advantage of having a 'multi-categories' definition is that it will assist in comprehensively encapsulating the concept of good faith. *Tomlin v Ford Credit Australia* provides an illustration of a 'multi-categories' definition of good faith whereby McDougall J claimed that:

The content of an implied duty to perform obligations and exercise contractual rights in good faith could be said to consist of an obligation to act honestly and reasonably.[108]

The 'multi-category' approach to the definition of good faith is consistent with certain influential legal texts in Australia. The 'multi-categories'

[106] Terry, A., & Cary. D. L. (2009). Franchising and the Quest for the Holy Grail: Good Faith or Good Intentions. *Melbourne University Law Review*, 33, 542–554.
[107] (1999) 153 FLR 236, 262.
[108] [2005] NSWSC 540, 540.

definitions given by Peden and Mason J were referred to as the two principal texts for the definition of good faith. Peden claimed that:

> *... it is suggested that the true meaning of good faith must be a requirement to behave honestly and to have regard to the interests of the other party without subordinating one's own interest.*[109]

Mason J's definition of good faith is more detailed, whereby good faith is defined in relation to three notions: (a) an obligation on the parties to cooperate in achieving the contractual objectives (loyalty to the promise itself), (b) compliance with honest standards of conduct and (c) compliance with standards of contract which are reasonable and have regard to the interests of the parties.[110] The definition formulated by Mason J has been cited in a number of cases, including *Burger King Corporation v Hungry Jack's Pty Ltd*[111] and *Hughes Aircraft Systems International v Airservices Australia.*[112]

Nevertheless, good faith is a difficult concept to define. The advantages of expressing the definition of good faith in a 'multi-categories' form is that it provides flexibility of definition, as illustrated by the two prominent scholars Peden and Mason J. The *Small Business Commissioner of South Australia* also supported a 'multi-categories' approach to the definition of good faith and submitted that 'good faith can be defined in plain English to mean acting fairly, honestly, reasonably and cooperatively'.[113] These definitions resonate with what the courts have held to be the underlying duties of the parties and the integral conduct imposed by the courts to a commercial contract.[114]

Based on the above discussion, the researcher proposes that good faith should be defined by a 'multi-categories' approach. The empirical

[109] Peden, E. (2003). *Good Faith in the Performance of Contract.* LexisNexis Butterworths. p. 170.

[110] Mason, A. (2000). Contract, Good Faith and Equitable Standards in Fair Dealing. *Law Quarterly Review*, 116, 66–69.

[111] (2001) 69 NSWLR 558, 570.

[112] (1997) 146 ALR 1, 37.

[113] Small Business Commissioner South Australia, Submissions to the Australian Government, *Review of the Federal Franchising Code of Conduct*, February 2013, 10.

[114] Small Business Commissioner South Australia, Submissions to the Australian Government, *Review of the Federal Franchising Code of Conduct*, February 2013, 10.

observation reveals that there are three popular notions of good faith: (a) honesty (b) reasonableness and (c) having regard to other's interests.

6.7 Conclusion

In this chapter, nine definitions or meanings of good faith were found in the literature and identified cases, as illustrated in Table 6.1. Out of nine, three of the definitions or meanings of good faith were found to have received greater support compared to other definitions. The three potential meanings or themes are: (a) honesty, (b) reasonableness and (c) having regard to other's interests, as illustrated by Fig. 6.17. These three thematic terms are also supported by empirical evidence, as shown in Table 6.3. The proposed definitions of good faith are consistent with the definition proposed by Competitive Foods Australia in its submission to a Parliamentary Joint Committee on Corporations and Financial Services, *Inquiry into Franchising Code of Conduct*, September 2008.[115] The proposed definition of good faith is by way of 'multi-categories', and the definition is assessed by reference to a 'non-discretionary reference criteria', which provides that:

> *Good faith in relation to conduct by a franchisor or a franchisee means that the party has acted:*
>
> (a) *honestly and reasonably; and*
> (b) *with regard to the interests of the other parties to the franchise.*

This definition was supported by a list of six factors which may be taken into account by a court in determining whether or not a conduct by a franchisee or franchisor has been in good faith:

> (c) *the commercial and business objects of the franchise;*
> (d) *the legitimate business interests of each of the parties, and what is reasonably necessary for the protection of those interests;*
> (e) *the respective financial and non-financial contributions made by each of the parties to the establishment and conduct of the franchised business;*

[115] A draft model amendment was included in Competitive Foods Australia, Submission No. 22 to Parliamentary Joint Committee on Corporations and Financial Services, *Inquiry into Franchising Code of Conduct*, September 2008.

(f) *the risks taken by each of the parties in the establishment and conduct of the franchised business;*
(g) *the alternative courses of action available to the parties in respect of the matter under consideration; and*
(h) *the usual practices in the industry to which the franchise relates.*

The proposed definition, which is 'multi-categories', received strong support in this study, as demonstrated by the literature and the empirical evidence discussed in Sects. 6.3 and 6.4. These definitions also received robust support from prominent experts in the area of good faith, namely, Peden and Mason J. Based on these findings, good faith may be best defined through a 'multi-categories' approach: (a) honesty and reasonableness and (b) having regard to other's interest. The proposed workable definition of good faith is supported by 'multi-categories', which assists in the definition of good faith. It also provides a wider room of flexibility for an abstract concept like good faith, which needs guidelines in determining its meaning. In addition, the 'multi-categories' approach is also significant to lawyers, judges and scholars as it provides a workable solution to the unsettled issue of the definition of good faith.

CHAPTER 7

Legislating a Good Faith Obligation in Australia

7.1 Introduction

This chapter examines the possibility of legislating a good faith obligation in Australia. To date, there remains no High Court decision that has decided on its application and definition. Despite its uncertain status, good faith has nevertheless played an important role in Australian contract law. The concept of good faith has recently received much attention in Australia by way of an attempt to enshrine it in legislation. In the specific context of franchising, there is a move to legislate good faith which was proposed to curb the unethical exploitative conduct of franchisors towards the franchisees. Suggestions have also been made to legislate good faith as a general obligation similar to the civil law code model. In the civil law code model, good faith is not defined but instead requires judicial interpretation. This chapter argues that good faith can be legislated in contractual performance similar to the experience in the context of franchising, which provides an opportunity to legislate good faith. Undoubtedly, the presence of an authoritative definition of good faith will resolve the issue of uncertainty. It is anticipated that this approach to the legislation of a good faith obligation will do away with the reservations arising from the issue of uncertainty.

N. Abdullah, *Good Faith in Contractual Performance in Australia*,
https://doi.org/10.1007/978-981-15-6078-1_7

7.2 Issues of Good Faith

In Australia, the issue of good faith is important, relevant and fast gaining recognition despite the absence of a definitive High Court decision regarding its application and definition. Good faith is an uncertain concept. It is a mutable concept as it 'means different things at different times and in different moods at different times and in different places'.[1] It has many meanings. Most of the meanings are confusing and contradictory to each other. Despite it being a problematic concept, good faith is widely known and used in contract law. Recently in Australia, attempts have been made to legislate good faith either as a general obligation or as a specific obligation. In regard to good faith being legislated as a general obligation, there is a preliminary discussion revolving around reforming Australian contract law by way of codification, which provides the opportunity to legislate good faith in a manner similar to civil law code models.[2] In this context, good faith is not defined but its interpretation is left to the judges. Instead of a definition of good faith, there are other approaches to defining good faith similar to the concept of unconscionability. Both unconscionability and good faith share a similar feature of being difficult to define. However, unconscionability was given a legislative effect in s 22 of the *Australian Consumer Law* as stated in schedule 2 of the *Competition and Consumer Act 2010* (Cth). Unconscionability is not defined but was instead understood in a manner of 'non-discretionary reference criteria'. The approach of 'non-discretionary reference criteria' provides legislative guidance to the judges. Therefore, because good faith is just as broad a concept as unconscionability, a legislative guideline is suitable to encapsulate such a concept.

In regard to the specific obligation, there has been a move to legislate an express obligation of good faith in specific businesses contexts, such as franchising. Franchising is a popular business model in Australia.[3] However, franchising has suffered problems due to the unethical behaviour of some

[1] Bridge, M. (1984). Does Anglo-Canadian Contract Law Need a Doctrine of Good Faith? *Canadian Business Law Journal*, 9, 385–413.

[2] Australian Government, Business Law Branch Attorney-General's Department, *Improving Australia's Law and Justice Framework: A Discussion Paper Exploring the Scope for Reforming Australian Contract Law*, 2012.

[3] Australian Government, *Commonwealth Government Response to the Report of the Parliamentary Joint Committee on Corporations and Financial Services*-Opportunity Not Opportunism: Improving Conduct in Australian Franchising (2009).

franchisors towards franchisees by taking advantage of any imbalance of bargaining power between both parties. This has caused problems in the franchisor-franchisee relationships. In this context, the previous Australian government commissioned Wein, an experienced franchisor operator and small business advisor, to conduct a review of the *Franchising Code of Conduct*. Wein recommended that the Franchising Code be amended to include an express obligation for both franchisees and franchisors (as well as prospective franchisees) to act in good faith in pre-franchise agreement negotiations, in the performance of the franchise agreement and in disputes. Wein proposed that such an obligation of good faith should not be defined; instead, good faith should be incorporated in a manner similar to the unconscionable conduct prohibition set out in s 22 of the *Australian Consumer Law*.[4] This means that good faith would be best understood by an assisted 'non-discretionary reference criteria' which provide a legislative guideline to the judges.

7.3 A General Obligation of Good Faith

In Australia, there had been suggestions from time to time to legislate good faith as a general obligation similar to civil law code models. In civil law countries, good faith is recognised as a general and pervasive principle. Good faith serves as a guideline for the contractual behaviour of the parties. Most European civil codes mention good faith.[5] However, despite its broad recognition in civil law countries, there is still a lack of definition of good faith. The interpretation of good faith depends on the facts of each case,[6] which requires judicial interpretation.

In 2012, a discussion paper was issued by the Australian Attorney General's Department on the possibility of reforming Australian contract law to make improvements which would be of the greatest benefit to users of contract law and the economy as a whole.[7] One of the aims of the reform would be to improve certainty in those areas of contract law that

[4] Australian Government, *Commonwealth Government Response to the Review of the Federal Franchising Code of Conduct-* Forward Looking Franchising Regulation (2013), 13.

[5] See Chap. 3 for further details.

[6] Woo, P. Y. (2001). Protecting Parties' Reasonable Expectations: A General Principle of Good Faith. *Oxford University Commonwealth Law Journal*, 1, 195–221.

[7] Australian Government, Business Law Branch Attorney-General's Department, *Improving Australia's Law and Justice Framework: A Discussion Paper Exploring the Scope for Reforming Australian Contract Law*, 2012.

are unsettled or unclear. In this regard, the concept of good faith was suggested as offering a number of benefits to contracting parties such as allowing contracting parties to allocate risk more efficiently, lessening the risk of disputation between the contracting parties and reducing costs for both parties and for the government. In addition, when the legal consequences of actions or omission are clear and predictable, individuals and businesses have the information they need to make informed choices and to develop long-term plans.

In view of its broad usage but lack of an agreed definition, the Discussion Paper recognised that the existence and content of an implied obligation of good faith is a controversial issue in Australia. It was suggested that codification may allow for greater emphasis to be placed on good faith, especially in facilitating 'long term contracts'.[8] Many submissions were made in response to the reform proposal to codify and include good faith in Australian contract law. Some commentators support the codification of contract law and the inclusion of good faith because of the benefits it offers to both legal practitioners and users of contract law. The *Australian Corporate Lawyers Association* agreed that an 'implied contractual duty of good faith' should be examined as part of any reform proposal in order to bring a degree of uniformity to Australian contract law.[9] This is because Australian contract law differs between Australian jurisdictions in several areas due to the existence of non-uniform Commonwealth, state and territory statutes. Therefore, having a codified contract law system will reduce the risk and costs associated with cross-border transaction. In the business context, many Australian business partners, such as China, Japan and Korea, have codified contract law systems. In the codified contract law systems, good faith is an important element to the contracting parties. Uniformity of the contract law system helps to align better business deals with business partners.

Commentators who opposed the codification of contract law and the inclusion of statutory good faith did so on the basis that it could potentially increase uncertainty and costs. For example, the peak professional body, the *Law Council of Australia*, argued that there would be uncertainty and inconsistency as to how a contractual obligation to exercise

[8] For example, franchising contract.

[9] The Australian Corporate Lawyers Association, Submission to Attorney-General's Department, *Improving Australia's Law and Justice Framework: A Discussion Paper Exploring the Scope for Reforming Australian Contract Law*, 20 July 2012.

good faith should be interpreted and the circumstances in which an obligation of good faith may be implied into a contract.[10] Good faith is an uncertain concept. It is a mutable concept because it 'means different things at different times and in different moods at different times and in different places'.[11] It has many meanings, most of which are confusing and contradictory. The definition of good faith depends on its particular context. McDougall J of the New South Wales (NSW) Supreme Court commented that the definition of good faith should 'look at the particular contract, to see what might be comprehended as a particular expression of the general concept of good faith, and then to inquire whether that particular term, or a term having that particular content, should be implied, or whether is excluded by express term or necessary implication from them'.[12]

The Chief Justice of the NSW Supreme Court, Honourable T.F. Bathurst, has observed that although a number of courts have recognised an implied duty of good faith, 'its existence has not been finally decided'.[13] As the *CPA Australia* policy adviser on environment, sustainability and governance had commented, 'codification in and of itself does not mean legal certainty, nor does it result in the end of the development phase'.[14] Purcell emphasised the importance of the role of the judges in seeking out the legislative's objective.[15] This comment is aligned with the nature of codification itself. In its general sense, codification is the 'systematic collection or formulation of the law, reducing it from a disparate mass

[10] Law Council of Australia, Submission to Attorney-General's Department *Improving Australia's Law and Justice Framework: A Discussion Paper Exploring the Scope for Reforming Australian Contract Law*, 20 July 2012.

[11] Bridge, M. (1984). Does Anglo-Canadian Contract Law Need a Doctrine of Good Faith? *Canadian Business Law Journal*. 9, 385–413.

[12] McDougall, R. (21 February 2006). The Implied Duty of Good Faith in Australian Contract Law. Retrieved from http://www.lawlink.nse.gov.au/lawlink/Supreme_Court/II_sc.nsf/vwPrint1/SCO-mcdougall210206.

[13] Bathurst, T. F. (20 July 2012). Submission to Attorney-General's Department Improving Australia's Law and Justice Framework: A Discussion Paper Exploring the Scope for Reforming Australian Contract Law.

[14] Purcell, J. (30 July 2012) 'Codifying Australia's Contract Law Is a Step in the Wrong Direction', Intheblack (Sydney). Retrieved from http://www.itbdigital.com/opinion?t=legal.

[15] Purcell, J. (30 July 2012) 'Codifying Australia's Contract Law Is a Step in the Wrong Direction', Intheblack (Sydney). Retrieved from http://www.itbdigital.com/opinion?t=legal.

into an accessible statement which is given legislative rather than merely judicial or academic authority'.[16] In this context, the Code contains only broad statements at a high level of abstraction that leaves a need for judicial interpretation to give meaning to the relevant provisions and to apply the meaning to the relevant situation. One obvious problem is that the broad statements will be of limited utility as a guide in a specific situation. Therefore, if the concept of good faith is to be adopted in a contract law code, it will cause uncertainty in two ways. Firstly, good faith will not be defined in the code, and secondly, when the interpretation of good faith is left in the hands of judges, many definitions will be produced because different judges will interpret the concept differently based on the peculiar circumstances of their respective cases.

Such were the concerns of Honourable T.F. Bathurst, who expressed his view that codification is not the appropriate mechanism to explain a broad and general concept like good faith. His Honour is of the view that:

> *The implication of a general duty of good faith into commercial contracts will be worked out on a case-by-case basis where the extent of its operation and its interaction with equitable doctrines such as unconscionability can be considered. Codification will not achieve this.*[17]

The attempt of the draft code to replace the entire Australian contract law will not help to achieve the aim to reduce complexity and ambiguity that exist in the existing contract law. Damian, a partner of Freehills, commented that:

> *it is, however, the stuff of pure fantasy to believe that those 29 sentences could govern the meaning of contracts, and future decisions on those few pages would be ignored and would have no influence on other decisions.*[18]

[16] Donald, B. (1973). Codification in Common Law System. *The Australian Law Journal*, 47, 160–161.

[17] Bathurst, T. F. (20 July 2012). Submission to Attorney-General's Department Improving Australia's Law and Justice Framework: A Discussion Paper Exploring the Scope for Reforming Australian Contract Law.

[18] Damian, T. (20 July 2012). Contract Code No Answer to Contract Law Reform. The Australian (Sydney). Retrieved from http://www.theaustralian.com.au/business/legal-affairs/contract-code-no-answer-to-contract-law-reform/story-e6frg97x-1226430355969#mm-premium.

To insert a general and broad concept like good faith in the code will lead to an undesirable lack of certainty in the contract.

CPA Australia argued that 'there is an absence of compelling evidence that Australian business is disadvantaged by the current scheme - a highly prescriptive codification may, in fact, be costly and counterproductive generating a lengthy period of judicial interpretation'.[19] An extreme submission from the *Australian Copyright Council* argued that at this stage, it is not necessary to reform Australian contract law as the current contract law is sufficient to handle any disputes pertaining to contract law issues.[20]

The current debate in Australia shows that there is no unanimous support to codify contract law, and as such, the opportunity to legislate good faith through this means is uncertain. In this context, legislating good faith as a general obligation similar to the civil law code model leads to uncertainty due to the lack of definition of good faith. Furthermore, there is the difficulty of formulating the appropriate judicial method under codified law, where each interpretation is based on a case-by-case basis, which also leads to uncertainty.[21] Without a legislative guideline, the judges will draw their own personal discretion, experience and knowledge in interpreting good faith. This situation may be costly, counterproductive and generate a lengthy period of judicial interpretation.

There is another approach of legislating good faith as a general obligation without having a definition. This approach is similar to the case of legislating unconscionability. Unconscionability is a concept similar to good faith and has become one of the significant themes in the Australian law of contract in relation to harsh and unfair contracts.[22] It is not a new concept in Australia and has been a feature of many cases in the country for years. Among the features it shares with good faith is that both concepts are difficult to define.

[19] CPA Australia, Submission to Attorney-General's Department: *Improving Australia's Law and Justice Framework: A Discussion Paper Exploring the Scope for Reforming Australian Contract Law*, 20 July 2012.

[20] Australian Copyright Council, Submission to Attorney-General's Department, *Improving Australia's Law and Justice Framework: A Discussion Paper Exploring the Scope for Reforming Australian Contract Law*, 20 July 2012.

[21] Donald, B. (1973). Codification in Common Law System. *The Australian Law Journal*, 47, 160–161.

[22] In *Renard*, Priestley J stated that 'there is a close association of ideas between the terms unreasonableness, lack of good faith and unconscionability' (1992) 26 NSWLR 234, 265. This statement by Priestley J confirmed that there is a relationship between the concept of good faith and unconscionability.

In *Antonovic v Volker*, Mahoney JA suggested that the concept of unconscionability was better described than defined because the principle is stated in very general terms.[23] Similarly for good faith, 'it would be preferable not to define the term exhaustively; any attempt to do so will result in exceptions and unsatisfactory outcomes in unusual situations'.[24]

Due to the problems surrounding the definition of unconscionability, attempts were made to codify unconscionability similar to the civil law code approach. In this approach, unconscionability is not defined but the interpretation of the concept is left to the judges. The issue of codification of contract law was tabled for consideration in a Discussion Paper in 1982 by the Victorian Law Reform Commission to provide a comprehensive and authoritative statutory framework similar to civil law code models. The realisation of this goal was premised on it being possible to achieve three basic features for the code: its level of generality, its lack of definitions and a central role for unconscionability.

The concept of unconscionability was considered an 'overriding article' in the draft code. The Victoria Law Reform Commission (VLRC) focused on unconscionability because the concept was becoming more frequently raised in contract disputes. One of the weaknesses of the concept of unconscionability, however, is the difficulty of legislating such a wide and vague concept.[25] The VLRC contract code did not define unconscionability. Article 27 stated that 'a person may not assert a right or deny an obligation to the extent that it would be unconscionable to do so'. It is argued that in this form, Article 27 simply encourages unnecessary litigation about the meaning of these new concepts. Therefore, the Kennett government rejected the proposal of codifying contract law which gives the opportunity to legislate unconscionability. Rather than minimising uncertainty and complexity, it was determined that codifying contract law which gives the opportunity to legislate unconscionability would add to uncertainty and result in additional expenses, which are both similar concerns to those raised in reference to the codification of good faith.

Currently, the concept of unconscionability is given a legislative effect in the form of the *Australian Consumer Law*. The unconscionability

[23] (1986) 7 NSWLR 151, 196.

[24] Spencer, E., & Young, S. (14 February 2013). Submission to Federal Government of Australia Review of the Federal Franchising Code of Conduct.

[25] See generally Senate Standing Committee on Economics, Parliament of Australia, *The Need, Scope and Content of a Definition of Unconscionable Conduct for the Purpose of Part IVA of the Trade Practices Act 1974*(Cth) (2008).

provisions are contained in s 20, 21 and 22 of the *Australian Consumer Law* as prescribed in schedule 2 of the *Competition and Consumer Act 2010* (Cth), which came into effect on 1 January 2011. Section 20 prohibits unconscionable conducts which enshrine the equitable concept. In this context, it means that actions relating to unconscionable conduct, which is a concept that has been developed in common law, and the principle of equity may be commenced under the *Australian Consumer Law*. Section 21 is a new and more liberal statutory regime which simply prohibits unconscionability. In this context, the meaning of unconscionability is not defined but in relation to which judges can have regard to 'non-discretionary reference criteria', assists its meaning as prescribed in s 22.

The precedent to the current *Australian Consumer Law* was the *Contracts Review Act 1980* (NSW). The *Contracts Review Act 1980* (NSW) had introduced the 'non-discretionary reference criteria' to determine unconscionability instead of providing a definition. The *Contracts Review Act 1980* (NSW) is a significant legislation in handling the issue of harsh and unconscionable contracts of general application to consumer contract. This legislation was based on the 'Report on Harsh and Unconscionable Contracts' (hereinafter referred to as the Peden Report). In October 1976, a series of reforms to the law of contract in New South Wales were recommended in a report commissioned by the Minister for Consumer Affairs and authored by Professor John Peden of Macquarie University. The Peden Report claimed that there was no remedy available in common law and statutory law for dealing with the issue of harsh and unconscionable contracts, resulting in significant potential for abuse in both consumer and other transactions.

Therefore, it is the aim of the *Contracts Review Act 1980* (NSW) to provide a wider power to the court in granting relief in respect of harsh and unconscionable contracts. This is to ensure that the judges are given the necessary flexibility to ensure justice by granting appropriate relief.[26] Section 7(1) provides the Supreme Court of NSW, and subject to its jurisdictional limit, relief to the district courts in respect of certain contracts found to be unjust in the circumstances relating to the contract at the time it was made. The term 'unjust' has a wider interpretation as expressed in s 4. The term 'unjust' includes unconscionable, harsh or oppressive (conduct), and injustice is to be construed in a corresponding manner.

[26] Peden, J. R. (October 1976). *Report on Harsh and Unconscionable Contracts*. Macquarie University: NSW.

The *Contracts Review Act 1980* (NSW) is more promising because the legislation sets out the specific criteria to be considered in determining unconscionability.[27] The *Contracts Review Act 1980* (NSW) assists the judges to achieve certainty in their judgement. The precedent legislation to the *Contracts Review Act 1980* (NSW), that is, the consumer credit legislation (moneylending, hire purchase and credit sales legislation), suffered from the use of language that is too general and a lack of legislative guideline for a workable doctrine of unconscionability,[28] which has led to uncertainty. Due to the lack of a legislative guideline, the judges are reluctant to use unconscionability provisions in the consumer credit legislation.

Concerning the concept of unconscionability, a similar problem was experienced by the US in s 2.302 of the *Uniform Commercial Code* dealing with unconscionable consumer contract. Section 2.302 of the *Uniform Commercial Code* provided that a court can grant relief from a contract or any term of a contract found to be unconscionable at the time it was made. However, it was argued that the general provision of unconscionability rendered the provision ambiguous. Moreover, it lacked suitable guidelines for the judges to determine its application. Therefore, s 2.302 of the *Uniform Commercial Code* was largely considered to be ineffective because of the absence of a 'specific unconscionability guideline' to guide the judges in interpreting the definition of unconscionability.[29]

The need to reform the previous legislation to the *Contracts Review Act 1980* (NSW) was raised by the Peden Report to ensure that the judges do fairly in 'exercising broad discretions and making value judgements'.[30] Therefore, 'a structured doctrine of unconscionability taking account of elements of substantive and procedural fairness in the context of the commercial setting does not threaten the fabric of commerce and offers greater

[27] Terry, A. (1982). Unconscionable Contracts in New South Wales: The Contracts Review Act 1980. *Australian Business Law Review*, 311–312.

[28] Terry, A. (1982). Unconscionable Contracts in New South Wales: The Contracts Review Act 1980. *Australian Business Law Review*, 311–312.

[29] Peden, J. R. (October 1976). *Report on Harsh and Unconscionable Contracts*. Macquarie University: NSW.

[30] Peden, J. R. (October 1976). *Report on Harsh and Unconscionable Contracts*. Macquarie University: NSW.

opportunity for an ordered and uniform development of the law than the present haphazard common law developments'.[31]

Section 9 expresses NSW's unconscionability doctrine. This NSW's unconscionability doctrine resulted from the Peden Report recommendation to introduce a general formula consisting of distinctive criteria that determine unconscionability, otherwise known as the 'non-discretionary reference criteria'. The 'non-discretionary reference criteria' are a general guideline to identify unconscionability by identifying its integral components. This assists the court by specifying 'guidance criteria',[32] which must be referred to by the court when determining whether a contract is unjust. The matters specified in s 9(2) provide a definite direction to the court based on the extent of their relevance to the circumstances of the case. By identifying the specific components of unconscionability, it is better suited to meet modern circumstances as opposed to a repetition of the general law or previous 'harsh and unconscionable' formula.[33] Such a guideline facilitates greater consistency by providing a uniform framework for judges to identify and decide on unconscionability, which will result in greater certainty in commercial transactions and planning.[34] Terry, in his article, argued that the approach to unconscionability by way of the 'non-discretionary reference criteria' provides a better way in understanding a broad concept like unconscionability. He states that 'this approach to unconscionability provides the flexibility that a workable doctrine of unconscionability demands while establishing the guidelines under which the individual matters specified can be organised and analysed'.[35]

As a whole, legislating good faith obligation without a definition similar to the civil law concept will cause uncertainty due to two reasons. The first reason is that codification of good faith will not produce a definition as the nature of the civil law code does not consist of a definition. The code contains only broad statements at high levels of abstraction that leaves a need for judicial interpretation. Secondly, it gives a wider power to the judges

[31] Terry, A. (1982). Unconscionable Contracts in New South Wales: The Contracts Review Act 1980. *Australian Business Law Review*, 311–312.

[32] NSW Parliamentary Debates 1980, 5894.

[33] Peden, J. R. (October 1976). *Report on Harsh and Unconscionable Contracts.* Macquarie University: NSW.

[34] Peden, J. R. (October 1976). *Report on Harsh and Unconscionable Contracts.* Macquarie University: NSW.

[35] Terry, A. (1982). Unconscionable Contracts in New South Wales: The Contracts Review Act 1980. *Australian Business Law Review*, 311–312.

to define its meaning, which is based on a case-by-case analysis. Judges' interpretations will undeniably be broad and flexible without a legislative guideline. This will lead to further uncertainty when the judges use their own understanding and knowledge in interpreting the definition.

Therefore, legislating good faith by way of 'non-discretionary reference criteria' similar to unconscionability, as illustrated in s 22 of the *Contract Review Act 1980* (NSW), is an intelligent manner that strategically avoids the problems associated with its definition. Hence, legislating good faith by way of s 22 of the *Contract Review Act 1980* (NSW) 'may promote rather than impede the cause of contractual certainty'.[36] The similar argument of endorsing contractual certainty was put forcefully by Harland in the submission of his draft of legislation of the *Contract Review Act 1980* (NSW), which states that:

> *It is, in fact, strongly arguable that one result of requiring the courts to consider explicitly the policy issues involved, instead of manipulating traditional rules for purposes for which they were never designed, will be in time to increase certainty.*[37]

This was achieved by ensuring that its key features are considered by judges in their judicial rulings by means of the 'non-discretionary reference criteria'.

The approach of 'non-discretionary reference criteria' provides a legislative guideline to identify good faith, which the judge can refer to and ensure some degree of uniformity in the content and direction of the interpretation of good faith. In addition to the benefit of the legislative guideline to identify good faith, it also yields certainty where it provides a definite direction to the court based on the extent of its relevance to the circumstances of the case. Terry, in his article, strongly supported the 'non-discretionary reference criteria' approach because the 'structure provides the necessary frameworks under which the individual factors specified in the "shopping list" can be analysed and applied and serves to advance the causes of both justice and certainty'.[38] Therefore, this study

[36] Terry, A. (1982). Unconscionable Contracts in New South Wales: The Contracts Review Act 1980. *Australian Business Law Review*, 311–312.

[37] NSW Parliamentary Debates 1979, 3057.

[38] Terry, A. (1982). Unconscionable Contracts in New South Wales: The Contracts Review Act 1980. *Australian Business Law Review*, 311–312.

supports the 'shopping list' approach by way of suggesting a 'multi-categories' approach in proposing a workable definition of good faith.

7.4 A Good Faith Obligation in a Specific Business Context

Rather than legislating generally, a narrower 'context-specific' approach can be attempted by legislating good faith in a specific business context like franchising. This is similar to the approach already taken by common law in regard to insurance contracts. In a specific business context like insurance, good faith is a well-known concept. The concept of good faith and its relationship to the insurance contract has been recognised for more than 250 years from the case of *Carter v Boehm*.[39] It is a fundamental principle of insurance law that both the insurer and the insured must observe a duty of utmost good faith towards each other. Later, the concept of utmost good faith was given statutory recognition in s 13 of the *Insurance Contracts Act 1984* (Cth), where it is stated that:

> *A contract of insurance is a contract based on the utmost good faith and there is implied in such a contract a provision requiring each party to it to act towards the other party, in respect of any matter arising under or in relation to it, with the utmost good faith.*

The acceptance of the concept of utmost good faith in insurance is well established and is relatively uncontroversial due to the long engagement of the subject. Good faith in insurance contract law is not defined, but it is a well-known expectation of behaviour that both parties, namely, the insurer and the insured, must possess in the disclosure of information to each other. Due to its long engagement, it is considered a norm in the insurance contract law to ensure a successful insurance contract law.

The good faith experience in the insurance context offers some comfort for legislating a good faith obligation in the franchising context. In Australia, franchising has proved a very popular business model.[40] A call for good faith in franchising is due to the allegations of unethical

[39] (1766) 3 Burr 1905, 1910.

[40] Australian Government, *Commonwealth Government Response to the Report of the Parliamentary Joint Committee on Corporations and Financial Services*-Opportunity Not Opportunism: Improving Conduct in Australian Franchising (2009).

behaviour by franchisors taking advantage of any imbalance of bargaining power between franchisors and franchisees. The form of opportunistic behaviour is as follows:

> *Franchisee opportunism may take the form of free-riding, unauthorised use of franchisor's intellectual property rights, underperformance, or failure to accurately disclose income. However, the franchisor's control over the provisions in the contract enables franchisors to address opportunistic behaviour of this kind by enforcing the terms of the franchise agreement. Franchisor opportunism has been described as 'predatory conduct' and strong-arm tactics by franchisors involving the exploitation of a pre-existing power relationship between the franchising parties, which makes the franchisee 'vulnerable' or economically captive to the demands of the franchisor. There is an inherent and necessary imbalance of power in franchise agreements in favour of the franchisor, but abuse of this power can lead to opportunistic practices including encroachment, kickbacks, churning, non-renewal, transfer, termination at will, and unreasonable unilateral variations to the agreement.*[41]

Franchising is recognised as a special kind of contract. In *Dymocks Franchise System (NSW) Pty Ltd v Todd*,[42] the Privy Council recognised that franchising was not an ordinary commercial contract: 'These were not ordinary commercial contracts but contracts giving rise to long-term mutual obligation in pursuance of what amounted in substance to a joint venture and therefore dependent upon coordinated action and cooperation.'[43] In this context, franchising may be regarded as a relational contract. A relational contract is a kind of contract which is exposed to the risk of uncertainty and unforeseen factors due to the long engagement between the parties. Spencer describes the characteristics of a relational contract as follows:

> *Relational contracts are defined by features of incompleteness and longevity. Relational contracts must be flexible, sometimes to the point of being vague. There is often a high level of discretion accorded to the parties, and such contracts, therefore, rely heavily on reciprocity and on trust that develops over time between the contracting parties.*[44]

[41] The *'Opportunity Not Opportunism Report'*, 101.

[42] [2004] 1 NZLR 289.

[43] [2004] 1 NZLR 289, 63.

[44] Spencer, E. (December 2008). Submission to the Parliamentary Joint Committee Inquiry into Franchising.

Franchising is considered to be a special kind of contract because it 'is a continuous commercial relationship' between the franchisor and the franchisee.[45] The relationship between the franchisor and the franchisee is imbalanced due to the inequality of bargaining power between them. The existence of inequality of bargaining power lies in the structure of the franchising contract itself. The franchising contract is drafted by the franchisor and offers a one-sided agreement 'benefiting the franchisor and providing the franchisees with few options to protect its own interest'.[46] Unlike other business formats, 'it is the right of the franchisor to protect his business interest and the consistency of the business format'.[47] For example, in a buyer-seller relationship, the success of the relationship is based on the consensual transactions in an agreement to buy as well as an agreement to sell. Sometimes, the drafted agreement made by the franchisor is unreasonable and causes injustice by not taking into account the interests of the franchisee. This reason is based on the financial strength and the ability to access information and legal service by the franchisor, which the franchisee will most likely not have. Apart from the structure of the franchising agreement, the franchisee is highly dependent on the franchisor. The franchisee is often an inexperienced businessperson, while the franchisor is usually experienced. This means that when the franchisee agrees to the franchising agreement, the franchisor has provided the franchisee 'a package of corporate services, a product with a proven track record and the advantages of a common trademark'.[48] Spencer comments that the nature of the franchising contract contributed to the uncertainty of the contract and allocates risk to the franchisee. Spencer further states that:

> *because franchise contracts employ flexible, open-ended terms and discretion to accommodate the longer term and relational nature of the relationship, uncer-*

[45] Iglesias, J. (2004). Applying the Implied Covenant of Good Faith and Fair Dealing to Franchises. *Houston Law Review*, 40, 1423–1429.

[46] Ibid., 1436.

[47] Zahira Mohd Ishan & Shaik Mohd Noor Alam. (2009). Unconscionability-Statutory Prevention of Unethical Business Practices. *International Journal of Economics and Management*, 3, 151–157.

[48] Hadfield, G. K. (1990). Problematic Relations: Franchising and the Law of Incomplete Contracts. *Stanford Law Review*, 42, 927–991.

> *tainty is closely related to flexibility in the contract, grants of discretion to a franchisor and concomitantly high levels of risk to a franchisee.*[49]

This situation inevitably causes the franchisee to follow the franchisor's directives in light of his business experience and knowledge.

In Australia, three parliamentary inquiries in Western Australia,[50] in South Australia[51] and at the Federal level recommended that an obligation to act in good faith is to be imposed on franchisors and franchisees.[52] At the Federal level, the report—*Opportunity, Not Opportunism: Improving Conduct in Australian Franchising*—prepared by the Federal Parliamentary Joint Committee on Corporations and Financial Services[53] stated the view that there is concern in the franchise sector about the absence of an explicit overarching good faith standard of conduct for parties to a franchise agreement. The Joint Committee argued that the optimal deterrent against opportunistic conduct in the franchising sector is to explicitly incorporate, in its simplest form, the existing and widely accepted implied duty of parties to a franchise agreement to act in good faith.[54] The Joint Committee recommended that the following new clause be inserted into the *Franchising Code of Conduct*:

> *Franchisors, franchisees and prospective franchisees shall act in good faith in relation to all aspects of a franchise agreement.*

This clause was intended to provide a standard of conduct for franchisors, franchisees and prospective franchisees to 'act in good faith' in

[49] *Spencer, E. C. (2008). Balance of Power, Certainty and Discretion in the Franchise Relationship: An Analysis of Contractual Terms. Bond University Electronic Journal of Law.* Retrieved from http://epublications.bond.edu.au/laws_pubs/250.

[50] Government of Western Australia, *Inquiry into the Operation of Franchise Businesses in Western Australia-Report to the Western Australian Minister for Small Business*, April, 2008.

[51] Economic and Finance Committee, Parliament of South Australia, Franchises: *Final Report of the Sixty-Fifty*, May, 2008.

[52] For the purpose of this thesis, discussion is focused at the Federal level—the report *Opportunity Not Opportunism: Improving Conduct in Australian Franchising* prepared by the Federal Parliamentary Joint Committee on Corporations and Financial Services 2008 until the current accepted recommendation by Wein Report 2013.

[53] Parliamentary Joint Committee on Corporations and Financial Services, Parliament of Australia, *Opportunity Not Opportunism: Improving Conduct in Australian Franchising*, December, 2008 (*The Opportunity Not Opportunism Report).*

[54] The *Opportunity Not Opportunism Report* 114.

relation to all aspects of a franchise agreement. It was intended that this standard would permeate all stages of the franchisee and franchisor relationship from pre-contractual arrangements to disputes. The Joint Committee made it clear that an express good faith obligation is likely to curb opportunistic conduct by the franchisor taking advantage of any imbalance of bargaining power between franchisors and franchisees.

Many submissions were made in the debate regarding the introduction of an express statement of good faith obligation in a franchising context. In this context, the express statement of good faith means that good faith is not defined in the *Franchising Code of Conduct*. Support for the inclusion of an express statement of good faith obligation in the *Franchising Code of Conduct* was expressed by Zumbo, who endorsed the idea of a statutory duty of good faith as promoting ethical business conduct. Zumbo further explained:

> *Indeed, this [good faith] is readily apparent from the growing judicial attention and support given to an implied duty of good faith in commercial contracts, especially in New South Wales. Such a statutory duty of good faith should operate generally within the franchising relationship, including requiring the parties to resolve disputes in good faith.*[55]

Piccolo, who has been a long-time advocate for franchisee rights, shared the same view with Zumbo. He claimed that the inclusion of an express term of good faith obligation in the *Franchising Code of Conduct* will provide clarity to the parties in a franchise agreement to act in good faith and would also promote 'business integrity and ethics'.[56] In addition, the *Motor Trades Association of Australia* claimed that an express statement of good faith obligation is consistent with the objective of the Code.[57] Hence, the proponents of an express statement of a good faith obligation claimed that there are many benefits that good faith would bring to the ethical standards of the contracting parties, such as it provides clarity of the

[55] Zumbo, F. (October 2008). Submission No 140 to Parliamentary Joint Committee in Corporations and Financial Services, Parliament of Australia, Opportunity Not Opportunism: Improving Conduct in Australian Franchising.

[56] Tony Piccolo MP, Economics and Finance Committee. (2008). Parliament of South Australia, Proof Committee Hansard, Melbourne.

[57] Motor Trades Association of Australia, Submission No 90 to Parliamentary Joint Committee in Corporations and Financial Services, Parliament of Australia, *Opportunity Not Opportunism: Improving Conduct in Australian Franchising*, 2008, 7.

expected behaviour of the contracting parties and it fulfils the objective of the franchising code.

Opponents of the inclusion of an express statement of good faith in the *Franchising Code of Conduct*, including the *Australian Competition and Consumer Commission*, opposed it on the basis that it would potentially increase disputes and conflict due to the difficulty in defining its meaning.[58] This is because good faith 'has not just one meaning but many meanings',[59] which renders the concept abstract and vague depending on the circumstances and context of the case. The *National Retail Association* argued that good faith is a difficult concept that depends 'on the circumstances of the case and the context of the contract as a whole'.[60] Similarly, DLA Philips, a law firm with a strong franchising practice, commented that introducing an express statement of good faith obligation in a franchising context is 'unnecessary but an unfortunate legislative indication that good faith has different meanings as currently understood, applied and continually further developed by our Court'.[61] There will be a negative impact on the franchising parties when good faith is not defined. Franchisors and franchisees will encounter problems of uncertainty and confusion about their rights and responsibilities, which may potentially increase controversy among franchising participants. In the context of franchising, the relationship between the franchisor and the franchisee is in a state of imbalance because of the inequality of bargaining power between them. The issue of uncertainty makes it more likely that the franchisor and franchisee will have a different opinion on whether a certain conduct was in good faith or not. In addition, it also makes it more difficult for franchisors and franchisees to know precisely what is required of them to comply with the law. This leads to an undesirable lack of certainty in commercial arrangements like franchising. In *Esso Australia Resources Pty Ltd v*

[58] Australian Competition and Consumer Commission, Submission No 60 to Parliamentary Joint Committee in Corporations and Financial Services, Parliament of Australia, *Opportunity Not Opportunism: Improving Conduct in Australian Franchising*, September 2008, 19.

[59] Lucke, H. K. (1987). Good Faith and Contractual Performance. In Finn, P. (Ed). *Essays on Contract*. The Law Book Co.

[60] National Retail Association, Submission No 109 to Parliamentary Joint Committee in Corporations and Financial Services, Parliament of Australia, *Opportunity Not Opportunism: Improving Conduct in Australian Franchising*, 12 September 2008, 10.

[61] DLA Philips Fox, Submission No 81 to Parliamentary Joint Committee in Corporations and Financial Services, Parliament of Australia, *Opportunity Not Opportunism: Improving Conduct in Australian Franchising*, 12 September 2008, 4.

Southern Pacific Petroleum NL, Warren CJ, Buchanan JA and Osborn AJA commented that 'If good faith is not readily capable of definition then that certainty is undermined'.[62] Hence, the opponents of the express statement of good faith obligation in a franchising context claimed that such legislation would introduce many problems, particularly the issue of uncertainty when good faith is not defined. At this point in time, these debates show that there is no unanimous support to legislate good faith in the franchising context.

On 5 November 2009, the previous Australian government released its response to the *Opportunity Not Opportunism Report*[63] almost a year after the report was submitted. The previous Australian government rejected the recommendation of the Joint Committee to introduce an express statement of good faith obligation in a franchising context. The government was concerned that uncertainty would increase by an express statement of good faith obligation in a franchising context. The government commented that there are several problems with the suggested approach:

> *The law on good faith is still evolving. The scope of the requirement is unclear. From a commercial perspective, uncertainty would be increased by an express statement of the requirement in the Franchising Code. Neither franchisors nor franchisees would be certain of the occurrence of a breach. Indeed it would require court proceedings to establish that.*
>
> *From an economic perspective, in any given situation it is almost certain that the franchisor's perspective on the scope of the concept will differ from that of the franchisee. While the franchisor may have ready access to legal service on what good faith means, a franchisee will not, so there will be an information gap.*
>
> *The extra uncertainty created by the inclusion in the Franchising Code of a general, undefined good faith obligation could be expected to have adverse commercial consequences for franchisees. Franchisors would seek compensation for the extra risk they faced through larger franchise fees and more onerous terms and conditions in other parts of the agreement. And banks and other finan-*

[62] [2005] VSCA 228 (Unreported, Warren CJ, Buchanan JA and Osborn AJA 15 September 2005).

[63] Australian Government, *Commonwealth Government Response to the Report of the Parliamentary Joint Committee on Corporations and Financial Services*-Opportunity Not Opportunism: Improving Conduct in Australian Franchising (2009).

ciers would be more reluctant to provide credit to the franchisees and franchisors in these more likely risky commercial circumstances.[64]

The previous Australian government's response to the Joint Committee's recommendation regarding good faith was to perform the following four acts: (a) amend the Code to deal specifically with end-of-term arrangements for all new franchising agreements entered into after the commencement of the amendments, (b) amend the Code to include a list of necessary and desirable behaviours to encourage parties to approach a dispute resolution process in a reconciliatory manner, (c) refer specific behavioural issues to an expert panel for advice on whether further specific amendments to the Code are required to address those behaviours and (d) amend the Code to provide that nothing in the Code limits any common law requirement of good faith in relation to a franchise agreement to which the Code applies, thereby explicitly preserving and drawing attention to the parties' potential ability to take action as a pursuant to the common law relating to good faith.[65]

Rather than introducing a general but uncertain solution, the previous Australian government appointed an Expert Panel to inquire and report on the need to introduce measures into the *Franchising Code of Conduct* to prevent specific behaviours that are not appropriate in a franchising agreement. Addressing the specific types of behaviour that had caused problems in franchising provides more certainty than an express obligation of good faith, which may cause ambiguity to the parties. Based on consultations, these specific types of behaviour that are not appropriate in a franchising agreement relate to end-of-term arrangements, dispute solutions, unforeseen capital expenditure, unilateral contract variation, attribution of legal costs, confidentiality agreements and changes to franchise agreements when a franchisee is trying to sell the business.[66] The Expert Panel supported the decision of the Australian government to not introduce a specific definition of good faith but recommended an express state-

[64] Australian Government, *Commonwealth Government Response to the Report of the Parliamentary Joint Committee on Corporations and Financial Services-*Opportunity Not Opportunism: Improving Conduct in Australian Franchising (2009), 13.

[65] Australian Government, *Commonwealth Government Response to the Report of the Parliamentary Joint Committee on Corporations and Financial Services-*Opportunity Not Opportunism: Improving Conduct in Australian Franchising (2009), 13.

[66] Australian Government, *Commonwealth Government Response to the Review of the Federal Franchising Code of Conduct-* Forward Looking Franchising Regulation (2013), 14–19.

ment into the *Franchising Code of Conduct*, providing that 'nothing in the Code limits any common law requirement of good faith'.[67] In this context, it will allow the common law principles to continue to develop. There has been a mixed reaction to the introduction of clause 23A to the Franchising Code in 2010, which stated that:

> *Nothing in this Code limits any obligation imposed by the common law applicable in a State or Territory, on the parties to a franchise agreement to act in good faith.*

Proponents argued that there are many benefits to the introduction of a common law obligation of good faith in the *Franchising Code of Conduct*. According to submissions of *Competitive Foods Australia Pty Ltd*, there has been a 'major step forward' in the debate since 2008, with both franchisors and franchisees acknowledging a duty to act in good faith.[68] In addition, the reference to 'the obligation to act in good faith' has changed the general culture within franchising where many franchisors and franchisees are open-minded to accept that good faith is a fundamental part of the franchising relationship.[69]

Law firm Minter Ellison submitted that clause 23A of the *Franchising Code of Conduct* is 'sufficient and effective at addressing concerns regarding conduct that would breach an obligation of good faith. As it is intended, clause 23A highlights to franchisors and franchisees that there is an obligation at common law of good faith that could apply. It also operates to alert parties to their ability to seek address should they consider there has been a breach. However, it does not state (quite correctly) that good faith will apply equally in all cases or encourage parties to act without considering their commercial position, their legal rights or seeking appropriate advice'.[70]

The opponents of the introduction of clause 23A to the Code in 2010 were sceptical of the common law evolution of good faith. The *Law Society*

[67] Expert Panel (Professor Bryan Horrigan, Mr David Lieberman, Mr Ray Steinwall), Parliament of Australia (February 2010). Strengthening Statutory Unconscionable Conduct and the Franchising Code of Conduct, Canberra.

[68] Competitive Foods Australia Pty Ltd, Submission to Federal Government of Australia *Review of the Federal Franchising Code of Conduct,* 15 February 2013, 11.

[69] Ibid.

[70] Ellison, M. (February 2013). Submission to Federal Government of Australia Review of the Federal Franchising Code of Conduct.

of South Australia doubts the effectiveness of clause 23A of the *Franchising Code of Conduct* due to the fact that 'common law does appear to be moving towards a general principle of good faith in contractual relationship, this will inevitably be determined on a case by case basis'.[71] *Competitive Foods Australia Pty Ltd* was concerned about the undefined good faith, which leads to the fact that 'the franchisor will be more able than the franchisees to pay for legal advice about what the unwritten law says in relation to good faith, the undefined nature of any obligation to act in good faith presents a "lawyers picnic" because parties have to get legal advice about what it means'.[72]

The previous Australian government reviewed the efficacy of the 2008 and 2010 amendments to the Franchising Code as part of their response to the Joint Committee report. The Australian government appointed Wein, an experienced franchisor operator and small business advisor, to conduct a review of the Franchise Legislation and *Franchising Code of Conduct*, under terms of reference which required Wein to make recommendations as to the efficacy of the current *Franchising Code of Conduct* and legislation in Australia. The terms of reference for the review focused on the 2008 and 2010 amendments to the Code, which were (a) good faith in franchising, (b) the rights of franchisees at the end of the term of their franchise agreements and (c) provisions for enforcement of the Code. For the purpose of this chapter, the discussion is focused on (a) good faith in franchising. Many submissions were received.

Of particular interest is the shift of views by the *Franchise Council of Australia* since the '*Opportunity Not Opportunism Report*'. Previously, the *Franchise Council of Australia* strongly opposed such an amendment. Currently, however, the *Franchise Council of Australia* is prepared 'to contemplate an amendment to the Franchising Code to expressly incorporate the current common law duty of good faith into all franchise agreements'.[73] The rules of good faith in common law are consistent with the industry code and previous Australian government policy in which codes set out clear obligations rather than aims or ideals. The *Franchise Council of Australia* also believes that the concept of good faith is not well under-

[71] Law Society of South Australia, Submission to Federal Government of Australia *Review of the Federal Franchising Code of Conduct*, 21 February 2013, 5–6.

[72] Competitive Foods Australia Pty Ltd, Submission to Federal Government of Australia *Review of the Federal Franchising Code of Conduct,* 15 February 2013, 12–14.

[73] Franchise Council of Australia, Submission to Federal Government of Australia, *Review of the Federal Franchising Code of Conduct*, February 2013, 5.

stood. Therefore, when the concept of good faith as it would be interpreted by the courts is carefully considered, it will no longer suffer from the problem of uncertainty.

The *Law Society of South Australia* supported the definition of good faith as assessed by way of the 'non-discretionary reference criteria'.[74] This approach was argued to be better than leaving its evolution under the common law, which will cause uncertainty, take too much time and cost franchisee litigants who often ill afford such debates.[75] One franchisor, *Bakers Delight Holdings Ltd*, supports the introduction of a statutory definition of good faith and clearly defined with examples what constitutes a lack of good faith to both franchisor and franchisee. A clear duty of good faith to both franchisor and franchisee is important to ensure the successful relationship of both parties. Currently, *Bakers Delight Holdings Ltd* suffers 'a severe disadvantage from former disgruntled franchisees who extensively use social media, traditional media outlets and local, state and federal politicians to influence their position prior to, leading up to, and throughout the mediation period. For this reason, good faith obligation must be imparted to both the franchisor and the franchisee.'[76] The proponents claim that there are many benefits of the statutory definition of good faith that will help overcome the issue of uncertainty to ensure a successful relationship between the franchisor and franchisee and facilitate successful business operations.

Opponents against the inclusion of a statutory good faith obligation in a franchising context argued that uncertainty is the main problem with the concept. Spencer, an associate professor from Bond University, and Young, a legal practitioner, commented that 'good faith has not been embraced by the courts or the legislatures of Australia. Whilst good faith is part of broad contracts and commercial codes in jurisdictions such as the United States and Germany, it is not part of the legal traditions of the UK or Australia.'[77] The *Shopping Centre Council of Australia* was concerned that

[74] Law Society of South Australia, Submission to Federal Government of Australia, *Review of the Federal Franchising Code of Conduct*, 21 February 2013, 5.

[75] Law Society of South Australia, Submission to Federal Government of Australia, *Review of the Federal Franchising Code of Conduct*, 21 February 2013, 5.

[76] Bakers Delight Holdings Ltd, Submission to Federal Government of Australia *Review of the Federal Franchising Code of Conduct* (2013), 14 February 2013.

[77] Spencer, E., & Young, S. (14 February 2013). Submission to Federal Government of Australia Review of the Federal Franchising Code of Conduct.

the uncertainty of good faith will bring problems to the business activity in Australia. This is well translated in their statement that:

> *Good faith is a concept which is generally impossible to define and is therefore not a legal standard suitable for insertion as a statutory provision. In neither Australia nor elsewhere is there a clearly defined well-understood, statutory doctrine of 'good faith'. This can only add to business uncertainty and put the conduct of many business affairs into the hands of the courts, therefore adding to the cost of doing business in Australia.*[78]

Opponents to the statutory definition of good faith fear the problem of uncertainty that would develop around the understanding of the concept itself and businesses at large. Despite the contradictory views from the proponents and opponents of the statutory definition of good faith, the weight of opinion supports the inclusion of such an obligation of good faith in the *Franchising Code of Conduct.*[79] Such obligation of good faith is not defined; instead, good faith should be incorporated in a manner similar to the unconscionable conduct prohibition set up in s 22 of the *Australian Consumer Law*.

On 24 July 2013, the previous Australian government released its response to the review of the Franchising Code of Conduct by Wein.[80] The report was presented to the government on 30 April 2013 and made various recommendations. One of the recommendations was that the government accepts that the *Franchising Code of Conduct* to be amended in order to include an express obligation to act in good faith. Wein recommended that the Franchising Code be amended to include an express obligation for franchisees and franchisors (as well as prospective franchisees) to act in good faith in pre-franchise agreement negotiations, in the performance of the franchise agreement and in disputes. According to Wein, such an obligation of good faith should not be defined; instead, good faith should be incorporated in a manner similar to that of the unconscionable conduct prohibition set out in s 22 of the *Australian*

[78] Shopping Centre Council of Australia, Submission to Federal Government of Australia *Review of the Federal Franchising Code of Conduct* (2013), 1.

[79] Wein, A. (30 April 2013). Submission to Federal Government of Australia Review of the Federal Franchising Code of Conduct.

[80] See generally Australian Government, *Commonwealth Government Response to the Review of the Federal Franchising Code of Conduct*-Forward Looking Franchising Regulation (2013).

Consumer Law.[81] Section 22 of the *Australian Consumer Law* prohibits unconscionable conduct in connection with the supply of goods or services or the acquisition of goods or services in business transactions. This means that the concept of unconscionable conduct in s 21 and s 22 of the *Australian Consumer Law* is not bound by common law and equitable principles. However, while courts may consider any relevant matters as illustrated in a list of 12 factors to assist the meaning of unconscionability, the *Australian Consumer Law* established a list of 12 factors that are 'non-discretionary reference criteria' factors which the court may take into account or use as a guideline in determining whether a conduct is unconscionable or not as illustrated in the *Australian Consumer Law* s 21 and s 22.

In the context of franchising, the Australian government made a major decision to accept the recommendation by Wein to legislate good faith in dealing with the allegations of unethical behaviour by franchisors taking advantage of any imbalance of power between the franchisor and the franchisee. The franchising debate simply provides a relevant contemporary opportunity to legislate good faith in the context of contractual performance. Therefore, it is argued here that legislating good faith in a franchising context offers some comfort to legislate good faith in contractual performance.

7.5 The Challenges of Legislating a Good Faith Obligation

The challenges of legislating a good faith obligation either as a general obligation or as an obligation in a specific context such as franchising rest in the uncertainty associated with its definition. Despite the difficulty of legislating a specific and precise definition of good faith,[82] good faith can

[81] Australian Government, *Commonwealth Government Response to the Review of the Federal Franchising Code of Conduct-* Forward Looking Franchising Regulation (2013), 13.

[82] B Reiter, 'Good Faith in Contracts' (1983), 17 *Valparaiso University Law Review* 705, 707; H K Lucke, 'Good Faith and Contractual Performance' in Paul Finn (ed) *Essays on Contract* (The Law Book Co, 1987), 155,160; The Hon Justice Steyn, 'The Role of Good Faith and Fair Dealing in Contract Law: A Hair-Shirt Philosophy?'(1991), 6 *Denning Law Journal* 131,140; and Roy Goode, 'The Concept of Good Faith in English Law' (1992) Paper delivered at the Centro di Syudi e Ricerche di Diritto Comparato e Straniero, Rome, 3 cited by T R H Cole, 'The Concept of Reasonableness in Construction Contracts' (1994), 10 *Building and Construction Law Journal* 7, 12.

be defined.[83] In *Esso Australia Resources Pty Ltd v Southern Pacific Petroleum NL*, Warren CJ, Buchanan JA and Osborn AJA commented that 'If good faith is not readily capable of a definition then that certainty is undermined'.[84] For example, in the absence of an authoritative definition, 'uncertainty and disputation are inevitable and the relationship between the franchisor and franchisee will be placed under stress'.[85] Due to the long relationship, unforeseen situations may cause problems to the franchisor-franchisee relationship. Inserting a definition of good faith, however, will help reduce uncertainty to regulate the potential conflict in franchise relationships.

Defining good faith is controversial due to its many meanings. Most of the meanings identified are complex, contradictory and unclear. Some of the expressions of good faith are a 'single category', and some of the expressions are 'multi-categories'. In the 'single category', only one element expresses the meaning of good faith, while instances in the 'multi-category' involve a combination of more than one element in the expression of the meaning of good faith. The empirical data in this study proved that good faith can be defined by way of 'multi-categories' in order to have a workable definition of good faith. The proposed 'multi-categories' definition of good faith in this study includes (a) honesty, (b) reasonableness and (c) having regard to other's interests.[86] The 'multi-category' approach is a more productive approach because it provides a guideline in understanding such a broad and abstract concept like good faith.

Honesty is the least controversial definition in defining good faith.[87] Generally, honesty is widely accepted to be a general requirement when acting in good faith.[88] This is the reason why honesty is the most cited term when defining the concept. In *Aiton Australia Pty Ltd v Transfield Pty Ltd*, Einstein J stated that 'Parties are subject to a universal duty to act

[83] See Chap. 8 for details discussion.

[84] [2005] VSCA 228 (Unreported, Warren CJ, Buchanan JA and Osborn AJA, 15 September 2005).

[85] Andrew Terry, Submission No 91 to Parliamentary Joint Committee in Corporations and Financial Services, Parliament of Australia, *Opportunity Not Opportunism: Improving Conduct in Australian Franchising*, 2008, 2.

[86] See Chap. 8 for details discussion.

[87] Terry, A., & Cary. D. L. (2009). Franchising and the Quest for the Holy Grail: Good Faith or Good Intentions. *Melbourne University Law Review*, 33, 542–554.

[88] Mason, above n.630, 69.

honestly in any case'.[89] In certain instances, honesty as a 'single category' can be combined with another 'single category' to constitute a 'multi-categories' definition. This is clearly demonstrated in *Tomlin v Ford Credit Australia*, in which McDougall J claimed that:

> *The content of an implied duty to perform obligations and exercise contractual rights in good faith could be said to consist of an obligation to act honestly and reasonably.*[90]

This proposed definition of good faith by way of 'multi-categories' is similar to the approach given by Peden and Mason J. The definitions given by Peden and Mason J is of a 'multi-categories' definition and was referred to as the two principal texts for the definition of good faith in Australia. Peden claimed that:

> *… it is suggested that the true meaning of good faith must be a requirement to behave honestly and to have regard to the interests of the other party without subordinating one's own interest.*[91]

Mason J's definition of good faith is more detailed and is defined in relation to three notions: (a) an obligation on the parties to cooperate in achieving the contractual objects (loyalty to the promise itself), (b) compliance with honest standards of conduct and (c) compliance with standards of contract which are reasonable and have regard to the interests of the parties.[92] The definition formulated by Mason J has been cited in a number of cases, including *Burger King Corporation v Hungry Jack's Pty Ltd*[93] and *Hughes Aircraft Systems International v Airservices Australia*.[94]

The advantage of expressing the definition of good faith in a 'multi-categories' form is that it provides flexibility and provides a comprehensive definition. Good faith is a broad concept and as such requires guidance in expressing the definition in order to encapsulate the underlying principle of good faith that all parties to the contract owe a duty to each other

[89] (1999) 153 FLR 236, 262.

[90] [2005] NSWSC 540, 540.

[91] Peden, E. (2003). *Good Faith in the Performance of Contract*. LexisNexis Butterworths.

[92] Mason, A. (2000). Contract, Good Faith and Equitable Standards in Fair Dealing. *Law Quarterly Review*, 116, 66–69.

[93] [2001] NSWCA 169 [187].

[94] (1997) 146 ALR 1, 37.

beyond those expressly provided by the terms of the contract. In this context, it is expected that the contracting parties take into account other parties' interests when exercising their contractual rights.[95] This approach gained support from the *Small Business Commissioner of South Australia*, who supported a 'multi-categories' approach to the definition of good faith and submitted that 'good faith can be defined in plain English to mean acting fairly, honestly, reasonably and cooperatively'.[96] A 'multi-categories' approach to the definition of good faith is found to be clear and easier to understand. These definitions also resonate with what the courts have held to be the underlying duties of parties and the integral conduct imposed by the courts on parties to a commercial contract.[97]

7.6 Conclusion

Legislating a good faith obligation is a highly debated issue in Australia. As discussed, there are two attempts of legislating a good faith obligation either as a general obligation or as a specific obligation. As a general obligation, legislating good faith is similar to the civil law code model, where good faith is not defined but judges are given a wider power to determine its meaning without any legislative guideline. This approach is not productive because the judicial interpretation without any legislative guideline in interpreting the meaning will cause uncertainty of the definition of good faith. Nevertheless, legislating good faith as a general obligation without a definition but by way of a 'non-discretionary reference criteria' similar to the legislation of unconscionability, as illustrated in s 22 of *Australian Consumer Law*, is much more productive and clearer as the process of interpreting the meaning of good faith is guided by uniform features that ensure a good degree of uniformity of any interpretation of good faith, thereby mitigating the issue of uncertainty surrounding the concept. Therefore, in this study, the proposed workable definition of good faith by way of 'multi-categories' gives greater certainty and justice. This is because a 'multi-category' approach acts like a 'shopping list' in which it serves as

[95] See Gava, J., & Kincaid, P. (1996). Contract and Conventionalism: Professional Attitudes to Changes in Contract Law in Australia, *Journal of Contract Law*, 10, 141–150.

[96] Small Business Commissioner South Australia, Submissions to the Australian Government, *Review of the Federal Franchising Code of Conduct*, February 2013, 10.

[97] Small Business Commissioner South Australia, Submissions to the Australian Government, *Review of the Federal Franchising Code of Conduct*, February 2013, 10.

a guideline in understanding the definition of a broad concept like good faith.

The recent major decision by the previous Australian government in the context of franchising signifies a shift in its view to the concept of good faith. It indicates that there is strong support for using good faith in dealing with specific issues in the franchising context. Therefore, it is argued here that the experience of good faith in the franchising context provides a valuable precedent for its consideration to be similarly legislated in the context of contractual performance.

CHAPTER 8

Conclusion

This study set out to explore the role and impact of the concept of good faith in contractual performance in Australia. Despite the absence of a High Court decision regarding its application and definition, the concept of good faith is gaining increased recognition and continues to have an increasing influence on many types of contracts in many contexts. In regard to its origin, the concept of good faith is rooted in civil law countries, but it is nevertheless gaining recognition in common law countries. The reception of good faith in both civil and common law countries is analysed to provide a clear understanding of the concept of good faith in both legal systems. In addition, the reception of good faith at the international level was discussed whereby good faith is recognised in many international trade instruments. The subsequent discussion is focused on understanding the concept of good faith in Australia from its initial introduction by means of the *obiter* comments of *Priestley J* in the *Renard* case in 1992. The emergence and historical development of good faith in Australia were discussed to provide an overall overview. The discussion revolved around the watershed decision case of *Renard*, the issue of 'implication' and 'construction' and the current developing position of good faith in Australia. The doctrinal discussion is not sufficient for a comprehensive view of how the concept of good faith has been received in Australia by the Australian judiciary and its role in contract law. An empirical analysis was carried out based on data collected for a period spanning two decades (1992–2009). From here, an empirical overview of good

N. Abdullah, *Good Faith in Contractual Performance in Australia*,
https://doi.org/10.1007/978-981-15-6078-1_8

faith was developed that offers a detailed review of the 'landscape' of cases decided based on the issue of good faith in contractual performance, which was accompanied with tables and graphs to aid in the understanding of the discussion. The attitude of Australian judges was gauged by using a four-point Likert-type scale to measure judicial support. In order to show the reliability and validity of the data, the basic statistical analysis 'average and standard deviation' was used.

There are numerous meanings of good faith in contract law. Most of the identified meanings are complex, contradictory and unclear. The wide range of meanings does support the argument made in this book that the concept of good faith has no specific or precise meanings. Given the problems associated with the definition of good faith, a taxonomic solution to its definition was proposed. This exercise concluded that a workable definition of good faith can be defined by way of 'multi-categories' wherein the multiple elements that make up the concept are included, thus ensuring that the fundamental components of its meaning are not ignored. This new approach to the definition of good faith assists judicial interpretation by ensuring that the necessary components that make up the concept are maintained in any interpretation while allowing some room for flexibility and certainty.

In regard to the legitimate acceptance of the concept of good faith within a legal framework, the previous Australian government accepted the recommendation by Wein, an experienced franchise operator and small business advisor, to include an express obligation to act in good faith in franchise agreements. Calls for good faith in franchising are due to the allegations of unethical behaviour by franchisors and franchisees. Wein contended that an obligation of good faith should not be defined; instead, good faith should be incorporated in a manner similar to the prohibition of unconscionable conduct set out in s 22 of the *Australian Consumer Law*.[1] Such an obligation of good faith is not defined; instead, good faith is understood by way of the 'non-discretionary reference criteria' to assist its meaning. The approach of 'non-discretionary reference criteria' will eliminate uncertainty due to the legislative guideline given to facilitate the judges in interpreting such a broad concept. The current development of good faith in the context of franchising showed that there are substantial amounts of support from the previous Australian government for the

[1] Australian Government, *Commonwealth Government Response to the Review of the Federal Franchising Code of Conduct*—Forward Looking Franchising Regulation (2013) 13.

concept of good faith in dealing with specific issues in the franchising context. Moreover, this may be seen as a legal precedent for its inclusion in contractual performance which has motivated this research to seek the possibility of legislating good faith in contractual performance.

In a specific context like franchising, there has been a move to legislate an express obligation of good faith to regulate the unethical behaviour of franchisors towards franchisees.

The research has implications for theory since very little progress has been made since *Renard*. There remains no High Court decision deciding the application and definition of good faith in Australia. In *Royal Botanic Gardens and Domain Trust v South Sydney City Council*, the High Court did not use the opportunity to discuss good faith, but Kirby J held that 'Whilst the issues respecting the existence and scope of a "good faith" doctrine are important, this is an inappropriate occasion to consider them'.[2] Previous research has nevertheless focused on the status and evolution of good faith in Australia. Despite the fact that past definitions of good faith have caused undesirable problems and tension, there remain many definitions of good faith.[3] This is perhaps due to the shortcomings of the single-category approach to understanding good faith, which fails to encompass the breadth of the concept, thus resulting in greater reservations in its use due to increased uncertainty.

This research has contributed to the literature on the definition of good faith by way of proposing a workable definition. The proposed taxonomic solution to the definition of good faith is a 'multi-categories' definition of good faith.[4] This solution is supported by empirical observation as discussed, where a rigorous thematic analysis of the meaning of good faith was conducted. The advantages of defining good faith by way of a 'multi-category' approach are that it is a more comprehensive approach. This approach will benefit the parties to the litigation, lawyers and judges by offering greater confidence and certainty. It will assist their interpretation of good faith by providing guidelines for its definition.

Parties in the litigation will have the option to argue on the grounds of good faith based on the clear understanding offered by the 'multi-categories' approach. Lawyers are also set to benefit through greater clarity of the concept. Since there is no High Court decision, now it is the

[2] (2002) 186 ALR 289, 312.

[3] See Chap. 6 for further details.

[4] See Chap. 6 for further details.

legislature's task to legislate good faith in the Australian contract law. Waiting for judges can be a lengthy, costly and counterproductive process that some parties may ill afford. Instead of assuming greater certainty when good faith is defined by way of 'multi-categories', it offers greater certainty, confidence and clear guidelines for the parties in the litigation, lawyers and judges.

Further research on good faith in contractual performance could be conducted over a longer period for further insight on the direction of good faith in contractual performance in Australian contract law, for example in long-term contracts, such as in the context of franchising and joint venture contracts, to provide another perspective to the concept of good faith. In this regard, an interview with Priestley J, who introduced good faith into the judicial agenda in Australia, would be another step forward towards a better understanding of his Honour's position on good faith despite his *obiter* comments. Furthermore, other judges who shared his Honour's view could be interviewed as part of the research.

Bibliography

Case Laws

Aiton Australia Pty Ltd v Transfield Pty Ltd (1999) 153 FLR 236 (2000) 16 BCL 70.

Alcatel Australia v Scarella (1998) 44 NSWLR 349.

Aldin v Latimer Clark, Muirhead & Co [1984] 2 Ch 437.

Ansett Transport Industries v Commonwealth (1977) 139 CLR 54.

Antonovic v Volker (1986) 7 NSWLR 151.

Archibald Barr Motor Company Ltd & Anor v ATECO Automotive New Zealand (High Court, Auckland, CIV 2007-404-5797, 26 October 2007).

Armstong v State of Victoria (No.2) (1957) 99 CLR 28.

Asia Pacific Resources Pty Ltd v Forestry Tasmania Unreported, Supreme Court of Tasmania, 4 September 1997.

Auag Resources Ltd v Waihi Mines Ltd [1994] 3 NZLR 571.

Australia Pty Ltd v Bruness Pty Ltd [2002] WASC 286 (Unreported, Hasluck J, 4 December 2002) 372.

Australian Competition & Consumer Commission v CG Berbatis Holdings (2003) 214 CLR 51.

Australis Media Holdings Pty Ltd v Telestra Corporation Ltd (1998) 43 NSWLR 104.

Automasters Australia Pty Ltd v Bruness Pty Ltd & Anor [2002] WASC 286.

Bilgola Enterprises Ltd v Dymocks Franchise Systems (NSW) Pty Ltd (2000) 3 NZLR 169.

Biotechnology Australia Pty Ltd v Pace (1988) 15 NSWLR 130.

Birmingham Dudley & District Banking Company v Ross (1888) 38 Ch D295.

N. Abdullah, *Good Faith in Contractual Performance in Australia*,
https://doi.org/10.1007/978-981-15-6078-1

Blomley v Ryan (1956) 99 CLR 362.
Bobux Marketing Ltd v Raynor Marketing Ltd [2002] 1 NZLR 506.
BP Refinery (Westernport) Pty Ltd v Shire of Hastings (1977) 180 CLR 266.
Breen v Williams (1996) 186 CLR 71.
Bropho v Human Rights & Equal Opportunity Commission [2004] FCAFC 16 [84].
Bryne Australia v Australian Airlines Ltd (1995) 185 CLR 410.
Burger King Corporation v Hungry Jack's Pty Ltd [2001] NSWCA 187.
Butt v McDonald (1896) 7 QLJ 68.
Byrne v Australian Airlines (1995) 185 CLR 410.
Carter v Boehm [1766] 3 Burr.1905.
Castlemaine Tooheys Ltd v Carlton & United Breweries Ltd (1987) 10 NSWLR 468.
Central Exchange Ltd v Anaconda Nickel Ltd [2001] WASC 128.
Chirnside v Fay [2007] 1 NZLR, 433.
Codelfa Construction Pty Ltd v State Rail Authority of New South Wales (1982) 149 CLR 337.
Commercial Bank of Australia v Amadio (1983) 46 ALR 402.
Commonwealth Bank of Australia Ltd v Spira (2002) 174 FLR 274.
Commonweatlh Development Bank of Australia v Cassagrain [2002] NSWSC 965,[210].
Comunale v Traders & General Insurance Co 50 Cal.2d 653, 328 P.2d (1958).
Council of the City of Sydney v Goldspar Australia Pty Ltd (2006) 230 ALR 437.
Director General of Fair Trading v First National Bank [2002] 1 All ER 97.
Director General of Fair Trading v First National Bank [2000] QB 672.
Dymocks Franchise System (NSW) Pty Ltd v Todd [2004] 1 NZLR 289.
Eastwood v Magnox Electric Plc [2005] 1 AC 503.
Esso Australia Resources Pty Ltd v Southern Pacific Petroleum NL [2005] VSCA 228 (Unreported, Warren CJ, Buchanan JA and Osborn AJA 15 September 2005).
Far Horizons Pty Ltd v McDonald's Australia [2000] VSC 310 (18 August 2000).
Gary Rogers Motors (Aust) Pty Ltd v Subaru (Aust) Pty Ltd (1999) ATPR ¶ 41-703.
Gateway Realty v Arton Holdings (No.3) (1992) 106 NSR (2d) 180 (SC).
Gibbons Holdings Ltd v Wholesale Distributors Ltd [2008] 1 NZLR 277.
GSA Group Pty Ltd v SiebePlc (1993) 30 NSWLR 573.
Harmerv Jumbil (Nigeria) Tin Areas Ltd [1921] 1 Ch 200.
Helmore v Smith (1886) 35 ChD 436.
Hospital Products Ltd v United States Surgical Corporation (1984) 156 ALR 417.
Hudson Resources Limited v Australian Diatomite Mining Pty Limited & Anor [2002] NSWSC 314.
Hughes Aircraft v Airservices Australia (1997) 146 ALR 1, 37.

Hughes Bros Pty Ltd v Trustees of the Roman Catholic Church (1993) 31 NSWLR 91.
Hurley v McDonald's Australia Ltd (2000) ATPR 41-741, 40, 585.
ICC Arbitral Award No 8611 of 1997, URL: http://cisgw3.law.pace.edu/cases/978611i1.htm.
Insight Oceania Pty Ltd v Philips Electronics Australia Ltd [2008] NSWSC 710.
Interfoto Picture Library Ltd v Stiletto Visual Programmes Ltd [1989] QB 433.
James Spencer & Co Ltd v Tame Valley Padding Co. Ltd (Court of Appeal, 8 April 1998, unreported).
JF Keir Pty Ltd v Priority Management Systems Pty Ltd (administrators appointed) (2007) NSWSC 789.
JLCS Pty Ltd v Squires Loft City Steakhouse Pty Ltd 78 IPR 319.
Kelly v New Zealand Insurance Co Ltd (1993) 7 ANZ Insurance Case 61-197 [78, 258].
Kirke La Shelle Co v Paul Armstrong Co 188 NE 163, 167.
Kiwi Gold NL v Propehcy Mining NL (Unreported 18 July 1991, Court of Appeal, CA/30/91).
Linfox v Ellul & Ors [2004] NSWSC 276.
Liverpool City Council v Irwin [1977] AC 239.
Livingstone v Roskilly [1992] 3 NZLR 230.
Mackay v Dick (1881) 6 App Cas 251.
Molton Builders Ltd v City of Westminster London Borough Council (1975) 30 P & CR 182.
Mona Oil Equipment Co v Rhodesia Railways [1949] 2 All E.R 1014.
Narni Pty Ltd v National Australia Bank [2001] VSCA 31 [16].
New Zealand Shipping Co. Ltd v A.M Satherwaite & Co Ltd [1975] Q.B 154.
Nuclear Tests Case (Australia v France) [1974] ICJ REP. 253, 268.
Overlook v Foxtel [2002] Aust Contract Reports ¶90–143. 91–972.
Pearce v Foster (1886) 17 QBD 536.
PRP Diagnostic Imaging Pty Limited (in its capacity as trustee for the Pittwater Radiology Trust) & Ors v Pittwater Radiology Pty [2008] NSWSC 701.
Renard Constructions (ME) Pty Ltd v Minister for Public Works (Renard) (1992) 26 NSWLR 234.
Royal Botanic Gardens and Domain Trust v South Sydney City Council (2002) 240 CLR 45, 63.
Secured Income Real Estate (Australia) Ltd v St Martin's Investments Pty Ltd (1979) 144 CLR 596.
Service Station Association Ltd v Berg Bennett & Associates Pty Ltd (1993) 45 FCR 84, 97.
Shelanu Inc v Print Three Franchising Corporation (2003) 64 OR (3d) 533.
Shepherd v Felt & Textiles of Australia Ltd (1931) 45 CLR 359, 378.

Shipping (London) Ltd v Polish Steamship Co (The Manifest Lipkowy) (1989) 2 Lloyd's Rep 138, 142.
Shirlaw v Southern Foundries [1939] 2 KB 206, 227.
Simonius Vischer & Co v Holt & Thompson [1979] 2 NSWLR 322.
State Bank of New South Wales Ltd v Currabubula Holdings Pty Ltd (2001) 51 NSWLR 399.
TarmacCanadaInc.vHamiltonWentworth(RegionalMunicipality)O.J.3273(1999).
The Mogul Steamship Co Ltd v McGregor, Gow & Co (1889) 23 QBD 598.
The Moorock (1889) 14 PD 64.
Thiess Contractors Pty Ltd v Placer (Granny Smith) Pty Ltd [.1999] WASC 1046.
Thiess Contractors Pty Ltd v Placer (Granny Smith) Pty Ltd [2000] WASCA 102.
Tomlin v Ford Credit Australia [2005] NSWSC 540.
Tymshare Inc v Covell 727 F2d 1148 (1984).
Union Eagle Ltd v Golden Achievement Ltd [1997] AC 514 [218–219].
United Dominions Corporation Ltd v Brian Pty Ltd (1985) 157 CLR 1.
Vero Insurance New Zealand Ltd v Fleet Insurance & Risk Management Ltd (High Court, Auckland, CIV 2007-404-1438, 21 May 2007).
Walford v Miles [1992] 2 AC 128.
Wallace v United Grain Growers [1997] 3 SCR 701.
Watseka First International Bank v Ruda 135 3d 140 (III, 1990).
Wessex Dairies Limited v Smith [1935] 2 KB 80.
Wheeldon v Burrows (1879) 12 Ch D 31, 49.
Wood v Lucy, Lady Duff-Gordon 222 NY 88,118 NE 214, 214(1917).

Statutes

Australian Consumer Law 2010.
City and Suburban Electric Railways (Amendment) Act 1967 (NSW).
Competition and Consumer Act 2010.
Contract Law of the People's Republic of China.
Dutch Civil Code.
Employment Relations Act 2000 (EERA).
Franchising Code of Conduct.
French Civil Code.
German Civil Code.
Greek Civil Code.
Insurance Act 2015.
Insurance Contracts Act 1984.
Insurance Contracts Act 2015 (Part 5).
International Institute for the Unification of Private Law (UNIDROIT).
Italian Civil Code.
Principles of European Contract Law.

Principles of International Commercial Contracts (UNIDROIT Principles 2004).
Quebec Civil Code.
Restatement (Second) of Contracts.
Restatements of the Law.
Swiss Civil Code.
Trade Practices Act 1974 (Cth).
Unfair Terms in Consumer Contracts Regulations 1999.
Uniform Commercial Code, Vol. 1 (4th ed.) 5, 187.
Vienna Convention on the Law of Treaties.

Journal Articles

Duncan, W. D. (1998). Non-Derogation from Grant and Tenant Mix. *Australian Property Law Journal*, 6, 2.

Adler, R. S., & Mann, R. A. (1995). Good Faith: A New Look at an Old Doctrine. *Akron Law Review*, 28, 31–34.

Allsop, J. (2011). Good Faith and Australian Contract Law: A Practical Issue and a Question of Theory and Principle. *Australian Law Journal*, 85, 342–344.

Arlen, D. (2007). A Universal Duty of Good Faith: An Economic Perspective. *Monash University Law Review*, 33, 182–199.

Bigwood, R. (2005). Symposium Introduction: Confessions of a Good Faith Agnostic. *New Zealand Business Law Quarterly*, 11, 371.

Bigwood, R. (2006). Conscience and the Liberal Conception of Contract: Observing Basic Distinctions Part 1. *Journal of Contract Law*, 16, Special Issue: 1–36.

Binh, N., & Terry, A. (2014). Meeting the Challenges for Franchising in Developing Countries: The Vietnamese Experience. *Journal of Marketing Channels*, 21(3), 210–221.

Braucher, R. (1958). The Legislative History of the Uniform Commercial Code. *Columbia Law Review*, 798–812.

Bridge, M. (1984). Does Anglo-Canadian Contract Law Need a Doctrine of Good Faith?. *Canadian Business Law Journal*, 9, 385–413.

Bristow, D. I., & Seth, R. (2000). Good Faith in Negotiations. *Dispute Resolution Journal*, 55, 16–18.

Burrows, J. F. (1968). Contractual Cooperation and Implied Terms. *Modern Law Review*, 31, 390.

Burton, S. J. (1980). Breach of Contract and the Common Law Duty to Perform in Good Faith. *Harvard Law Review*, 94, 369.

Burton, S. J. (1984). More on Good Faith Performance of a Contract: A Reply to Professor Summers. *Iowa Law Review*, 69, 497–499.

Burton, S. J. (1993). Good Faith in Articles 1 and 2 of the UCC: The Practice View. *William and Mary Law Review*, 35, 1533–1536.

Burton, S. J., & Andersen, E. G. (1990). The World in Contract. *Iowa Law Review*, 75, 861.

Carlin, T. M. (2005a) The Rise (and Fall) of Implied Duties of Good Faith in Contractual Performance in Australia 25 *University of New South Wales Law Journal*, 25, 99–124.

Carlin, T.M & Chau, L (2005) Good Faith-Time to Put the Genie Back in the Bottle, *Journal of Law & Financial Management*, 3, 22–30.

Carlin, T.M (2005b) Good Faith in Contractual Performance - Smoke without Flame?, *Journal of Law & Financial Management*, 4(2), 18–37.

Carter, J. W., & Peden, E. (2004). Good Faith in Australian Contract Law. *Australian Construction Law Newsletter*, 94, 6–8.

Carter, J. W., & Stewart, A. (2002). Interpretation, Good Faith and the True Meaning of Contracts: The Royal Botanic Decision. *Journal of Contract Law*, 18, 182–190.

Cohen, J., & Weinberg, L. (2002). Good faith and Fair Dealing: A Primer on the Differences between the United States and Canada. *Franchise Law Journal*, 22, 37–40.

Cole, T. R. H. (1994). The Concept of Reasonableness in Construction Contracts. *Building and Construction Law Journal*, 10, 7–12.

Damian, T. (20 July 2012). Contract Code No Answer to Contract Law Reform. The Australian (Sydney). Retrieved from: http://www.theaustralian.com.au/business/legal-affairs/contract-code-no-answer-to-contract-law-reform/story-e6frg97x-1226430355969#mm-premium.

Davies, J. (2002). Why a Common Law Duty of Contractual Good Faith is Not Required. *Canterbury Law Review*, 8, 529–530.

Dixon, B. (2007). Can the Common Law Obligation of Good Faith be Contractually Excluded?. *Australian Business Law Review*, 35, 110–113.

Dixon, B. (2011). Good Faith in Contractual Performance and Enforcement-Australian doctrinal Hurdles. *Australian Business Law Review*, 39, 227–231.

Dobbins, T. J. (2005). Losing Faith: Extracting the Implied Covenant of Good Faith from (Some) Contracts. *Oregon Law Review*, 84, 227–230.

Donald, B. (1973). Codification in Common Law System. *The Australian Law Journal*, 47, 160–161.

Dubroff, H. (2006). The Implied Covenant of Good Faith in Contract Interpretation and Gap-Filling: Reviving a Revered Relic. *St. John's Law Review*, 80, 559–587.

Easterbrook, F. H., & Fischel, D. R. (1993). Contract and Fiduciary Duty. *Journal of Law and Economics*, 36, 425–438.

Farnsworth, E. A. (1963). Good Faith Performance and Commercial Reasonableness under the Uniform Commercial Code. *University of Chicago Law Review*, 30, 666–667.

Farnsworth, E. A. (1995a). Duties of Good Faith and Fair Dealing Under the UNIDROIT Principles, Relevant International Conventions and National Laws. *Tulane Journal of International and Comparative Law*, 3, 47–55.

Ferrari, R. (1994). Uniform Interpretation of the 1980 Uniform Sales Law. *The Georgia Journal of International and Comparative Law*, 24, 183–210.

Finn, P. (1989). Contract and the Fiduciary Principle. *University of New South Wales Law Journal*, 12, 76–84.

Finn, P. (1994). Unconscionable Conduct. *Journal of Contract Law*, 8, 37–38.

Finn, P. (2001). Equity and Commercial Contracts: A Comment. *AMPLA Yearbook*, 414–418.

Fitzgerald. P. J. (1970). Are Statutes Fit For Academic Treatment. *Journal of Society of Public Teachers of Law*, 142–144.

French, R. S. (1989). A Lawyer's Guide to Misleading or Deceptive Conduct. *Australian Law Journal*, 63, 250.

Gava, J., & Kincaid, P. (1996). Contract and Conventionalism: Professional Attitudes to Changes in Contract Law in Australia, *Journal of Contract Law*, 10, 141–150.

Goff, R. (1984). Commercial Contracts and the Commercial Court. *Llyod's Maritime and Commercial Law Quarterly*, 382–391.

Goff, R. (1992). Opening Address (Second Annual Journal of Contract Law Conference in London in September 1991). *Journal of Contract Law*, 5, 4.

Goode, R. (1997). International Restatements of Contract and English Contract Law. *Uniform Law Review*, 2, 231–240.

Hadfield, G. K. (1990). Problematic Relations: Franchising and the Law of Incomplete Contracts. *Stanford Law Review*, 42, 927–991.

Hillman, R. A. (1979). Policing Contract Modifications Under Uniform Commercial Contract: Good Faith and the doctrine of economic duress. *Iowa Law Review*, 64, 849–877.

Holmes, E. M. (1977). A Contextual Study of Commercial Good Faith: Good Faith Disclosure in Contract Formation. *University of Pittsburgh Law Review*, 39, 381–408.

Holmes, E. M. (1980). Is There Life after Gilmore's Death of Contract – Inductions from a Study of Commercial Good Faith in First-Party Insurance Contract. *Cornell Law Review*, 65, 330–377.

Hunter, O. H. (1992). Book Reviews: Good Faith in English Law. [Review of the book *Good faith in English Law*]. *Journal of Contract Law*, 5, 172.

Iglesias, J. (2004). Applying the Implied Covenant of Good Faith and Fair Dealing to Franchises. *Houston Law Review*, 40, 1423–1429.

Kirby, M. (1988). Bold Spirit of the Law. *Quadrant 16*, 32(3).

Klein, J., & Bachechi, C. (1994). Precontractual Liability and the Duty of Good Faith Negotiations in International Transactions. *Hous Journal International Law*, 17, 1–17.

Koneru, P. (1997). The International Interpretation of the UN Convention on Contracts for the International Sale of Goods: An Approach Based on General Principles. *Minnesota Journal of Global Trade*, 6, 105–140.

Leonhard, C. (2010). A Legal Chameleon: An Examination of the Doctrine of Good Faith in Chinese and American Contract Law. *Connecticut Journal of International Law*, 25, 305–306.

Mason, A. (2000). Contract, Good Faith and Equitable Standards in Fair Dealing. *Law Quarterly Review*, 116, 66–69.

McDougall, R. (21 February 2006). The Implied Duty of Good Faith in Australian Contract Law. Retrieved from: http://www.lawlink.nse.gov.au/lawlink/Supreme_Court/II_sc.nsf/vwPrint1/SCO-mcdougall210206.

McKendrick, E. (1997). English Contract Law – A Rich Past, an Uncertain Future?. *Current Legal Problems*, 50, 25–35 & 42–44.

Musy, Alberto M. "The Good Faith Principle in Contract Law and the Precontractual Duty to Disclose: Comparative Analysis of New Differences in Legal Cultures." *Global Jurist Advances*, vol. 1, no. 1, 2001, https://doi.org/10.2202/1535-1661.1007.

Nicholas, B. (1974). Rules and Terms – Civil Law and Common Law. *Tulane Law Review*, 946.

O'Byrne, S. K. (1995). Good Faith in Contractual Performance: Recent Developments. *Canadian Bar Review*, 74, 70–73.

O'Byrne, S. K. (2007). The Implied Term of Good Faith and Fair Dealing: Recent Developments. *Canadian Bar Review*, 86, 194–195.

Palmieri, N. W. (1993). Good Faith Disclosures Required During Precontractual Negotiations. *Seton Hall Law Review*, 24, 70, 200–201.

Pargendler, M. (2008). Modes of Gap Filling: Good Faith and Fiduciary Duties Recognised. *Tulane Law Review*, 82, 1315–1318.

Paterson, J. M. (1998). Terms Implied in Fact: The Basis for Implication. *Journal of Contract Law*, 13, 103–106.

Paterson, J. M. (2000). Duty of Good Faith Does It Have a Place in Contract Law?. *Law Institute Journal*, p. 48.

Paterson, J. M. (2001). Good Faith in Commercial Contracts? A Franchising Case Study. *Australian Business Law Review*, 29, 270–291.

Peden, E. (2000). Co-operation in English Contract Law – To Construe or Imply. *Journal of Contract Law*, 16, 56.

Peden, E. (2002). The Meaning of Contractual Good Faith. *Australian Bar Review*, 22, 235–247.

Peden, E. (2003a). Good Faith in the Performance of Contract Law. *Law Journal Society*, p. 64.

Peden, E. (2005). When Common Law Trumps Equity: The Rise of Good Faith and Reasonableness and the Demise of Unconscionability. *Journal of Contract Law*, 21, 226–248.

Peden, E., & Carter, J. W. (2003). Good Faith in Australian Contract Law. *Journal of Contract Law*, 19, 155–162.

Peden. E. (2001). Incorporating Terms of Good Faith in Contract Law in Australia. *Sydney Law Review*, 23, 222.

Perrigot, R., Terry, A & Lernia, C. D. (2019) Good Faith in Franchising The Perceptions of Franchisees, Franchisors and Their Lawyers in the French Context, *International Journal of Retails & Distribution Management* (47)(3), 246–261.

Phang, A. (2000). Security of Contract and the Pursuit of Fairness. *Journal of Contract Law,* 16, 158.

Powell, R. (1956). Good Faith in Contracts. *Current Legal Problems*, 16–20.

Powers, P. J. (1999). Defining the Undefinable: Good Faith and the United Nations Convention on the Contracts for the International Sale of Goods. *Journal of Law and Commerce*, 18, 333–337.

Purcell, J. (30 July 2012) 'Codifying Australia's Contract Law is a Step in the Wrong Direction', Intheblack (Sydney). Retrieved from: http://www.itbdigital.com/opinion?t=legal.

Reitier, B. (1983). Good Faith in Contracts. *Valparaiso University Law Review*, 17, 705–707.

Rickett, C. E. F. (2001). *Some Reflections on Open-Textured Commercial Contracting*. AMPLA Yearbook, 372–383.

Riley, J. (2003). Mutual Trust and Good Faith: Can Private Contract Law Guarantee Fair Dealing in the Workplace? *Australian Journal of Labour Law*, 16, 1–4.

Schlechtriem, P. (February 1996). Good Faith in German Law and in International Uniforms Law. Retrieved from: http://www.uniromal.it/idc/ventro/publications/24sclectriem.pdf.

Spencer, E. C. (2008a). Balance of Power, Certainty and Discretion in the Franchise Relationship: An Analysis of Contractual Terms. *Bond University Electronic Journal of Law*. Retrieved from: http://epublications.bond.edu.au/laws_pubs/250.

Staughton, C. (1994). Good Faith and Fairness in Commercial Contract Law. *Journal of Contract Law*, 7, 193.

Steyn, J. (1991). The Role of Good Faith and Fair Dealing in Contract Law: A Hair-Shirt Philosophy?. *Denning Law Journal*, 6, 131–140.

Steyn. J. (1997). Contract Law: Fulfilling the Reasonable Expectations of Honest Men. *Law Quarterly Review*, 113, 442.

Summers, R. (1968). Good Faith in General Contract Law and the Sales Provision of the Uniform Commercial Code. *Virginia Law Review*, 54, 195–196.

Summers, R. S. (1982). The General Duty of Good Faith-Its Recognition and Conceptualization. *Cornell Law Review*, 67, 810–819.

Sykes, J. (2009). Taken for Granted on the Scope of the Doctrine of Non-Derogation from Grant. *New Law Journal.*

Terry, A. (1982). Unconscionable Contracts in New South Wales: The Contracts Review Act 1980. *Australian Business Law Review*, 311–312.

Terry, A., & Cary. D. L. (2009). Franchising and the Quest for the Holy Grail: Good Faith or Good Intentions. *Melbourne University Law Review*, 33, 542–554.

Terry, A. (2005). Franchising, Relational Contracts and the Vibe 33. Australian Business Law Review, 289.

Terry, A., Zhang, Y. (2011). The power and information imbalance in franchising: The role of prior disclosure under the Franchising Code of Conduct. *Australian Business Law Review*, 39(4), 245–259.

Terry, A., & Huan, J. (2013). Franchisor Liability for Franchisee Conduct. *Monash University Law Review,* 39(2), 388–410.

Terry, A., & Ba Binh, N. (2013). Impact of the legislation on franchise to the development of franchising in Vietnam. *Journal of Legislative Research*, 21(253).

Terry, A., & Chetwin, M. (2015). Issues at the end of a franchising relationship. Australian Business Law Review, 43(2), 152–166.

Teubner, G. (1998). Legal Irritants: Good Faith in British Law or How Unifying Law Ends Up in New Divergence. *Modern Law Review*, 61, 11.

Thigpen, R. (1981). Good Faith Performance under Percentage Leases. *Mississippi Law Journal*, 315–320.

Turpin, C. C. (1965). Bonae Fidei Judicia. *The Cambridge Law Journal*, 260–262.

Van Zyl Steyn, J. (1991). The Role of Good Faith and Fair Dealing in Contract Law: A Hair-Shirt Philosophy?. *Denning Law Journal*, 6, 131–140.

Vigneau. C. (2010). The Obligation of Good Faith in France. *Comparative Labor Law & Policy Journal*, 32, 593–594.

Waas, B. (2010). Good Faith in the Law of the Employment Relationship: Germany. *Comparative Labor Law & Policy Journal*, 32, 603–605.

Wang, L., & Xu, C. (1999). Fundamental Principles of China's Contract Law. *Columbia Journal of Asian Law*, 13, 1–16.

Wang, Z., Terry, A. (2012). The Impact of China's Regulatory Regime on Foreign Franchisors' Entry and Expansion Strategies. *Asian Journal of Comparative Law*, 7(1), 1–30.

Woo, P. Y. (2001). Protecting Parties' Reasonable Expectations: A General Principle of Good Faith. *Oxford University Commonwealth Law Journal*, 1, 195–221.

Zaccaria, E. C. (2004) The Dilemma of Good Faith in International Commercial Trade. *Macquarie Journal of Business Law*, 1, 101–110.

Zahira Mohd Ishan & Shaik Mohd Noor Alam. (2009). Unconscionability-Statutory Prevention of Unethical Business Practices. *International Journal of Economics and Management*, 3, 151–157.

Zhang, Y., & Huang, D. (2000). The New Contract Law in the People's Republic of China and the UNIDROIT Principles of International Commercial Contracts: A Brief Comparison. *Uniform Law Review*, 5, 429–431.

Unpublished Papers

Davis, J. L. R. (1993). *Good Faith in Building Contracts and Construction*. Paper presented at the Construction Law Committee's Construction Law Seminar.

Goode, R. (1992). *The Concept of Good Faith in English Law*. Paper presented at the Centro di Studi e Ricerche di Diritto Comparato e Straniero, Rome, 3.

Unpublished Thesis

Carlin, T. M. (2005c). A Critical Analysis of the Burgeoning Good Faith Performance Doctrine in the Australian Contract Law (Unpublished master dissertation). University of Sydney, Sydney, Australia.

Books

Abdullah Alwi Haji Hassan. (1997). *Sales And Contracts In Early Islamic Commercial Law* (1). DELHI: Kitabbhavan.

Adams, J. N., & Brownsword, R. (2004). Understanding Contract Law. In Brownsword, R (Ed.). *Understanding Contract Law* (4th ed., p. 116). Sweet & Maxwell.

Atiyah, P. S. (2005a). Atiyah's Introduction to the Law of Contract. Oxford University Press.

Atiyah, P. S. (2005b). Implied terms (A Duty to act in Good Faith?). In *Atiyah, P. S. Atiyah's Introduction to the Law of Contract* (pp. 1–168). Oxford University Press.

Beatson, J., & Friedmann, D. (Eds.). (1995). *Good Faith and Fault in Contract Law*. Oxford University Press.

Bonell, M. H. (1987). Article 7: Interpretation of the Convention. In Biance, C. M., & Bonell, M. J. (Eds.). *Commentary on the International Sales Law- The 1980 Vienna Sales Convention*. Milan.

David, R. (1972). *French Law, Its Structure, Sources and Methodology*. Louisiana State University Press.

Farnsworth. E. A. (1995). Good Faith in Contract Performance. In Beatson, J., & Friedmann, D. (Eds.). *Good Faith and Fault in Contract Law* (p. 158). Oxford University Press.

Farnsworth. E. A. (2004). *Farnsworth on Contracts* (3rd ed.). Aspen Publishers.

Harrison, R. (1997). *Good Faith in Sales.* London: Sweet & Maxwell.

Healey, D., & Terry. A. (1995). *Misleading or Deceptive Conduct* (pp. 19–20). Australia: CCH Australia Limited.

Hesselink, M. (1998). Good Faith. In Hartkamp, A., Hesselink, M., Hondius, E., Joustra, C., du Perron, E. (Eds.). *Towards a European Civil Code* (2nd ed., revised and expanded) (p. 87). Kluwer Law International.

Hird, N. J., Howells, G. G., Brownsword, R. (Eds.). (1999). *Good Faith in Contract, Concept and Context.* Ashgate.

Hutchinson, D. (1999). Good Faith in the South African Law of Contract. In Brownsword, R., Hind, N. J., Howells, G. (Eds.). *Good Faith in Contract, Concept and Context* (p. 215): Ashgate.

International Law Commission. (1964). *Report of the International Law Commission Covering its 16th Session, 727th Meeting (20 May 1964).* Yearbook of International Law Commission.

Kötz, H. (1998). Towards a Europe Civil Code. In Cane, P., & Stapleton, J. (Eds.). *The Law of Obligation; Essays in Celebration of John Fleming* (pp. 243–244). Oxford University Press.

Lando, O. (1995). Article 1.201: Good Faith and Fair Dealing. In Lando, O., & Beale, H. (Eds.). *The Principles of European Contract Law, Part 1: Performance, Non-Performance and Remedies* (p. 113). Martinus Nijhoff Publishers.

Lando, O., & Beale, H. (Eds.). (1995). *The Principles of European Contract Law, Part 1: Performance, Non-Performance and Remedies.* Martinus Nijhoff Publishers.

Lucke, H. K. (1987). Good Faith and Contractual Performance. In Finn, P. (Ed.). *Essays on Contract.* The Law Book Co.

Norrie. G. (1984). *The Development of Consumer Law and Policy-Based Spirit and Timorous Souls.* Steven & Sons.

O'Connor, J. F. (1990). *Good Faith in English Law.* Dartmouth Publishing Company.

Oldham, J. (2004). *English Common Law in the Age of Mansfield, Contract and Quasi Contract.* The University of North California Press.

Paterson, J., Robertson, A., Heffey, P. (2005). *Principles of Contract Law* (2nd ed.). Law Book Co.

Peden, E. (2003b). Construction Distinguished from Implication in Fact. In Peden, E. *Good Faith in the Performance of Contract.* LexisNexis Butterworths.

Peden, E. (2003c). *Good Faith in the Performance of Contract.* LexisNexis Butterworths.

Peden, E., Tolhurst, G. J., Carter, J. W. (2007). *Contract Law in Australia, Good Faith*. LexisNexis Butterworths.

Peden, J. R. (October 1976). *Report on Harsh and Unconscionable Contracts*. Macquarie University: NSW.

Schermaier, M. (2000). Bonae Fides in Roman Contract Law. In Zimmermann, R., & Whittaker, S. (Eds.). *Good Faith in European Contract Law* (pp. 81–82). Cambridge University Press.

Seddon, N., & Ellinghaus, M. (2002). *Cheshire & Fifoot's Law of Contract* (8th ed.). LexisNexis Butterworths.

Slapper, G., & Kelly, D. (2006). *The English Legal System* (8th ed.). Cavendish.

Styles, S. C. (1999). Good Faith: A Principled Matter. In Forte, A. D. M. (Ed.), *Good Faith in Contract and Property* (pp. 157–158). Oxford: Hart Publishing.

Summers, R. (2000). The Conceptualisation of Good Faith in American Contract Law: A General Account. In Zimmermann, R., & Whittaker, S. (Eds.). *Good Faith in European Contract Law* (pp. 118–119). Cambridge University Press.

Wandlungen, R. E. (1930). Wissenschaft and Lehre. In Schoch, M. M. (Ed.), *Jurisprudence of Interests: Selected Writings* (pp. 17–18).

Wang, C., & Zhang, X. (Eds.). (1997). *Introduction to Chinese Law*. Sweet & Maxwell.

Watkin, T. G. (1999). *An Historical Introduction to Modern Civil Law*. Ashgate Publishing Company.

Whittaker, S., & Zimmermann, R. (2000). Good Faith in European Contract Law: Surveying the Legal Landscape. In Zimmermann, R., & Whittaker, S. (Eds.). *Good Faith in European Contract Law* (pp. 7–45). Cambridge University Press.

Governmental Reports and Documents

Australian Bureau of Statistics. (Dec 2011) http://www.abs.gov.au/ausstats/abs@.nsf/mf/3101.0/.

Australian Government, Business Law Branch Attorney-General's Department. (2012). Improving Australia's Law and Justice Framework: A Discussion Paper Exploring The Scope for Reforming Australian Contract Law.

Australian Government. (2009a). Commonwealth Government Response to the Report of the Parliamentary Joint Committee on Corporations and Financial Services-Opportunity Not Opportunism: Improving Conduct in Australian Franchising.

Australian Government. (2009b). Commonwealth Government Response to the Report of the Parliamentary Joint Committee on Corporations and Financial Services-Opportunity Not Opportunism: Improving Conduct in Australian Franchising.

Australian Government. (2009c). Commonwealth Government Response to the Report of the Parliamentary Joint Committee on Corporations and Financial Services-Opportunity Not Opportunism: Improving Conduct in Australian Franchising.

Australian Government. (2013a). Commonwealth Government Response to the Review of the Federal Franchising Code of Conduct- Forward Looking Franchising Regulation.

Australian Government. (2013b). Commonwealth Government Response to the Review of the Federal Franchising Code of Conduct- Forward Looking Franchising Regulation.

Australian Government. (2013c). Commonwealth Government Response to the Review of the Federal Franchising Code of Conduct- Forward Looking Franchising Regulation.

Australian Government. (2013d). Commonwealth Government Response to the Review of the Federal Franchising Code of Conduct- Forward Looking Franchising Regulation.

Bakers Delight Holdings Ltd. (14 February 2013). Submission to Federal Government of Australia Review of the Federal Franchising Code of Conduct (2013).

Bathurst, T. F. (20 July 2012). Submission to Attorney-General's Department Improving Australia's Law and Justice Framework: A Discussion Paper Exploring The Scope for Reforming Australian Contract Law.

Competitive Foods Australia. (2008). Submission No.22 to Parliamentary Joint Committee on Corporations and Financial Services, Inquiry into Franchising Code of Conduct.

CPA Australia. (20 July 2012). Submission to Attorney-General's Department: Improving Australia's Law and Justice Framework: A Discussion Paper Exploring The Scope for Reforming Australian Contract Law.

DLA Philips Fox (12 September 2008). Submission No 81 to Parliamentary Joint Committee in Corporations and Financial Services, Parliament of Australia, Opportunity Not Opportunism: Improving Conduct in Australian Franchising.

Economic and Finance Committee, Parliament of South Australia. (May, 2008). Franchises: Final Report of the Sixty-Fifty,

Ellison, M. (February 2013). Submission to Federal Government of Australia Review of the Federal Franchising Code of Conduct.

Expert Panel (Professor Bryan Horrigan, Mr David Lieberman, Mr Ray Steinwall), Parliament of Australia. (February 2010). Strengthening Statutory Unconscionable Conduct and the Franchising Code of Conduct, Canberra.

Franchise Council of Australia. (February 2013). Submission to Federal Government of Australia, Review of the Federal Franchising Code of Conduct.

Government of Western Australia. (April, 2008) Inquiry into the Operation of Franchise Businesses in Western Australia-Report to the Western Australian Minister for Small Business.

Law Council of Australia. (20 July 2012). Submission to Attorney-General's Department Improving Australia's Law and Justice Framework: A Discussion Paper Exploring The Scope for Reforming Australian Contract Law.

Law Society of South Australia. (21 February 2013). Submission to Federal Government of Australia, Review of the Federal Franchising Code of Conduct.

Motor Trades Association of Australia. (2008). Submission No 90 to Parliamentary Joint Committee in Corporations and Financial Services, Parliament of Australia, Opportunity Not Opportunism: Improving Conduct in Australian Franchising.

Tony Piccolo MP, Economics and Finance Committee. (2008). Parliament of South Australia, Proof Committee Hansard, Melbourne.

National Retail Association. (12 September 2008). Submission No 109 to Parliamentary Joint Committee in Corporations and Financial Services, Parliament of Australia, Opportunity Not Opportunism: Improving Conduct in Australian Franchising.

NSW Parliamentary Debates (1979), 3057.

NSW Parliamentary Debates (1980), 5894.

Ontario Law Reform Commission. (1979). Report on Sale of Goods (1979), Vol. 1, 163–71.

Opportunity not Opportunism: Improving Conduct in Australian Franchising prepared by the Federal Parliamentary Joint Committee on Corporations and Financial Services 2008 until the current accepted recommendation by Wein Report 2013.

Senate Standing Committee on Economics, Parliament of Australia. (2008). The Need, Scope and Content of a Definition of Unconscionable Conduct for the Purpose of Part IVA of the Trade Practices Act 1974 (Cth).

Senate Standing Committee on Economics, Parliament of Australia. (2008). The Need, Scope and Content of a Definition of Unconscionable Conduct for the Purpose of Part IVA of the Trade Practices Act 1974(Cth).

Shopping Centre Council of Australia. (2013). Submission to Federal Government of Australia Review of the Federal Franchising Code of Conduct.

Small Business Commissioner South Australia. (2013). Submissions to the Australian Government, Review of the Federal Franchising Code of Conduct.

Spencer, E. (December 2008b). Submission to the Parliamentary Joint Committee Inquiry into Franchising.

Spencer, E., & Young, S. (14 February 2013). Submission to Federal Government of Australia Review of the Federal Franchising Code of Conduct.

Terry, A. (2008). Submission No 91 to Parliamentary Joint Committee in Corporations and Financial Services, Parliament of Australia, Opportunity Not Opportunism: Improving Conduct in Australian Franchising.

Wein, A. (30 April 2013). Submission to Federal Government of Australia Review of the Federal Franchising Code of Conduct.

Zumbo, F. (October 2008). Submission No 140 to Parliamentary Joint Committee in Corporations and Financial Services, Parliament of Australia, Opportunity Not Opportunism: Improving Conduct in Australian Franchising.

Index

N. Abdullah, *Good Faith in Contractual Performance in Australia*,
https://doi.org/10.1007/978-981-15-6078-1

The manufacturer's authorised representative in the EU is Springer Nature Customer Service Centre GmbH, Europaplatz 3, 69115 Heidelberg, Germany. If you have any concerns regarding our products, please contact ProductSafety@springernature.com

Printed and bound by CPI Group (UK) Ltd, Croydon, CR0 4YY

23/09/2026

02221520-0006